Charles Hallock

Our New Alaska

Charles Hallock

Our New Alaska

ISBN/EAN: 9783337715939

Printed in Europe, USA, Canada, Australia, Japan

Cover: Foto ©Andreas Hilbeck / pixelio.de

More available books at **www.hansebooks.com**

OUR NEW ALASKA;

OR,

THE SEWARD PURCHASE VINDICATED.

BY

CHARLES HALLOCK,

AUTHOR OF THE "FISHING TOURIST," "SPORTSMAN'S
GAZETTEER," "CAMP LIFE IN FLORIDA," ETC.

———

*ILLUSTRATED FROM SKETCHES BY
PROF. T. J. RICHARDSON.*

———

NEW YORK:
FOREST AND STREAM PUBLISHING CO.,
1886.

PREFACE.

"Man has not found Alaska yet," says Edwards Roberts in the *Overland Monthly.* "Alone in the North she rests upon the bosom of her seas, waiting patiently for her deliverance."

The special object of this book is to point out the visible resources of that far off territory, and to assist their laggard development; to indicate to those insufficiently informed the economic value of important industries hitherto almost neglected, which are at once available for immediate profit; to elucidate the vexed problem of labor supply; to impress upon Congress the advantage, as well as the duty, of providing proper protection for the people, and granting them representation through a chosen delegate, who shall be competent and conscientious to instruct and advise, and efficient to push their claims and their necessities, so that they may voice the needs of this great integer of the republic, and contribute without let or hindrance to its wealth and prosperity ; and finally to prove conclusively that the " Seward Purchase " was not so bad a bargain after all. At the same time attention is directed to those extraordinary physical phenomena whose marvelous combination makes Alaska the most attractive region in the world for sojourners and summer tourists. I would fain divert a portion of the travel which habitually goes to Europe to this new field of commerce and adventure. I would popularize home excursions among our votaries of fashion—Yosemite, Alaska, and the Yellowstone—as the primary and proper thing to "do " before attempting the Old World tour ; and so make it incumbent upon every American citizen, who would claim consideration abroad, to be duly accredited at the home office as competent to travel.

Hitherto our new possession has seemed almost a myth too vague and intangible to tempt even the Argonauts. Like an unexpected legacy, its magnificence and value have not yet been comprehended; but the time is close at hand

when her mighty forests will yield their treasures, her mines
will open out their richness, her seas will give of their
abundance, and all her quiet coves will be converted into
busy harbors.   Her grassy islands, her rounded foot-hills
and her bounteous table-lands will pasture goodly herds,
and her exuberant soil teem with vegetables and fruit.   The
gelid out-put from her glacier fronts—the crystal ice-floes
which fill her most sequestered channels—will be harvested
where they float, for transportation to the semi-torrid latitudes below; pleasure yachts will thread the intricacies of
her studded islands, and no retreat for invalids and summer
saunterers will be half so popular.   Already the vibrations of
the pending boom begin to agitate the air.   The favorable
reports of government explorers sent out to investigate the
interior as well as the coast, are re-assuring.   Letters of
inquiry from intending settlers come from every section.
Official departments are getting down to systematic work.
New industries have been established within the present
year.   Capital will no longer be withheld grudgingly from
enterprises waiting to be developed ; and by the time this
book is ready to leave the press, a tide of emigration will
set strongly in the direction of the Aleutian Isles.

Talk of the sterility of Alaska, and its inhospitable soil !
Why there are eleven kinds of edible berries which mature
in August, and strawberries grow in lavish profusion right
under the breadth of the glacier fields in latitude sixty
degrees.   The mightiest giant of our eastern pineries is
but a pigmy in diameter beside the average conifer of
Alaska, where the undergrowth is so dense, and the "slash"
so intricate, below the snow-line, that progress through it is
almost impossible, and three miles a day is a difficult feat
to accomplish.

Alaska has been egregiously misconceived, maligned and
misrepresented.   The very encomiums which enraptured
tourists have bestowed upon her Alpine scenery, have served
to discourage settlement or adventure; men forgetting that
the forbidding Alps do not constitute the whole of Switzerland.   Frigid impressions of her climate and agricultural
capabilities have been reflected from her glacier fields and
snow-clad peaks.   Beneath her dazzling drapery fancy
apprehended a stark dead body instead of a living force.
What poets admire to paint as " The land of the midnight
sun," matter-of-fact folks accept as the polar world.   And
so Alaska is misjudged.

Alaska has been belied.   Not only are her marvelous
resources generally ignored, but they have been systemati-

cally and semi-officially denied. Authentic statements of disinterested investigators have been sedulously contradicted in the interest of parties whom it *paid* to keep the possibilities of the country close. It was so during the Russian occupation, and has been so ever since, and from kindred motives. No conscientious person ever dared affirm that the country was absolutely worthless; that a region with 2,000 miles of breadth and 25,000 miles of coast line (!) had absolutely nothing in it worth having; but the Russian government, which yielded its prerogatives to the fur companies, could itself get nothing out of it, and so, perhaps, it came to be for sale. Only within a few years past has the light of truth begun to gleam steadfastly through the fog, inasmuch as the country had been previously inaccessible to us; but now, with a regular bi-monthly steamer to principal ports, and the omnipotent fact published broadcast by the Sitka paper, that milk is sold at ten cents a quart, and lettuce is given away in the local market, some caution must be observed in pronouncing the territory valueless, incapable and agriculturally worthless. The scope and fitness of Alaska for agriculture and stock raising are not yet recognized, simply because they have not been extensively tested.

The illimitable wheat region of the British North-west, once supposed to be a desert, it has been proved can feed the world. The intense cold of winter, instead of being a drawback, acts in the farmer's interest. The deeper the frost goes the better. As it thaws out gradually in the summer, it loosens the sub-soil and sends up the needed moisture to the roots of the grain. The Canadian explorers in Rupert's Sound, in the interest of a railway to Hudson's Bay, claim that the country is not only densely forested but contains valleys and plains which promise rich wheat harvests when once they shall have come under cultivation. The interior of Alaska seems to be equally assuring, since all the witnesses in nature, there indigenous, rise up and testify to it. The geese which fly north in April and return in November, the grouse which brood in May, the flowers which bloom in June, the uncounted herds of caribou, the abundance of moose, bears, mountain goats, birds and other animal life, the exuberance of wild fruits and forest growth, the expansive prairies and moss-covered plains, and the almost tropical heat of mid-summer, all attest the presence of conditions, climatic and otherwise, upon which to predicate deductions altogether favorable.

And Alaska " is waiting for deliverance." She holds her

arms outstretched, and her lap filled with offerings, bidding us come and take them as our recompense, if we will but set her free from isolation and introduce her to the com-mercial world.

My unpretentious sketch may not add any great amount of information to what has already been written of this strange country, but what I have contributed is mainly from my own personal observation, unaided by reports and reference books, which I have purposely refrained from con-sulting. Its south-western coast line for a distance of one thousand miles has become already pretty well known, and is now being thoroughly surveyed by the government. My illustrations show some of its characteristics. It will take years to develop its visible resources, to say nothing of those which do not yet appear ; and, therefore, we need not care at present to speculate much upon what lies inland, back of the coast range. It is better to utilize the oppor-tunities at hand than to search for others which may not exist. The territory is vast, and centuries of systematic investigation will hardly suffice to reveal its fullest capa-bilities. Population will penetrate into the interior as soon as economic industries are fairly introduced along the sea-board, and if there be any land fit for cultivation it will be promptly brought into requisition to supply local demands. Those who know, and have raised fine potatoes one hundred and fifty miles up the Stickeen River, which matured in August, affirm that Alaska can supply her home people from the outset, and *pari passu* with their numerical increase, with fresh meat, and vegetables, game and berries, fish and dairy products, leaving the lower latitudes to supply the cereals and groceries. If minerals are found as widely distributed as indications suggest, the process of develop-ment and occupation will be rapid. Upon the whole, our people have shown considerable energy in taking hold to make something of what appeared to be "no good." They have done fairly well with their cumbersome acquisition, and events are likely to prove that the " Seward Purchase " was not only dirt cheap, but a remunerative investment.

I am pleased to add that the pages of this volume have been read by the specialists of the Smithsonian Institution and by the government officials most familiar with Alaska, and by them approved.

CHARLES HALLOCK.

Washington, D. C.,
    April 13, 1886.

CONTENTS.

CHAPTER I.

CHAPTER II.

CHAPTER III.

CHAPTER IV.

CHAPTER IX.

CHAPTER X.

CHAPTER XI.

CHAPTER XII.

CONTENTS.

CHAPTER XIII.

CHAPTER XIV.

ILLUSTRATIONS.

ITINERARY.

Twice a month a fairly good ocean steamer, with comfortable appointments for excursionists leaves Portland, Oregon, for Alaska, carrying the mails, freight and passengers,
and returning makes the round trip in about thirty days. It
connects at Port Townsend, the United States port of entry
for Puget Sound waters, with the regular steamer from San
Francisco. The excursion season extends from June to
September inclusive, but trips are made the whole year
round. The best route to Portland for passengers from
California and the South is by rail and stage. The 900
miles between San Francisco and Portland, is full of delightful experiences all the way. It used to make the heart ache
to contemplate the journey, and the bones ache to accomplish it ; but now almost seven-eighths of the distance are
done by steam, and for the rest, it is but a charming epi-
sode on wheels, taking the tourist through the most delightful scenery of the west coast, that he may be the better prepared to compare it with what is superlative beyond. All
the scenic attractions of the coast range, of the San Joa-
quin and Sacramento valleys, the Sierra Nevadas just within
view, Mt. Shasta in its isolated grandeur, the Siskiyou
Mountains, just across the Oregon line, and the Rogue River
and Willamette Valleys, are vouchsafed to us within the
limit of three days. How we bridge the mighty intervals
of space, and handicap old time in this modern race of
life !
For elegant comfort, without sight-seeing, the magnificent
Steamers of the Pacific Mail Company, running from San
Francisco to Portland, and Port Townsend on Puget
Sound, afford an incomparable service. The boats of the trans-
Atlantic routes to Europe are hardly more luxurious ; and
those dwellers of the Pacific to whom the beauties of the inland journey are familiar, generally choose the water route.
Excursion tickets which are good for 40 days from date of
issue, enable the tourist to accomplish both the inside and
the outside routes. Eastern people choose the Union
Pacific or Northern Pacific railroads, and Canadians the

Canadian Pacific, according as geographical location meets
their convenience. Those of the Southwest find their
objective point most accessible by the Southern Pacific.
Happy is he whose course leads across the northern tiers,
where the phenomenal solar heat of midsummer is always
tempered by a vitalizing atmosphere which cools when the
sun goes down. It would do your honest hearts good to
see the complaisance with which our Canadian neighbors
regard their completed transit—a stupendous accomplish-
ment whose engineering difficulties take precedence in comparison with the mightiest of our own, and whose passage
through the rugged gaps of *three* successive mountain
ranges makes our single cut across the Rockies, seem almost
common-place. Yet the Northern Pacific is a more interesting route, and the most desirable for all whose convenience permits a choice. It traverses a more diversified and
populous country, and is besides the great continental
artery whose pulsations are destined to keep the life-blood
warm in all our Alaskan extremities. It will presently become
the great feeder and factor of our Alaskan commerce, and
the popular thoroughfare of two-thirds of those who, by and
by, will regard the tour as imperative, as they have done the
stereotyped tour of Europe, now becoming a familiar and
effete experience.

I recall with pleasure my journey over this great thoroughfare, and the vague anticipations of my first Alaska trip.
My thoughts were full of the unknown land. The outlook
seemed without a horizon. I felt more than ever "foot-
loose,"—like a candidate blind-folded for a first degree, or
a novice after the preliminary toss of a blanket—not guess-
ing what was coming next, but feeling that all would turn
out right in the end. I fared sumptuously in the dining
car ; and my time was agreeably divided between reverie
and repletion.

"*Going to Alaska! Going to Alaska!*"

For three consecutive nights I had lain in my Pullman
berth, traveling westward, and between the hours of som-
nolence and semi-wakefulness, I would listen to the cadence
of the car wheels as the train rumbled on, and each mono-
tonous iteration, seemed always to repeat, with a repetition
which made me tired : " Going to Alaska—*going* to Alaska
—going to Alaska—going to *Alaska*—going to *Alaska !* "
Sometimes it would drop into a subdued refrain, and anon
increase to a rattling emphasis when the train ran through a
cut, and this continuous admonition was broken only whenever we came to a full stop and all the waste air in the

brakes blew off with a prolonged sigh and a fizz. Of course
I had started from St. Paul with that intention (to go to
Alaska) and it was perhaps well to know that I had made
no mistake in the passage ; nevertheless, it was a rest to all
the senses when daylight came to relieve the night-watch,
and unfold the wondrous revelations of the trans-continen-
tal trip. How impotent have been the attempts of pen
and brush to impress the comprehension with the reality of
things seen. In vain I hold up my hands and cry " *'mira-
bile.''* No two days' experiences were alike. Each succeeding view and extended panorama was altogether different from its predecessor, and one had hardly time to be
amazed at this, before he was lost in new admiration of the
other. " There is one glory of the sun, another of the
moon, and another glory of the stars." Across the illimitable grain fields and the prairie, through the mysterious
" Bad lands," over the pine-clad and snow-capped mountains, past the far-reaching sage plains, and down the tran-
scendent Columbia to the portals of the broad Pacific—
every division of the grand thoroughfare we traversed was
crammed full of novelty and absorbing interest. The
delicious warmth of an August atmosphere lay over all, and
delightful anticipations continually gave place to blissful
realization.

The tourist no sooner strikes the Columbia River than he
seems to have gotten into a new kingdom of creation. The
sudden transition from an interminable sage plain of more
than one hundred miles in breadth to vertical cliffs and pal-
isades which rise to fifteen hundred feet sheer out of the
river—this unexpected step from the unlimited horizontal to
the unattainable perpendicular—is of itself phenomenal.
Then the architecture of the rocks and hills is different from
any thing east. The rivers flow in mighty volume, green as
emerald, and plunge into black rifts and chasms, churning
their sides with foam. Shifting sands in their exposed beds
blow into fantastic dunes and bury the underbrush along
the shores until only their leafy tops protrude. Waterfalls
leap from dizzy heights, emulating the Yosemite. The
vegetation is luxuriant, and all the field of flora is new.
Every thing is gigantic. The common alder bush grows to
merchantable wood, and the principal forest trees into giant
columns six feet thick. The orchards break down with
redundant fruitage, and whenever there is a neglected garden patch the sweet briars and wild vines overrun the inclosing fences and bury them out of sight. Mosses cling to
the limbs of trees in solid masses and festoons, and cover

prostrate trunks ten iaches deep.   All along the route from
the Dalles to Portland are gangs of Chinese, section-hands,
at work along the railroad with costumes quaint and scanty,
and features bland and child-like. It was against those vertical walls which overhang the Columbia, that they swung
the indomitable heathen from the heights aloft, to drill and
blast a passage for the railroad out of the solid rock.   I
know not how many dozens lost their lives in the dangerous
exploit, but inasmuch as they stood substitute and proxy for
supposed better men, this little trifle can hardly enter into
the " Chinese Question."

Of course all tourists rhapsodize the notable points of
view along the river—the Dalles, Cape Horn, the Cascades,
Pillars of Hercules, Rooster Rock and Multnomah Falls,
each of which, if isolated and apart, instead of contiguous
to each other, would constitute an attraction which tourists
would travel far to visit.   Not the least interesting novel-
ties are the fish-wheels along the shores, both portable and
stationary, which scoop up the running salmon from March
to August by the tens of thousands, looking for all the
world like the obsolete mill-wheels of New England.
Occasionally little groups of Oregon Indians come in view,
seeming one-third civilized and two-thirds blank.   In vain,
however, we look for the spectral outlines of Mount Hope
and other notable peaks, for all the atmosphere is thick
with smoke of forest fires which have spread all over the
country ; and for six weeks past no one has drawn a breath
of pure air, so that the inhabitants of this notoriously moist
and fog-ridden region pray for rain. In course of time we
come to a comfortable halt at the romantic little station of
Bonneville, where a breakfast is served with more than
Oriental profusion of melons, fruits and vegetables in every
grown variety, and with milk and eggs, poultry, fish and
meats, and every thing else toothsome and edible, piled on
platters three tiers deep until the table holds no more—
and still the waiters come with reinforcements, hands full,
and loaded to the " gunnel." It seemed to the parched
and dusty travelers from the arid sage plain, just now left
behind, as if they had suddenly struck an oasis and every
thing had been knocked into " pi " by the collision. The
markets of Oregon and California were emptied out upon
the board ; Ceres and Pomona sat helpless with their laps
full. With this wide-open welcome the brief additional
run to Portland was made without apprehension, although
the approaching city could not be distinguished through
the murk.

There is a reputable tradition that when the atmosphere is clear, a view can be had from points of vantage whose unfolding is like a revelation of the celestial realm. Afar off in the horizon, just where the intense blue firmament seems to flank the spirit land, a trio of snowy peaks loom up from the somber plain in clear cut whiteness against the sky, like pyramids of crystal, Mt. Hood conspicuous and majestic above the rest. Rising in their purity to the very dome of heaven, and gleaming with a translucence supernatural, positive yet most intangible, they stand, as it were, the embodiment of the Eternal Trinity—not mere reflections of this material world. It is seldom that this beatific vision comes, even to patient watchers ; for fogs and mists obscure them in the spring, and clouds of smoke hang over them all the summer long ; but if, perchance, September rains should purify the air and lift the lowering veil, they appear momentarily to the world as the reflex of the divine transfiguration. As such, I beheld as one privileged. The time-favored denizens of Portland could not appreciate it more.

I don't know why tourists prefer to take the Alaska steamer to Portland *via* the Columbia River, and its distressful bar, with the supplementary and outside passage to Victoria, instead of choosing the Puget Sound route, except that they can thereby secure their berths for the voyage and survey serenely the subsequent scramble for places when the overland passengers arrive on board. The consideration is certainly important, but the experienced voyager can secure equal comforts by correspondence with the officials of the steamship company. One who took the river route writes :

" The Lower Columbia has none of the grand and sublime scenery of the Upper Columbia, where it breaks its way through the Cascade Mountains, but it has a picturesque beauty all its own, wooded isles and bold headlands, the river banks being high, wooded bluffs, with mountains in the background. We had an occasional picture of lovely level farms lying along the river and stretching back for miles, but such glimpses of cultivation were rare. Settlements were few. At about four in the afternoon we reached Astoria, which is fifteen miles from the sea ; and to-day we climbed to the top of a high hill, from which we could see the breakers on the bar. Astoria is quite a pretty town, has a population of five or six thousand, and its chief industries, fish and lumber, remain the same in kind as when John Jacob Astor established his trading post here.

The best part of the town, in regard to residence, is back
on the hills, which rise steep and near to the shore, while
the business part is built on piles over tide water."

An eight hours' ride by rail is a moderate journey, and
while the steamer is buffeting the waves of the outside passage, the overland tourist from Portland to Tacoma is permitted to enjoy the comforts of the superb hostelry at the
head of the sound, and perchance to view the snow-crested
peak of Mt. Tacoma, standing out in its virgin purity, like
a spirit of retrospection against the deep blue background
of sky. On it there are glaciers equal in size to those
found among the Alps. He may also observe the humble
houses under the hill by the cove, where the presence of a
half dozen Chinese small merchants was permitted for
years to vex the equanimity of 7,000 people, but now having been charitably wiped out, is obnoxious no more.
From Tacoma to Victoria there is a six hours' sail across a
long reach of the sound by the splendid steamer " Olym-
pian," palatial as any in the east, and electric-lighted in
every apartment. On the route is Seattle, a goodly brick-
built city of some ten thousand souls, already made historical by its four days' war with a "barbarian horde" of
Chinese 140 strong ; then Port Townsend, the lands' end
of our western possessions before Alaska, perched high
upon a perpendicular bluff whose top is reached by a hundred steps, with the mercantile traffic properly bestowed
upon the flat below. At every intermediate hamlet and
landing there is a saw-mill, with the primitive forest for a
background and reminder of its purpose. On every side
there are intimations of the country's recent settlement and
the presence of the wilderness. Indian dug-out canoes of
fantastic shapes with carved prows, steal quietly along the
shadowy shores, or cross the open water between the
embowered islands. Up and down, with every sweep of the
eye, this notable Mediterranean stretches its majestic length
of two hundred miles ; at times a broad expanse, anon no
wider than a river, with many a point and promontory
and curve of shore, roadsteads tortuous, channels narrow,
and water bluer than the reflected skies, dotted with
islands, indented with umbrageous recesses .where the
unsuspicious fish breaks the quiet surface, and offering in
every littoral dell and sweep of forest such delights as
sportsmen covet and endure long journeys to enjoy. And
yet, on every side are budding hamlets and thrifty settlements with airs of comfort, farms and hop-fields, and busy
saw-mills, and great ships sailing filled with surplus wheat,

and steamboats plying hither and yon—all significant of
energetic industry and a prosperous future. It is said that
a hundred steamboats ply the waters of the sound.

But the speculative tourist, looking far beyond, Alaska-
ward, is not content to abide. Victoria, the entrepot of
British Columbia, claims direct attention, and there is not a
surer refuge or resting place for the sea-worn and wayfar-
ing than the land-locked basin which forms its harbor.
While the good ship which is to take us onward waits at
her dock, and the purser and steward are making out their
lists, we have two days on shore to see the town. There is
a commodious hotel, called the " Driard," where the most
exacting guest can be made comfortable. It is quite up to
the modern standard, built of stone, and occupies half a
square ; containing within its walls a creditable Opera
House, which alone cost $50,000 to construct. Its landlord
is a dapper Louisiana Frenchman, acquainted with every
body in the two countries, and therefore a companionable
host for strangers to meet, having no race prejudices and
providing plenty to eat.

This far-western city is as substantial as it is charming.
Started originally as a fur company's post, and afterward
boomed into importance by the Fraser River mining excitement of 1858, time has proved that other than even extran-
eous causes have contributed to its prosperity and growth.
All the steamer lines of the Province center at Victoria,
whence they reach all coast ports where settlements have
been made, and penetrate far into the interior by ascending
the Fraser River and other water-ways ; and trade increases
constantly in proportion as the tributary settlements and
industries expand. The flags were all at half mast the day
I arrived, in commemoration of the Grant obsequies, and
my heart warmed toward the good people for their respect
shown to our great captain. Travelers say the town is
intensely English in its composition. If so, it has a warm
corner for its neighbors, and the " English of it " is good
will. A considerable portion of the town-site has been set
aside and designated as " Beacon Hill Park," with winding
drives, gentle undulations, conspicuous eminences, majestic trees, and a wonderful outlook toward the seas where
some small earthworks and great guns frown imperiously ;
but to me the entire location seemed like a natural park,
with its numerous bridges and points of rock, its picturesque bays and inlets, its islands and bits of beach, its
clusters of trees and luxuriant gardens, every eminence
crowned with a modern villa, every cove cuddling a cosy

cottage, and all the well-built business blocks occupying a curve of the land-locked harbor, constituting a picture of solid comfort and natural beauty which grew more and more attractive as it became familiar. There was just enough shipping to give the place an air of importance—some square-rigged vessels, some steamers, and a few old hulks which were well nigh past service. Here lay the old Hudson Bay steamer "Beaver," which crossed the ocean in 1832. It is said she has cheese aboard now which she brought then. Here was the "Otter," which laid the submarine cable, and the "Wilson G. Hunt," once plying in New York waters. Up the gorge, where the tide flows furiously, except at slack and flood, is a famous place for catching sea-trout with rod and fly. Everywhere about the bay Indian canoes were plying, and there were groups of tents on shore, with hectic salmon spread on neighboring rocks to dry. The dusky groups carelessly disposed about the grass, men, women, and children, in motley dress, sitting on native mats, and skins of mountain goats, knitting, mending clothes, plaiting baskets, lounging, or lazily turning the half-cured fish, resemble a gypsy camp or holiday picnic, so civilized are their appearance and surroundings. Few visible traces of aboriginal barbarism remain, only some rude lip ornament, or cherished habit almost obsolete, or amulet, or knick-knack, transmitted from their remote progenitors. Red, black and yellow colors predominate in their rustic fancy,—yellow scarfs for the head or neck, red for shawls or jackets, and black for frocks and skirts of women. In the city streets we see the girls in pairs loll up to the shop windows with the easy abandon of habitues, laughing outright with delight at the glittering objects displayed, as much enraptured and absorbed as a cat in catnip. Three generations of intercourse with white people whose policy has been justice and humanity and tempered with firmness, have won their confidence. They were treated kindly from the start, and no white man was permitted to do them an injustice without being punished for his conduct. At the same time they were made to understand that they were equally amenable to wrong doing. They were also given employment in pursuits suited to their proclivities and aptitude, which brought them food, trinkets, and clothing they had before been destitute of, whereby they learned the value of friendly relations with the new-comers. Henceforth we shall find them an omnipresent quantity along the coast, varying somewhat in features, habits, disposition and intelligence, but all well-disposed and tractable. Here in

Victoria the tourist can pick up much information of Alaska, together with curios, photographs of scenery, maps of route and itineraries, not to omit a " Chinook " dictionary which will be useful to him at all times, and indispensable if he wishes to make the most of his opportunities to trade with the natives and learn the ways of the people ; all of which he can buy cheaper for cash than up the coast.

The most interesting and æsthetic part of Victoria is the Chinese quarter, which is a cleanly business suburb of solid red brick blocks, with buildings two and three stories high ornamented with green verandas. Some of the stories and shops are very spacious, with superb fittings of gilt, tapestry and carved work, comprising stocks of general merchandise, drugs, spices and specialties. One of these Chinamen is said to own real estate within the limits worth $200,000. I took occasion to go through all parts of their reserve, into their theaters, joss houses and houses of pleasure, into their opium joints and their squalid and poverty-worn tenements where a dozen persons are herded together in a single room, and was compelled to change the impression which I had formed from popular hear-say. The worst I saw was not half as foul and repulsive as the slums of some populous eastern cities, outside of New York. They have a comfortable building where they board and lodge their kinsfolk when they first arrive, or when sick, or out of work, or on a visit from the interior. It is a sort of hotel-hospital. There are no Chinese beggars, for " John " takes care of his own in purse and person, and will even return their dead bodies to China, *if desired.* The impression that the return of dead Chinamen is imperative, is a myth, and absurd on the face of it ; but the prejudiced will believe any thing. I found them engaged in every kind of occupation, except the very highest, and was amazed at their general thrift, sobriety, and intelligence. The policy of the Canadians toward these Mongolians is much more liberal than ours,—as it has been with the Indians,—and in course of time they will surely profit by it. In British Columbia the occidental section of the Flowery Kingdom blooms and blossoms as the rose—a *tea* rose, as it were, whose fine points, not all of thorns, might be studied with advantage if we would only take the *cue.* But it is whispered in the inner chamber that the days of the cue are numbered. The conditions of a mighty dispensation are about to be fulfilled. The time is near at hand when the Chinese will be at liberty to cut off their cues and dispense with their large sleeves.

They say that according to a prophecy in one of their

sacred books, the reigning dynasty that imposed, centuries ago, the custom of dress now in vogue, will come to an end, and the new government will make the abolishment of both permissible—an act devoutly hailed by Chinamen. Thenceforth, these insignia of race distinctions will not be any more imperatively imposed. Obstacles to naturalization and American citizenship will be removed. Indeed, the days of immunity are already being anticipated, and scores of Chinese here and in the United States are taking out papers. Leading celestials assert that the movement will soon become general, and that most of their people in the southwest will soon proceed to become American citizens and permanent residents ; that they will then bring over their wives and children and spend their earnings here ; and that all the money which has hitherto been sent abroad for their support will be " blowed into " the treasury of the United States. Truly, the patience and long-suffering of the " heathen," in consequence of their two-fold religious and political disabilities, are worthy of admiration. For a free country such inflictions are hard to bear.

It was at Victoria that I first noticed that exuberance of vegetation which surprised me still more when I reached Alaska. The maple leaves were larger than I could span ; alders grew into trees ; fruit-trees broke under the weight of fruitage ; honeysuckles grew rank, and moss clung to the trees in great masses ; ferns were several feet in length ; water melons as big as a barrel ; growing pines ran up into the air indefinitely. Everything on this coast is gigantic, from the rocks and mountains and " big trees " to the Chinese immigration, the forest fires, and the ambition of the politicians. No wonder that the people of the Pacific coast claim to be the most favored in the world ; they absorb the beneficence of the Creator.

Three miles from Victoria, at Esquimault, there is a naval station, with arsenal, hospital, dock-yard, and powder magazine, the latter located on an island. The dry-dock is substantially built of concrete faced with sandstone, and will cost when fully completed a half million of dollars. The harbor is one of the deepest and securest in the world.

It is no small task to equip and provision a steamer, carrying two hundred persons, and get her under way for a
month ; but finally all the pigs, and poultry, and cabbages,
and crates of fruit, and ice, and carcasses of beef, are trundled aboard and stowed conveniently for the steward's daily
deal ; the sheep and hay are snugly housed between decks,
and the last reluctant steer is forced up the gangway by a
twist of the tail so excruciating that it wrings out a suggestion of ox-tail soup for next day's bill of fare.   Then the
hawsers are cast off, and the good ship swings bravely into
the stream on the hope of her new departure—bound for
Alaska.

First, there is an eight hour's run of 70 miles to the British port of Nanaimo for coal, in the course of which, if the
atmosphere be clear, the snow-clad peaks of the Cascade
range of mountains will appear like a crystal rampart across
the sea.   There is a succession of them, rising one above
the other, and looking as unreal and ethereal as a vision of
fairy-land. Enchantment of the voyage begins at the very
threshold of departure, and the first outlook is exhilarating
with satisfying promise. Nanaimo is the headquarters of
the Vancouver Coal Company, and the distributing depot
of a large coal district.   The coal areas of this province are
widely spread, of whose product San Francisco alone takes
150,000 tons per annum.   Departure Bay and Nanaimo are
twin harbors connected by a deep narrow channel of ample
width for navigation.   The town lies along the bay, with
streets quite irregular in conformity with the sinuosities of
the indented shore line.   A dense and continuous pine forest, underlaid by coal measures, occupies the back ground.
There is an octagonal block house three stories high, which
years ago did duty for the Hudson Bay Fur Company.
Hence, through the picturesque Strait of Georgia to the
head of Vancouver, 300 miles or more, there are islands all
the way, with a good deal of scrub cedar and fir ; now and
then a farm house and clearing.   Every body on board the
steamer busily studies charts, picking out the course of the

ship in advance, and locating her hourly whereabouts. Hour
after hour there succeeds an alternation of deep narrow
channels hemmed in by mountains, and long reaches of
open water which glisten with the scintillations of the sun.
Deep bays reach far into the land, and projecting points
invite the lambent breezes of the sea. Here and there are
shoals with warning beacons, and tide-rips churned by
counter-currents into foam, into which if a vessel without
steam be caught, she drifts on dangers, powerless to escape.
Of such mischances we see some victims now and then high
and dry on sunken reefs, keeled over. Sometimes, when
running close to land the jutting ledges seem about to pour
their leaping waterfalls bodily upon the deck, and over-
reaching boughs almost brush the taffrail as we pass. All
the shores are lined with drift-wood and stranded trunks of
enormous trees, weather-worn and naked. The average
rise of tide is eighteen feet, and on the ebb and flow, its
velocity through the narrow channels reaches nine miles an
hour, so that vessels have to make intelligent forecast of
time of tide, of fogs, and hours of moonlight. To attempt
the passage except on flood and slack is to court destruction, for although the mean depth of water is sometimes
seventy fathoms, the tortuous straits are filled with hidden
rocks. The first and worst of these is " Seymour Rapids,"
a passage less than a quarter of a mile wide, about nine
hours run from Nanaimo ; and here in the awful swell and
vortex which lashes each broken shore with the rage of
Niagara's whirlpools, the U. S. man of War " *Saranac*" went
down, shivered on a sunken rock ; and in the self-same
place, by an extraordinary coincidence of mischances, the
steamer " *Grappler* " was burned and sunk. She was carrying Chinese coolies, of whom seventy vainly struggled
momentarily with the surging waves, and disappeared ; but
they do say that their bodies periodically come to the surface, and pitch about the eddies, with pigtails streaming
wildly in their wake, though the more matter-of-fact opinion
is that the objects seen are only strings of kelp drifting on
the tide. Other dangerous passages are Grenville Strait
and Peril Strait. For the rest, the journey is at present
without risk or peradventure, and with ordinary seamanship and prudence, depending much upon experienced
pilots, may be made with less discomfort than the passage of Long Island Sound ; for the sweep of the ocean
blasts seldom reaches these sheltered by-ways. Fogs are
chronic, however, for eight months of the year, and apt to
occur at early morning, all the summer long, though they

do not interrupt travel ; for navigators have learned to evoke the echoes from the enfilading walls and headlands by resonant blasts of the steam whistle, and so estimate their courses, whereabouts, and distances.

By the time passengers have been two or three days at sea, they get to know many of the tricks of the ship, as well as of their fellow-voyagers. They have topics in common which promote familiar intercourse ; and so, between the scenery, the log, the bill of fare, and themselves, they find strong ties of mutual sympathy. Furthermore, the sailors had a bear aboard, named " Pete," which was raised on bilge water and was very tame; a black setter, a companion of the bear ; a toy terrier ; and a fine tom-cat; all of whose intellects had been largely developed by their association with tourists and shipmates. I know of no better training-school for bears than a voyage of this kind.

From the head of Vancouver Island to the Alaskan frontier, the coast maintains the same indented and tortuous line, flanked by innumerable islands. The mountains gradually increase in height, and at Grenville Narrows they rise to fully 3,000 feet, directly out of the sea ; some of them with snowy peaks, and numerous water-falls tumbling from their aerial reservoirs, but wooded at the base with conifers. As the civilization of this region is mainly apart from the route of the steamer, and unseen by tourists who imagine it all unsettled, I venture to prompt the reader from the pages of the *West Shore Magazine*, so that erroneous impressions may not obtain. Some may be astonished at the proficiency of the Indians, not long since savage.

We read : " The population of this region is chiefly Indian, and they are both intelligent and industrious ; performing nearly all the labor of the two industries—salmon canning and lumbering—which have gained a foothold there. In going north, Rivers Inlet is the first reached where industries have been established. At its head is situated the village of Weekeeno. On the inlet are two salmon canneries and a saw-mill. Bella Coola is situated at the head of Burke Channel, on the North Bentinck Arm. It is the site of a Hudson's Bay company post, and years ago was the landing place for the Cariboo mines. Bella Coola River is a considerable stream entering the arm from across the mountains. Here is a tract of some 2,000 acres of rich delta land, which is partially cultivated by the Indians. Bella Bella is a Hudson's Bay post on Campbell Island, near the head of Milbank Sound, 400 miles north of Victoria. There are three Indian villages, with a combined

population of 500. The next important point is the mouth
of Skeena River, a large stream flowing from the interior.
It is a prolific salmon stream, and there are three canneries
on its banks ; one at Aberdeen, another at Inverness Slough,
and a third at Port Essington, near its mouth, where there
is a small village of traders, fishermen and Indians. The
river is navigable for light draught steamers as far as
Mumford Landing, sixty miles inland, and 200 miles further
for canoes. There are two missionary stations on the river,
and along its course are many spots favorable for settlements.

"Sixteen miles beyond the mouth of the Skeena is the
town of Metlakahtla, on the Tsimpsheean Peninsula. There
are a store, salmon cannery, a large church and school-
house. This is an Indian missionary station, about which are
gathered fully 1,000 Tsimpsheean Indians, who have been
taught many of the mechanical arts. They have a saw-
mill, barrel factory, blacksmith shop ; live in good wooden
houses; do the work at the cannery, and are industrious in
many other ways ; the women having learned the art of
weaving woolen fabrics. Fifteen miles beyond Metlakahtla,
on the northwest end of the same peninsula, is the important station of Fort Simpson, separated from Alaska Territory by the channel of Portland Inlet. This is one of the
finest harbors in British Columbia, and was for years the
most important post of the Hudson's Bay Company in the
upper country, furs being brought there from the vast interior. Besides the company's post, the Methodist Mission
has buildings valued at $9,000. There are about 800
Indians in the village, most of them living in good shingled
houses and wearing civilized costumes. They are governed
by a council, and have various organizations, including a
temperance society, rifle company, fire company and a brass
band. They earn much money in the fisheries. Forty
miles up the Portland Channel is the mouth of Nass
River, a very important stream in the fishing industry,
being the greatest known resort of the oolachan. Two salmon canneries, a saw-mill, store, two missionary stations
and several Indian villages are situated along the stream.
The climate is favorable to the growth of fruit, cereals and
root crops near the coast, and there are a number of quite
extensive tracts of bottom lands, requiring only to be
cleared to render them fit for agriculture or grazing.
Further up the stream there are a number of good locations,
and several settlements have been made. Gold is found in
small quantities along the river.

" A special feature of the province is the outlying group of large islands known as the Queen Charlotte Islands, the upper end lying nearly opposite the southern extremity of Alaska. They are three in number—Graham, Moresby and Provost—and are about 170 miles long and 100 wide. They are mountainous and heavily timbered, and the climate is more genial and the rainfall less than on the mainland coast, Along the northern end of Graham, the most northerly of the group, is a tract of low lands thirty-five miles in extent, and much level, arable land is to be found elsewhere, which only requires clearing. There are also many extensive marshy flats requiring drainage to render them fit for cultivation. The mineral resources of the islands are undoubtedly great. The only industry now established is the factory of the Skidegate Oil Company, on Skidegate Island in a good harbor at the southern end of Graham Island. In connection with this is a store. The Hudson Bay Company has a store and a trading post at Massett, near the upper end of Graham's Island, where there are a Protestant Mission and a large Indian village.

" There are several villages on each of the islands of the group which are occupied by Hydah Indians, the most intelligent of the aboriginal inhabitants of the coast. Their origin, in the absence of any written record or historical inscriptions, is an interesting subject for speculation. Their features, tattooing, carvings and legends indicate that they are castaways from Eastern Asia, who, first reaching the islands of Southern Alaska, soon took and held exclusive possession of the Queen Charlotte group. Their physical and intellectual superiority over the North Coast Indians, and also marked contrasts in the structure of their language, denote a different origin. They are of good size, with exceptionably well developed chests and arms, high foreheads and lighter complexion than any other North American Indians.

" Massett, the principal and probably oldest village of the Hydah Nation, is pleasantly situated on the north shore of Graham Island at the entrance to Massett Inlet. Fifty houses, great and small, built of cedar logs and planks, with a forest of carved poles in front, extend along the fine beach. The house of Chief Weeah, is fifty-five feet square, containing timbers of immense size, and planks three feet and one-half in width and eighteen inches thick. The village now has a population of about 250, the remnants of a once numerous people, the houses in ruins here having accommodated several times that number. Massett is the shipyard of the Hydahs, the best canoe-makers on the continent, who supply them to the other coast tribes. Here may be seen in all stages of construction these canoes, which, when completed, are such perfect models for service and of beauty. This is the abode of the aristocracy of Hydah land. Other villages are the offshoots from the parent colony, caused by family and tribal feuds and quarrels."

Although not included within the limits of Alaska, being some fifteen miles south of its frontier, I am pleased to be able to give fair sketches of the remarkable Indian settlement of Metlakahtla, above referred to, not only as an instance of the advanced state of civilization to which some of the Pacific coast Indians have already been brought, but because it is an earnest of the enviable results which must surely crown our own endeavors, if properly applied, and therefore an encouragement to persevere.

Metlakahtla is truly the full realization of the missionaries' dream of aboriginal restoration. The population is 1,200, and there are but six white persons in the place. Like the mission Indians at Fort Simpson, its residents have also a rifle company of forty-two men, a brass band, a two gun battery, a cooper shop, and a large co-operative store where almost any thing obtainable in Victoria can be bought. We visited this port on our return trip from Sitka, and were received with displays of bunting from various points, and a five-gun salute from the battery, with Yankee Doodle and Dixie from the band of thirteen pieces. The Union-Jack was flying. The church is architecturally pretentious and can seat 800 persons. It has a belfry and spire, vestibule, gallery across the front end, groined arches and pulpit carved by hand, organ and choir, Brussels carpet in the aisles, stained glass windows, and all the appointments and embellishments of a first class sanctuary; and it is wholly native handiwork! This well ordered community occupy two-story shingled and clap-boarded dwelling houses of uniform size, 25x50 feet, with three windows and gable ends and door in front, and inclosed flower gardens, and macadamized sidewalks ten feet wide along the entire line of street. The chief peculiarity of these houses is, that none of them have chimneys, the apartments being heated by fires built on hearths in the center of the ground floor, and the smoke passing out through a flat cupola in the roof, after the fashion of Indian tenements in general. These people have also a large town hall or assembly room of the same capacity as the church, capable of accommodating the whole population. It is used for councils, balls, meetings, and for a drill room.

It is warmed by three great fires placed in the center of the building, and lighted by side lamps. The people dress very tastefully in modern garb, and I am not sure but they have the latest fashions. The women weave the cloth for all the garments, and there are gardens which afford vegetables and fruit in abundance. It is as cleanly and orderly as the most punctilious Shaker settlement. A fine assortment of Hydah utensils, plaques, and carved work is on sale here. For exquisite beauty and quaint designs, there is nothing like Hydah ware to be found on the whole coast. A most beautiful table service of many pieces is on view at the U. S. National Museum in Washington, carved from black talcose slate. Miniature totem-poles two or three feet high, wrought of the same material, may also be bought at $5 to $7, American or Canadian money, both being current.

From this point to American soil the distance is short. *"Decensus Averno."* The transition from the neat and thrifty settlements left behind to the dilapidated and half-deserted line of buildings—formerly a Russian trading post of rank, but now the U. S. port of entry of Alaska, is not flattering to spread-eagle pride. When the weather-stained Custom House officer formally comes on deck, conscientious American citizens " go below." It was said that nothing remunerative to any body ever followed his official visits. Usually it was "too foggy" for him to discover the vessel, and this fog became so constitutionally prevalent in all that district that smuggled goods were nowhere apparent until, one unpropitious day last February, Collector Beecher by some timely hint conveyed through the circumlocution office, was enabled to unearth at Tongass no less than $45,000 worth of opium packed in casks purporting to cover furs. However, the Territorial regime is full of irregularities, affecting other things than revenue, all of which will be speedily corrected whenever domestic order shall succeed official chaos. But I shall venture no reflections. I will hold no " mirror up to nature," for never did nature see herself to better advantage than upon that early morn at Tongass. There was no fog then ; the early sun had scarcely risen ; and all the morning lights which painters find it so difficult to limn, filled the firmament with their transparency. Not only the trees and rocks, and mountains, the moss, the kelp, the gulls on wing, the reek of the smoke-stack, and the rosy glow of morn, but even the fleecy films of vapor which, in voluptuous summer float high in the upper air—the lace-

like canopy embroidered on the blue—were mirrored on
the water ; and each individual wave upturned by the cleaving prow formed reduplicating mirrors, like the facets of a
gem, reflecting a consummate picture in each one.   It was
a moment of perfectly earthly peace.   The impressionable
young ladies on board declared that it was "just too lovely
for any thing."   These little maids from school all keep
faithful diaries of the happenings aboard ship, nautical and
social, the distances run each day, the places called at, what
the steward laid for dinner, how many chickens there are
left in coop, what the captain told them *sub rosa*, and all
the special and private information to be picked up in the
purser's state-room, and the "after-run."   They make
themselves "solid" with the officers, tip the steward and
waiters, and even button-hole the first officer for best boats
when little side excursions are afoot, for on those Alaska
journeys frequent opportunities are offered to go ashore at
the regular landings,of which there may be ten, besides special trips to places of universal interest ; after each visit the
cabins and state-rooms are littered with ferns, mosses, wild
flowers, clam shells, bits of mineral, slippery kelps, Indian
curios and souvenirs of all sorts brought aboard.   One of
these little exploring parties once came across a member of
the ship's crew digging a hole in the ground on a secluded
point, and when he told them he was to get three dollars for burying a dead Chinaman who had been sent over
from the steamer in the yawl, they were paralyzed.   The
body lay on the ground beside him, covered with a coat.
In their view such a summary disposal of a corpse was not
at all in accordance with civilized customs, but it seemed to
be approved in Alaska.   This incident was of course duly
noticed in the diaries, with comments.   So also was the adventure of the "rooster and the cook."   The chicken coop,
it seems, stood on the hurricane deck in the lee of one of
the paddle-boxes, and passengers would often stop on their
matutinal turns aloft to inspect or feed the feathered
inmates, and speculate upon the uncertainties and vicissitudes of galley life.   On these occasions the chickens were
always inclined to be sociable and would scuffle with each
other for donations ; but it was remembered that whenever
the cook or his assistant, both of whom were Chinamen, approached the coop, the apprehensive flock fled to the rear
and bunched up in the corners.   They knew the difference,
and no wonder !   One by one the fatted victims were summarily withdrawn and served as soup or fricassee, until at
last the cutest of them all, an old rooster who had hitherto

evaded the intruded hand, was fairly cornered ; yet he did not succumb nor faint. Watching his chance, he slipped John's grip, and getting free on deck, at last he gave both the Chinamen a desperate chase around the texas and the smoke-stacks, this way, and that way, and back again, headed off at every turn, feathers flying, pig-tails streaming, all hands cackling and squawling, and every passenger look-ing on quite interested. At last, utterly exhausted, the rooster was neatly coraled in a bunch of life-preservers (which were nothing to him then), when he suddenly took wing, and with one defiant and despairing shriek, flew over-board and was drowned ! He deliberately committed sui-cide rather than go to pot ; so he escaped the ignominy, but the passengers lost their salad.

I am quite sure, if I desired a complete epitome of the voyage, with no details omitted, I could find it in one of these same records; but as I am not likely to meet any of these " Vassar Girls Abroad," it only remains for me to re-cite the bare fact of our due arrival at Wrangell, which was fifteen years ago a town of considerable importance, where large parties fitted out daily for the Stickeen mines located nearly three hundred miles inland across the country in British Columbia. There the whole region is even now filled with deserted cabins. There was a temporary glim-mer of brightness for Alaskan prospects, in the first dawn of the new " purchase," when no less than 3,000 people congregated here to " outfit." Then there were many shops and stores, and warehouses on the wharf, and all sorts of rude places of amusement, and a motly and unruly crowd such as always gathers at a frontier town. Even old hulks were improvised as boarding-houses. But the prospects " petered out," not for lack of mineral so much as lack of suitable mechanical appliances, and so both the mines and the town are now almost dead. There is a picturesque block-house on a convenient hill, and a grassy plaza with barracks where troops were quartered then, and a couple of small churches, Catholic and Protestant, on the crest of a ridge, with plank walks leading to them, but the barracks are now occupied by the Indian Mission of Mr. Young, and the bethels and brothels are boarded up. Everything is dilap-idated and worn of paint, and spacious hostelries where board was once $3.00 per day, have already tumbled into ruins, with the walls collapsed and the roofs fallen in. There are about 500 people left, chiefly Indians, whose better houses, many of them painted, occupy a picturesque curve of the shore and a point of land which projects into the harbor. A foot bridge also leads across an estuary to what is an island when the tide is full, and here are some of the best built houses and elaborate totem-poles. This part of the town has at least the charm of supreme novelty, and I dare say there is nothing like it to be seen in all Alaska; a hint of which visitors should take due note and govern themselves accordingly. I suppose that there will be a better civilization ere many years have passed, but this peculiar architecture and ornamentation stand to-day, not only as striking illustrations of the idiosyncracies of a peculiar people, but of their native capabilities, made more creditable and more conspicuous from lack of superior tools with which to cut, hew, carve and smooth. When it is borne in mind that their boards are split from hemlocks, riven with an ax, and planed with adzes, and that shaping and finishing is done with rude knives, it is apparent that the impartial judge will allow them many points for ingenuity and skill. This special subject I leave for a future chapter.

Wrangell lies at the mouth of the Stickeen. One of these days not distant, a steamboat excursion up the Stickeen River through the great cañon which it has cut for its passage through the mountains, will be one of the most popular and exciting of all the experiences on this continent. There is steamboat navigation for one hundred and sixty miles from its mouth to Glenora, up to which point the river is usually clear of ice by the middle of April. There the Dominion custom-house is located on the supposed boundary line, and the scenery is of the most romantic character all the way, the wonderful creations of nature being diversified by trading posts, stores, and mining stations along the banks. Several fine glaciers are to be seen en route, and a number of tributary streams or branches flow into the main river. From the head of navigation there are canoe routes and overland trails for pack trains which lead to the gold mines at Deese Lake, eighty miles further, and to the noted quartz lodes and placers of Cariboo and Cassiar in British Columbia. The strip of territory owned by the United States and lying along the coast is only ten leagues wide by the Russian Treaty of 1828 with Great Britain ; and the continual difficulties which arise between customs officials along an indeterminate boundary line, makes its speedy official establishment in every respect very desirable.

The distance between Victoria and Wrangell is a little less than eight hundred miles, the whole route so land-locked that not a qualm of sea-sickness is permitted to come

U. S. TRIPODS IN CHANNEL.

aboard, and all the emissaries of Neptune lie low among the grottoes of the deep. The further northward ones goes the grander the scenery becomes, the higher and more rugged grow the mountains, the whiter their caps of snow, the denser the surrounding forests, and the more numerous the streams which leap from the lips of the crags. There are fjords deeper and blacker than the Saguenay, open chan- nels greener than Niagara. Peaks are piled on peaks in most tumultuous forms. Outlines serrated and sharp cut the upper sky. Black ravines and dazzling patches of snow alternate. Scars seam the entire sides of lofty moun- tains, where the spring avalanches have scathed them of every vestige of soil and vegetation. The inlets are often enveloped in fogs, but when they lift, the surprises are bewildering. Sometimes it is the bases of the mountains which are revealed, and sometimes the peaks, with a filmy drapery floating athwart their sides, or a golden fleece hung gracefully over their broad shoulders. At Kasaan there is a wharf and cannery with an annex of Indian cabins like an old time negro quarter. There is a fleet of splendid canoes employed in the fishery, drawn high and dry upon the beach ready for use, but now tenderly covered with sails and mats to protect them from the alternate damp and sunshine. The hulk of an old sloop long since past usefulness, lies on the shore cracked, seamed, dismantled and keeled over. She has a history, for once she smuggled goods for the old Russian magnate, Carl V. Baronovick, and carried many a goodly cargo through the intricate water-ways which it did not pay to watch. Out in the stream the U. S. sur- veying steamer lies at anchor, with every thing taut and trim and her brass aglow with polish, like the " knocker of a big front door." She has done lots of work on the coast, and marked out the intricate and dangerous channels with tripods and can-buoys. Some twelve miles off is a Hydah village—one of the few to be found in Alaska—which excursionists sometimes visit for the collection of curios. Its head chief, " Scowl," who was quite a celebrity in his day, died two years ago, leaving a good house and an hon- orable pedigree, vouched for by no less than four totem- poles set up inside, and a tall one in front, outside, made of yellow cedar, which grows abundantly in the vicinity, and is exceedingly beautiful, taking a finish like satin wood, with an odor as distinctive as that of sandal-wood. At Salmon Bay the steamer stopped at another cannery to receive some three hundred barrels of salted salmon, and again at Naha Bay, near which there is a beautiful lake

connecting with the ocean by a tidal passage, into which
the salmon were crowding to spawn.   There is a double fall
at the outlet of this lake ; the fresh water pouring out when
the tide is low, and the salt water flowing in when the tide
is high.   Here the salmon were wedged so tightly for the
whole length of two miles that they could not move at
times.   The rise of the tide is some eighteen feet and the
entire channel, from the surface to the bottom, was jammed
and packed solid, so that if a plank were laid upon the living mass, a person might have walked dry shod across it.
This is hard to believe, but easy to understand when it is
known that during the salmon "run," from early spring to
August, the vast schools which swarm along the shores and
fill the bays and inlets, swim in compacted masses six feet
thick, so that it is impossible to thrust a spear or lift a boat-
hook without impaling a fish.   In rivers of Oregon the
salmon often obstruct a ford so that horses can not pass,
but in Alaska the astounding aggregate is infinitely greater,
and large rivers being few, they crowd into available inlets
as frightened sheep were never known to block a gangway.

   Juneau, or Harrisburg, is the metropolis of Alaska—a
town of several streets and shops, stores and restaurants, with
a trading-post, a dance-house, a brewery, a barber-shop, and
a dramatic company.   It is the depot for the rich placer
mines behind the mountains back of it, and the live center
from which radiates whatever of excitement there is in the
territory, outside of " government circles " at Sitka.   Gold
ore was first discovered on Douglas Island, opposite, where
there is to-day in operation the largest stamp mill in the
world ; but it has since been found to exist in paying quantities on the main-land in the mountains back of Juneau.
An Indian revealed the secret, for a consideration, to two
prospectors named Harris and Juneau, who at once staked
out claims and began to pan out pay dirt and nuggets of free gold handsomely.   The town is named for each
of them respectively, though the post-office is now called
Harrisburg.   It is growing rapidly and is orderly.   The
miners themselves are temperate, industrious, and well-
behaved, and are gradually gathering around them a community of good citizens.   One of the best of the miners,
Michael Powers, with two others, was unfortunately killed
last winter by an accidental cave in the " basin " where the
placers are being worked.   The population of Juneau in
winter, when the mines are idle, is fully 1,500.   The laborers
employed are chiefly Indians, with a few Chinese.   There
are two villages of Indian huts built along the shore, one

on either side of the town. They belong to different tribes who are traditional enemies—the Auks and the Takus—but they live amicably enough with the white settlement sandwiched in between them. Fleets of canoes ornament the sloping shores in front of the cabins, and wolfish dogs, brindled and yellow, with bushy tails and pricked ears, doze and loll in front of every door. As a general rule their bark is not dangerous. Beyond these dusky suburbs there are burying grounds, with strips of white and colored muslin tied to the tips of poles to indicate the graves, which would otherwise be lost in the teeming undergrowth that overruns them in a single season. It is a motley throng which crowds the wharf on "steamer day," but not altogether so savage as might be imagined. It is purely cosmopolitan, and one may land and move about the throng or through the streets of the town and not be stared at as he would be in any equal village of New England. It may be accepted for granted that there is not a white man in all the lot as "fresh" and "tender" as the tourist who supremely contemplates him with his eye-glasses, quite aloof. All of them have "traveled." Some of the stores are branches run by leading merchants of Oregon and San Francisco, and I doubt not one could find the latest cut of trowsers at the tailor's shop. Baths there are, hot and cold, and shaving-parlors with veritable black men behind the chairs, quite comfortable and luxurious to observe and enjoy. There were no less than five negroes in Juneau last year. Verily, the African is as widely scattered as the Israelite! Here the tide falls twenty-five feet, and when it is dead low water all the piles of the wharf stand out in stark alignment, crusted with barnacles hung with sea-weed and bored by teredos. So destructive is this well-known sea-worm that piles have to be renewed every two years at a great deal of labor and inconvenience, and it is not unusual to find them actually eaten in two below the water-line. A ferry boat runs half hourly from Juneau to Douglas Island, where there is a saw-mill and a considerable settlement connected with the stamp-mill and ore-beds. In the center of the harbor is a pretty island, with a point stretching out from the mainland half the distance to meet it, on which there is an artificial marble monument. Back of the point is a ravine with a goodly stream tumbling out of it in a series of cascades, discolored with the tailings of the sluices back in the mountains which have contributed to swell its volume. Up the timbered slope which skirts it a precarious foot-path leads to the "basin," along the edges of steep precipices and through thickets of "devil's club" and luscious salmon-berry bushes.

From Juneau to Chilkat and Pyramid Harbor, so called from a wedge-shaped island in the center of the channel, it is a twelve hours' run. Here are the two largest salmon canneries in the territory, together employing over one hundred hands. From this place a novel excursion may be made in canoes or boats to the Chilkat village, where the famous blankets are made. This tribe numbers a thousand souls at least. The women are expert manufacturers of baskets and mats, as well as blankets. The first are made from grass and the dried fiber of sea-kelps; the blankets from the wool of the mountain sheep and goats, woven by hand and dyed with native dyes in strangely wrought designs of blue, black and yellow. These are chiefly used in dances and on fete days. From Chilkat to Kilisnoo is the next stage. Here there is a cannery and phosphate works—phosphate made from the scraps of herring after the oil is extracted.

With a run through Lynn Channel to Glacier Bay, where a day is passed in viewing the greatest wonder of the coast, and thence through Cross Sound, we finally reach Sitka, which is usually the terminal objective point of the long voyage, but is really a considerable distance on the home stretch, accomplished by a long detour to the northward, for Sitka lies in latitude fifty-seven degrees, while Chilkat is in latitude fifty-nine degrees, thirty minutes. In the gray of the early morn we can faintly discern the spectral summit of Mount Edgecumb right before us, and trace the dusky out-lines of the rambling town, the outlying islands, and the hull of the *Pinta*, U. S. man-of-war lying restfully at anchor a few cables length from the government pier.

Thus hastily touching at points of interest, I have attempted to give the tourist a general idea of what he is to see. In a general way also, he will like to know what to take for the voyage. Presumably he will not require an evening dress, even should a ball be given at the "Castle of the Governor." Indispensible, however, are great-coats and gossamers, heavy shoes, warm underclothing, and short skirts for ladies, as well as light wraps and thin garments of all sorts, traveling caps, and stout canes for glacier-climbing. Those who are fond of fishing and hunting may carry shot-guns and tackle for both salt and fresh water use. A blue-fish outfit, with heavy sinker, and a black-bass rod, with reel and line, will be sufficient. Steamer chairs may be bought at any port before leaving Victoria, and a half-dozen books will afford exceptionable pastime. Finally, if the officers of the line would only provide a steam launch, forty feet long, with a compound engine, to burn both wood and coal, and half a dozen skiffs for trolling, the service would be quite complete, and the passengers correspondingly happy.

KLOOTCHMAN'S.

There is undoubtedly a tendency on the part of enthused and susceptible visitors to turn the bright side of Alaska always toward the light, for surely there was never scenery more grand, or climate more delectable. From the first of June to the end of September, throughout the whole excursion season, the temperature is equable. One needs not perspire without exercise. He is always cool and needs never be cold. Morning fogs burn off by ten o'clock ; rain seldom falls ; there is scarcely wind enough to fill a sail ; and the headway of the steamer makes a grateful breeze. On shore there are few insects or flies, no reptiles, and scarcely a butterfly or beetle. The whole excursion of fully 2,000 miles is one long blithesome holiday without a blemish. The thermometer ranges imperturbably and conscientiously between sixty degrees and seventy degrees.

Looking back over my past sojourn on the North Pacific, and my saunterings along its extended coast, I am at first bewildered by the retrospect. Remote from other men, and from evidences of the very existence of men, except when intermittent glimpses are vouchsafed, I seem to have been adrift in a new creation, such as is sometimes outlined in our dreamland. I am lost in the height of the mountains, the depth of the sea, and the immensity of space. Every thing is on so enlarged a scale that there is no familiar standard of comparative measurement. When I stand in the heart of the Rockies I am impressed by the environment of mountain chains and snow-clad peaks. I am appalled by the rugged grandeur of their height, and the interminable depth of their cañons and chasms. The senses are crushed and oppressed by their overwhelming weight. But in this archipelago of mountains and land-locked seas, objects individually so magnificent in themselves as to startle the senses are multiplied and reduplicated until they paralyze one's comprehension ! Looking forward from the deck of the steamer, through a long vista of headlands, whose clear-cut outlines are set against the sky in graduated shades of blue, I see a *chevaux de frise* of snow-

capped peaks so high that Mount Washington or White
Top would seem like hills beside them. Astern, or on
either side abeam, the same stupendous view looms up in
wondrous counterpart. Between the wave-washed foot-hills
in the foreground close at hand, the sea is placid like a
mirror, and all the gigantic firs which clothe the mountain
side, the scores which the avalanche has made on the rocks,
and the waterfalls which fall from perpendicular heights,
higher than Yosemite, are pictured there in sublime reflections. At night the glory of the stars and constellations is
repeated from infinite heights to infinite depths, and the
round, full moon seems regent of the whole universe. In
land-locked basins, so small that the ship could scarcely
turn, great whales disport, and all the battles of the brine
are fought, like combats in a prize ring. It is funny to see
whales playing in what seems to be a mountain lake, and, of
course, all the sea lions rear up on the adjacent rocks and
smile. Occasionally there are nights when the crests of all
the waves are luminous, and the lustrous phosphoresence
piles up under the prow in lumps of liquid light, and streams
off in the receding wake of the vessel. Looking over the
bow, a watchful eye will detect large fish darting aside to
avoid the advance of the vessel, leaving the scintillations
and curves of fire as they double and turn. The passengers
watch these submarine pyrotechnics by the hour.

Points and curves, headlands fiords and bays, sea-worn
rocks and wooded islets, rocks and reefs awash at low water,
narrow channels ·and precipitous heights, towering peaks
and shadowy valleys, luxuriant forests and kelp-covered
shores, waterfalls projected from dizzy heights, glaciers
pressing toward the sea, and splitting off with thunder
tones and roaring splash—these characterize the scenery
and the landscape throughout the entire voyage. Occasionally an Indian village of huts or tents is seen on shore, or a
canoe load of natives sweeps by under pressure of blanket-
sail and paddle. Of course, throughout this extended
coast-line, there are many islands of many different
phases—some of them mere rocks, to which the kelps
cling for dear life, like stranded sailors in a storm ;
while others are gently rounded mounds, wooded with
fir ; and others still, precipitous cliffs standing breast
deep in the waves. Steaming through the labyrinths
of straits and channels which seem to have no outlets ;
straining the neck to scan the tops of snow-capped peaks
which rise abruptly from the basin where you ride at anchor ;
watching the gambols of great whales, thresher-sharks and

herds of sea-lions, which seem as if penned up in an aquarium, so completely are they inclosed by the shadowy hills—one watches the strange forms around him with an intensity of interest which almost amounts to awe.

In this weird region of bottomless depths, there are no sand beaches or gravelly shores. All the margins of mainland and islands drop down plump into inky fathoms of water, and the fall of the tide only exposes the rank yellow weeds which cling to the damp crags and slippery rocks, and the mussels and barnacles which crackle and hiss when the lapping waves recede. When the tide sets in, great rafts of algæ, with stems fifty feet long, career along the surface ; millions of jelly fish and anemones crowded as closely as the stars in the firmament ; great air bulbs, with streamers floating like the long hair of female corpses ; schools of porpoises and fin-back whales rolling and plunging headlong through the boiling foam ; all sorts of marine and mediterranean fauna pour in a ceaseless surge, like an irresistible army. Hosts of gulls scream overhead, or whiten the ledges, where they squat content or run about feeding ; ducks and sandpeeps, eagles, ospreys, fish-crows and kingfishers, the leaping salmon and the spouting whales, fill up the foreground with animated life. Here and there along the almost perpendicular cliffs the outflow of the melting snow in the pockets of the mountains leaps down in dizzy waterfalls. From the cañons which divide the foot-hills, cascades pour out into the brine, and all their channels are choked with salmon crowding toward the upper waters. I could catch them with my hands as long as my strength endured, so helpless and infatuated are these creatures of predestination. At the heads of many of these rivulets there are lakes in which dwell salmon trout, spotted with crimson spots as large as a pea; the rainbow trout with its iridescent lateral stripe; and his cousin germain, the ‘cut-throat trout,’ slashed with carmine under the gills. And there is another trout, most familiar to the eye in eastern waters, and doubly welcome to the sight in this far-off region—the *Salvelinus Canadensis* or ‘ sea trout,’ which I have recognized these many years as a separate species. Here he is in his garniture of crimson, blue and gold, just like his up stream neighbors of New England and the Provinces, only here he is no “ brook trout run to sea,” for all the denizens of Alaska brooks are *Salvelinus irideus*, and not at all like him! and no naturalist claims that these last two are identical.

Sometimes we cross the mouth of a sound open to the sea, where the full force of the Pacific waves rolls in to swell the symphony of the inshore surf. There is a stretch of thirty miles across Queen Charlotte's sound, and of fifteen miles at Millbank, where even in ordinary weather passengers show the effects of the motion ; but these disagreements are brief. Some of the cloud effects are very grand, stretching, as they do, for scores of miles half-way up the mountain sides, overhanging the peaks or piled on top. Sometimes a blue pyramid or cone will be seen projected above a mass of clouds which has obscured the whole landscape, just as the glory appeared to Jacob when he slept. Fogs are of almost daily occurrence. In the chilly mornings the hills are wrapped in a thick mantle, and all the little foothills are cuddled like bantlings in the fleecy vapors ; but when the warm sun mounts, the fogs disappear and the day comes out almost cloudless.

After all one can not epitomize Alaska in a brief synopsis or *resumé*. There it stands before you in its inimitable wilderness of forest-clad mountains, eternal and snow-capped, outlined by the clouds and circumscribed by the sea : and one scarcely knows more of what lies on the surface of the one than under the billows of the other. The marvelous and the amazing are combined with startling effect wherever we go. Many of the wonders of the Yellowstone country are reduplicated here. We have in Alaska hot springs, lava beds and volcanoes as well; a volcano on Chernabura island, Cook's inlet, is said to be in active and sulphurous operation ; and these together with the unique interest of Russian and Indian life added, and the apparently incongruous juxtaposition of arctic and tropical features, which are continually presented, render the experiences of the tourist so delightful, and so novel withal, that it needs no artificial adjuncts to give them expression, and no new lights and shades in the coloring to make them attractive. The answering mirror held up to nature reflects on every side a goodly picture. It forecasts a future replete with promise.

ECONOMICALLY CONSIDERED.

But what of Alaska that is practical? Is it frigid? sterile? God-forsaken? a land of perpetual ice? Will any thing grow there? Can any considerable population, apart from the coast, subsist on the country? Are the natives any less savage than the seals and bears they hunt? Are the traces of Russian occupation Siberian or barbarian? Did the Muscovites leave any thing at all which Uncle Samuel wants? Is there any gold or other mineral there? Any thing which the Creator does not regret having made? In a word, is our new possession good for any thing at all, except for another " National Park ? " a resort for tourists and mid-summer ramblers? I answer in my preface with a broad declaration, and with equal emphasis on the title page.

Years ago, when we gathered in the Louisiana purchase for the sum of $15,000,000—a tract in itself nearly as large as Europe—there were immense areas of it which were deemed absolutely worthless; and these were set off, in the transaction, against the more fertile tracts, with their diversity of climate, soil and vegetation. Especially, that very considerable portion of it which is now known as the Territory of Dakota—although a population of more than half a million have made it the peer of any state in every thing but privilege—was disregarded; it "didn't count." On the maps it was marked " American Desert." At the best, in the opinion of merely superficial observers, it was only an illimitable buffalo range, rainless and treeless, whose russet-colored grass dried up in June for lack of moisture, and was worthless. Now it is the most valuable and productive portion of the entire Louisiana purchase; capable of feeding the world with grain; subsisting domestic herds as countless as the buffalo which once grazed over its broad expanse; munificent in its out-put of precious metals; underlaid with coal measures which form the subsidiary reserves of the region lying west of the Mississippi River; seamed and interspersed with out-croppings of the finest building stone yet discovered; flowing with milk and the richness of its dairy products. Even the " Bad Lands " which were designated pre-eminently so, in contradistinction from others esteemed not quite so bad, have become the chosen grazing ground of herds which supply the East with beef, and of horses which bid fair to rival the swiftest and sturdiest stock of Kentucky and Vermont. So far from being sterile, the soil of the " Bad Lands " has been proved actually better for general farming than the heavy tenacious loam of the Red River Valley, just because it is lighter.

Not less erroneously regarded was the illimitable territory of the British Northwest, whose agricultural possibilities are now ascertained to be co-extensive with her boundaries. This impression of incapacity was founded on its hyperborèan situation. But practical men who had to deal with practical measures, upon which the very life and perpetuity of the Canadian Dominion depended, went forward in advance of the projected railroad through the country, and ploughed and planted at intervals of every twenty miles, to test the quality of soil and climate; and when without tillage or protection, the answering grain came up in bounteous profusion and ripened before the autumn frost, no better assurance of the future was desired ; and now the directors of the Canadian Pacific Railroad confidently predict that the new Northwest will have fifty millions of people a century hence, with capacity to feed themselves and the rest of the world, if need be. Indeed, it seems incredible, and altogether unaccountable, to those who infer that the climates of all high latitudes are rigorous and inhospitable, to read in the current newspaper telegrams of the day, that spring wheat-sowing commenced at Maple Creek on February 4th, 1886, six hundred miles west of hyperborean Winnipeg, on the same parallel of latitude ; that the temperature ranged from fifty-four to fifty-seven degrees at Fort McLeod during the corresponding week ; and that the trains of the Canadian Pacific Railroad were all running on time through the snowdrifts of the mountain division.

Maple Creek, lying at the east base of the rocky mountains, feels the influence of the Chinook winds which are wafted from the warm bosom of the Kuro Siwo, or Japan current, although they have to pass over four great mountain ranges—the Cascades, Gold, Selkirk and Rockies, each of which helps to cool and condense the atmosphere—whereas access to the interior of Alaska is obstructed only by the single barrier of the coast range.

I have traveled over a great part of the British Northwest and British Columbia, and have read the official reports of their geological surveys, railway engineers, Hudson Bay officials and Indian inspectors ; I have gathered together all the facts I could find in books, and listened to the tales of miners and traders, and old settlers whose lives have been passed in the *ultima thule ;* and I have supplemented the whole with the observations photographed on the eye ; and having gotten together all this testimony, and discovered that the physical features of this vast region and Alaska are much alike with each one's advantages and objections reciprocally counterbalanced by the vagaries of isothermal lines, I am prepared to believe that Alaska is worth all that was paid for it, and to predict that in due course of time it will surprise the expectations of its purchasers more than despised Dakota or the Northwest has done. The elements of wealth pervade it ; they are through, above and around it.

Misconceptions of the productive capabilities of a country spring from imperfect diagnosis. No mere superficial observation will suffice ; no hasty conclusions predicated' upon general appearances. Nothing but a thorough examination of the soil, flora and fauna will furnish testimony of an absolute character that can be relied on Dakota was condemned because her summer rain-fall was meager, and the dry and arid appearance of every thing contrasted most unfavorably with the verdant green of eastern localities. The Northwest was condemned for like reasons—with the inferential objection of high latitude added ; but there were hidden influences underneath the soil, begotten by the very conditions which seemed adverse, that served to counteract them. The book of nature was left wide open, but men neglected to turn its pages. A high latitude is very naturally suggestive of cold, but in the code of climatology latitude is less arbitrary than isothermal lines. Even in countries truly frigid there is a season of respite from inexorable congelation. Most people imagine Iceland to be ice-clad and ice-bound the whole year round, and yet its summer lawns are verdant with rich grass, and the meadows are spangled with buttercups and daisies ; pigeons congregate upon the house-roofs, and the cows come home from pasture with the same straggling gait as the kine of other lands. Nine-tenths of the children at school believe the Arctic zone to be a realm of perpetual darkness and intolerable frigidity without a break, and would hoot with incredulity if told that its inhabitants swelter in the heat of her mid-summer sun, and that nothing but its brief duration prevents a high development of ver-

dure.   But, compared with Alaska, the blessings and
fruition of other northern lands in either hemisphere are
insignificant—British Columbia alone excepted.

Of course the modifying influence of the Japan Current,
or Pacific Gulf Stream, which projects its vast volume of
tepid water athwart the Aleutian Isles, is already well
understood, but the results one sees there are hard to realize, and the reports we hear are listened to as mariners'
tales.   The effect of this warm current is equivalent to
twenty degrees of latitude, that is to say, the same products
which are found in latitude forty degrees on the Atlantic
thrive in latitude sixty degrees on the Pacific, which is
but little north of the location of Sitka, and on a scale far
more generous.   Fruits, vegetables, plants, and trees are
not only of greater size, but their yield is manifold, though
it is fair to say, that the quality of flavor is not always as
good.   Oranges, which do not mature in the East above
the latitude of Port Royal, S. C., grow to perfection in
Shasta, California, in latitude forty-one degrees, which is a
little higher than the latitude of New York City. Shasta also
produces cotton, limes, soft-shell almonds, and superb
prunes.   By the same ratio of climatic progression, tomatoes,
musk-melons and grapes ripen in the latitude of Victoria,
but better back of the coast-range than on the seaboard,
because of the higher temperature and immunity from exces-
sive fogs and rain.

The influence of ocean currents in distributing heat
throughout the globe, and especially of the warm currents
which modify the climate of the polar regions, is set forth
very intelligibly in Croll's *" Climate and Climatology,"* published by the Appletons.   By that influence, places which
are now buried under permanent snow and ice were once
covered with luxurious vegetation, and arctic regions
enjoyed a comparatively mild and equable climate ; and
vice versa.   Hitherto this influence seems to have been
enormously underestimated.   Really, the amount of heat
borne north by the Gulf Stream, whose volume and temperature have been ascertained with an approach to certainty,
is computed to be more than equal to all the heat received
from the sun within a zone of the earth's surface extending
thirty-two miles on each side of the equator.   Or, in other
words, as a little calculation will demonstrate, the amount
of equatorial heat carried into temperate and polar regions
by this stream alone is equal to one-fourth of all the heat
received from the sun by the North Atlantic from the
Tropic of Cancer up to the Arctic Circle.   But there

are other great oceanic currents, especially the Kuro-Siwo,
which, though not yet subjected to as careful mensuration,
are believed to convey as much heat poleward as the Gulf
Stream.   Evidently, then, comparatively slight changes in
the oceanic circulation would increase or decrease glacial
conditions.   The severity of climate, in Mr. Croll's view, is
about as much due to the cooling effect of the permanent
snow and ice as to an actual want of heat.   An increase in
the amount of warm water entering the Arctic Ocean, just
sufficient to prevent the formation of permanent ice, is all
that is really necessary to make the summers of Greenland
as warm as those of England."   It is obvious that a large
decrease in its temperature and volume would lead to a state
of things in northwestern Europe approaching to that which
now prevails in Greenland.   The causes which he assigns
for changes in the volume and temperature of ocean currents, he declares are actual and explicable, and by no
means based on mere hypotheses ; all of which are set forth
in a most intelligible and interesting manner in the volume
referred to.   Briefly epitomized, they may be stated in Mr.
Crolls own words, as follows :

" The causes of these changes may be found in physical
agencies, stimulated or checked by changes in the eccentricity of the earth's orbit, provided the heat-transferring
power of such agencies is suffered to be operative by such
geographical conditions as now exist, and which there is
not an atom of evidence for believing have been materially
altered since the glacial epoch.   It is unnecessary to postu-
late the submergencies or the elevation of continents, or the
existence of extra inter-continental channels, transporting
northward additional heat currents, and thus contributing to
ameliorate the climate of the pole.   The geographical conditions and the physical agencies which actually exist are amply
sufficient to account for all the facts.   When the eccentricity
of the earth's orbit is at a high value, and the northern winter solstice is in perihelion, agencies are brought into operation which make the southeast trade-winds stronger than
the northeast, and compel them to blow over upon the
northern hemisphere as far probably as the Tropic of Cancer.   The result is that all the great equatorial currents of
the ocean are impelled into the northern hemisphere, which
thus, in consequence of the immense accumulation of warm
water, has its temperature raised and snow and ice to a
great extent must then disappear from the Arctic regions.
When, contrariwise, the precession of the equinoxes brings
round the winter solstice to aphelion, the condition of

things on the two hemispheres is reversed, and the north-east trades then blow over upon the southern hemisphere, carrying the great equatorial currents along with them. The warm water being thus wholly withdrawn from the northern hemisphere, its temperature sinks enormously, and snow and ice begin to accumulate in temperate regions."

Mr. Croll is also at pains to show that the mean interval between two consecutive interglacial periods (correspond-ing to the time required by the equinoctial point to pass from perihelion round to perihelion) is not, as is commonly assumed, 21,000, but 23,230 years. At intervals, therefore, of from 10,000 to 12,000 years the north pole will experi-ence the extreme of cold and the extreme of heat compat-ible with the coincident geographical conditions, and with the coincident eccentricity of the earth's orbit, the latter factor being ascertainable from Croll's tables.

The final result, therefore, to which Mr. Croll would lead us is that those warm and cold periods which have alter-nately prevailed during past ages are simply the great secu-lar summers and winters of our globe, depending as truly as the annual ones do upon planetary motions, and like them also fulfilling some important ends in the economy of nature.

It is needless to say that in a country as vast as Alaska the climate varies greatly ; but taken as a whole, it is more moderate and equable than that of any region of a corres-ponding latitude west of the Rocky Mountains—enjoying summers cooler, and winters much more mild. On its mountains there is perpetual snow, but not perpetual cold. There are large tracts of country where the mean yearly tem-perature is higher than that of Stockholm or Christiana of Europe, and where it is milder in winter, with a less fall of both rain and snow than in the southern portion of Sweden. Along the southern seaboard, which is the most habitable portion, the average temperature is forty-two degrees, with a common range between the zero point and a maximum of eighty degrees. Winter breaks up in March. Even in January, showers, such as we of the north have in April, alternate with the sunshine of May.

John J. McLean, the U. S. Signal Officer at Sitka, has kindly furnished me the following synopsis of meteorological data for the winter of 1885–6.

Date.	Mean Temp.	Precipitation inches.	Max. Temp.	Min. Temp.
Nov. 1885.	40.2	9.65	50.	29.5
Dec. "	36.8	11,70	50.5	30.5
Jan. 1886.	29.2	7.36	48.	4.
Feb. "	37.1	18.84	52.5	24.

In the region fully subject to the influence of the equatorial current, flowers bloom and vegetation remains green and
bright the winter through, with only a temporary suspension
for rest and recuperation, and there is little save the
almanac to remind the stranger that winter is in transit,
though the native knows it from the increased rainfall. The
warm air coming off from the Gulf Stream meets the colder air
from the north and evokes precipitation, more abundant on
the main land coast than on the islands, or in the interior.
And it is this steaming moisture which clothes the mountains
to the height of more than a thousand feet with their dense
growths of spruce, pine, alder, hemlock, and cedar. But it is
not always calm and mild and delectable in that region ; for
the Custom House officer who keeps his lonesome watch at
the tumble-down post at Tongass, which is the southernmost
limit of our possession, tells how the winds begin to blow
about the 1st of November and sometimes hard enough to
upset the crow's nest at the look-out, and whisk the shingles
off the roof. Frequently he is weather-bound for weeks,
and once he did not taste fresh meat for four months. In
mid-winter snow sometimes falls as deep as four feet, an
immense precipitation, but it seldom remains unmelted for
more than a fortnight, and the temperature rarely falls to
zero. In January, 1886, it reached five degrees, the coldest
of the season for many years. Capt. L. A. Beardslee, commanding the U. S. Steamer, *Jamestown*, on the Alaska Station, in his official report for 1879, made at Sitka, mentions
the appearance of robins, sparrows and buntings in March,
with ducks flying north. He gives four hundred and sixty-
nine hours of blue sky out of a total of seven hundred and
forty-four hours for the thirty-one days of the month. In
April about one day in seven is cloudy. The summer up to
September is uniformly dry, with an equable temperature.
September temperature is sixty degrees in the shade, and
seventy degrees in the sun, with a good deal of rain generally. It is these early rains which prevent the ripening of
grains on the coast. Cereals would do better in the interior
despite the short summer. All kinds of vegetables mature

on the coast, and potatoes grow large and keep through the winter as seed for the next year's planting. As testimony to the dryness of the climate, the captain says : " Our guns (vessel of war) do not suffer as on our own coast." Halibut and herring fishing occurs in April. Salmon fishing begins May 1. Coots, teal, widgeon and sprigtail ducks arrive in September ; canvas-backs and mallards in October; geese fly in November.

A great deal more has been written about Alaska than the public imagines. A whole library of information is available among the shelves of the Smithsonian Institution at Washington, and all the traits and industries and social life and religious belief of its peculiar peoples are illustrated in the cabinets of the U. S. National Museum. The reports of Prof. Dall alone, whose research covers a period of seventeen seasons in Alaska, published under Government auspices, afford such explicit information that no one need be ignorant of its capabilities. But such valuable emanations as Government reports and " pub. docs." are usually consigned to the archives, to be presently forgotten, or perhaps exhumed in exigency for special reference, while the imperfect and baser effusions of irresponsible contributors find universal currency. Mr. Bancroft, in his exhaustive " History of Alaska," comprising seven hundred and fifty pages, has also given us all the information which research can unearth, from the earliest discovery of the country to the present day. The volume comprises a most valuable and authentic repertory of facts, geographical, historical and economical, coast-wise and in-board, all of which are sufficient to demonstrate and prove that the difficulty to be encountered in the agricultural development of Alaska, is not a climatic one, but rather lies in the extremely rugged and mountainous character of that portion which is most salubrious and accessible, rendering the agricultural areas comparatively small and remote from each other. It can not be conjectured that the far-off interior will be available for generations, except for the very limited local demand which may possibly arise from the fortunate discovery of mines. Notwithstanding the habitable and cultivable modicum is relatively but little, it is of far greater extent and importance than would be supposed by those who fail to appreciate the magnitude of the territory as a whole; and it must ever be borne in mind that the area of Alaska is greater than that of the original thirteen states, and poor indeed must be that plat of earth, so magnificent in sweep and superficies, which does not contain the value inherent

of $7,500,000, the equivalent of the "Seward Purchase."
What real or tangible foundation is there for the impression
that it can not decently support more than a handful of
population, when other countries, which resemble it in
climate and character, support large numbers ? The con-
tributory causes of a false impression have already been
hinted at in the preface of this volume, and will presently
be made more clearly to appear.

In the latter years, with the discovery of the fertility of
our illimitable prairies and their boundless capacity for
grain, men's ideas of farm dimensions expanded in proportion, until an area of less than 10,000 acres came to be
regarded as small. But the era of bonanza farms has now
passed away ; the great wheat fields are being subdivided ;
mixed industries are being introduced, and with constantly
diminishing areas it will be possible presently to conceive
of a farm no larger than those they have in Scotland or
New England ; and a country may be considered agricultural that is not wholly an alluvial level destitute of trees and
stones. Nay, it may even come within the grasp of thought
to imagine acres tucked away in the folds of the Alaska
mountains or spread out like blankets upon the waste terraces of the upper Yukon. No lands were ever more fruitful than the hill counties of Judea, where the desert
encroached very nearly upon the fertile tracts, and there
are few countries where the climatic conditions are better
adapted to diversified crops than the mountainous seaboard
of Alaska. With regard to its local or indigenous products,
let me recite the testimony of Captain Beardslee, of the U.
S. Navy, given in 1879, soon after his arrival on the station,
to wit : "We have been here three months, and during that
period have been plentifully supplied with a variety of good
vegetables, among which have been radishes, lettuce, car-
rots, onions, cauliflower, cabbage, peas, turnips and potatoes, and have a prospect during the coming month of beets,
parsnips and celery, all of which look well in the gardens.
The cauliflower and cabbage are as good as I ever ate ; the
potatoes are just coming on, and are not quite ripe yet. I
had this day (Sept. 17th) at my dinner, a potato grown here
which was seven inches long, three inches thick, and weighed
one pound five ounces, and it was one of many I have seen
which would average from one-half to three-quarters of a
pound in weight. Its flavor was good, and I shall, as do
all other people here, depend upon this market for my
winter's supply. There are many small gardens which
return crops, as in all other countries, in proportion to the

care and skill displayed in their cultivation. I have seen plenty of 'the watery walnuts dubbed potatoes,' but they came from gardens belonging to people so excessively pious that they trusted God for every thing, and put in no work themselves. Some of these gardens are over a single acre in extent, and have supplied good crops annually for quite a while. On Japonski and Biorka, and Survey and other islands there are hundreds of acres which could be cultivated with profit, if the population were great enough to furnish customers. On Biorka, an island about twelve miles from here, there is now under cultivation a thriving vegetable garden of several acres, and these acres have been under annual cultivation for some years. So we eat and grow fat, when we thought to have had short commons."

The captain is writing at Sitka, two hundred and forty miles up the coast from the southernmost boundary of the territory, where the climate may be supposed to be less favorable to perfect maturity of esculents. There are some good vegetable gardens at Wrangell and Tongass. Mr. and Mrs. Young, who have charge of the mission at Wrangell, have a ranch of 1,600 acres at the mouth of the Stickeen River, on which they have successfully raised barley and oats, but that is ninety-five miles southeast of Sitka. At the village of Haines, further up the Stickeen, there is another good ranch. Red raspberries are cultivated at Tongass. In the stores at Wrangell, I have seen fine potatoes on sale in the month of August ; but these were not raised on the coast, but up the Stickeen River, one hundred and fifty miles back in the interior. As a matter of fact, the whole coast region is so like a vapor-bath or hot-house, that vegetation grows too exuberantly. There is no room for it, and indigenous plants crowd the economic products. If you fence a garden, or a grave-plot, the fence disappears from view the second year among the overgrowth. The same vegetable phenomena pertain to the interior, but there the summer temperature is inordinately higher, the skies are cloudless, and the supply of moisture derived from the reeking sub-soils and underlying strata of ice, abundantly sufficient. Wild hops, wild onions and wild berries grow in profusion; crab-apples, gooseberries, currants, black and red whortleberries, raspberries, cranberries, strawberries, red and white salmon berries (like raspberries, only four times the size), checker berries, pigeon berries, and angelica, furni•h the native fruit supply. At berries we have to draw the line between Alaska and Southern British Columbia, which can supply the Dominion with choicest apples, pears,

plums, peaches, grapes, cherries, etc.   One curious feature
of Alaska vegetation is that nearly every flower is succeeded
by a berry.   In the same latitude of Labrador on the
Atlantic side, the only solitary fruit is a little yellow berry,
locally known as " baked apple," which grows among the
grass and lichens ; and spruce sticks, no more than eight
inches in diameter, illustrate the best forest growth.   Why
don't the Canadian Government remove its two thousand
pinched and starving population from Labrador to British
Columbia at the public expense?   They would earn their
transportation in a year.

As stock raising is the remunerative complement of every
well constituted farm, it could be prosecuted by the Alaskan granger with marked advantage.   Certainly the climate
is vastly more propitious than in Northern Minnesota and
Dakota, where the grazing of fine sheep and the best
blooded cattle is now prosecuted with signal profit.   Like
the bonanza wheat fields of the Northwest, so the illimitable
cattle ranges of the further west are being sub-divided.
Diversity of industry has become a necessity and a watch-
word.   Gradually the wheat fields and the cattle ranges
are over-lapping and dove-tailing into each other.   Very
rapidly the farmer of the West is driving the desert before
him.   The developments of each succeeding year make it
more and more obvious that the encroachment of the home-
steader upon the grazing lands can not be checked.   The
Denver Tribune says :—" Men have stood in line a hundred
deep at the Land Offices waiting their turns to enter land
upon which as little rain falls as in the most arid spot east
of the Rocky Mountains.   If this move can be made to
pay them it simply means that all the plains will be homesteaded within a few years.   It means that the large herds
will disappear and that the lands will be fenced by their
real owners.   In short, it forebodes another change in the
evolution of the arid cattle-grazing business greater than
any that has gone before."

Finally when all the land is homesteaded, men will look
to Alaska.   And why not?   Says Bancroft :—" Grasses
thrive almost everywhere on the low-lands.   Kodiak is a
good grazing country, capable of sustaining large droves of
cattle.   On the Aleutian Islands trees do not grow, but the
grasses are luxuriant."   Lieutenant Schwatka in his report of
the interior, speaks enthusiastically of the upland meadows
and the grass-grown bluffs.   Capt. Beardslee says :—" I am
not sufficiently posted in the mysteries of a granger's profession to undertake to speak very positively as to the num-

ber of stock of any kind which any given amount of land would support, but that there is land here which will support some stock, I will also prove by facts. * * * While the army was here Japonski Island was used as a stock ranch. There has been kept on it as many as sixty head of cattle, over one hundred of sheep, and over three hundred of hogs ; all of which obtained their own food for a much greater portion of the year than they could have done in any state north of Alabama ; and there was no difficulty in getting good hay. Twelve miles north of here are the Katliansky and Nesquasarisky bays and plains, which, having been planted with timothy some years ago by a settler named Doyle, furnished to the troops an average of sixty tons of good hay, cured during the heated spell of July, when the temperature goes up into the nineties ; and this year those who cut a little for their own supply estimate that there was at least one hundred tons. In the immediate vicinity of Sitka there are three thousand acres of arable land, much of which is now well grassed and covered with white clover. And on the summits of some of the foot-hills there are plateaus now covered with wild grasses, where innumerable deer obtain pasturage and where goats and mountain sheep would thrive."

These references are to limited areas which have come within a circumscribed scope of observation. They illustrate the coast region, just as arable places illustrate Switzerland ; and Switzerland is a good country, if not strictly agricultural. With regard to the Yukon River country, Captain Wm. H. Dall, of the United States Coast Survey, says, in his report made to the Commissioner of Agriculture in 1867 :—" Among the more valuable grasses, of which some thirty species are known to exist in the Yukon territory, is the well-known Kentucky blue grass, which grows luxuriantly as far north as Kotzebue Sound, and perhaps to Point Barrow.

" The wood meadow-grass is abundant. The blue joint-grass (*Calamagrostis canadensis*) also reaches the latitude of Kotzebue Sound, and grows on the coast of Norton Sound with a truly surprising luxuriance, reaching in very favorable localities four or even five feet in height, and averaging at least three. Many other grasses enumerated in the list of useful plants grow abundantly, and contribute largely to the whole amount of herbage. Two species of *Elymus* almost deceive the traveler with the aspect of grain-fields, maturing a perceptible kernel which the field-mice lay up in store.

"The grasses are woven into mats, dishes, articles of clothing for summer use, such as socks, mittens, and a sort of hats, by all the Indians, and more especially by the Esquimaux.

"In winter the dry grasses, collected in the summer for the purpose, and neatly tied in bunches, are shaped to correspond with the foot, and placed between the foot and the seal-skin sole of the winter boots worn in that country. There they serve as a non-conductor, keeping the foot dry and warm, and protecting it from contusion.

"Grain has never been sown on a large scale in the Yukon territory. Barley, I was informed, had once or twice been tried at Fort Yukon, in small patches, and the grain had matured, though the straw was very short. The experiments were never carried any further, however, the traders being obliged to devote all their energies to the collection of furs."

Respecting the Aleutian islands, he states that "The climate is better adapted for haying than that of the coast of Oregon. The cattle were remarkably fat, and the beef very tender and delicate ; rarely surpassed by any well-fed stock. Milk was abundant. The good and available arable land lies chiefly near the coast, formed by the meeting and mingling of the detritus from mountain and valley with the sea sand, which formed a remarkably rich and genial soil, well suited for garden and root-crop culture. It occurs to us that many choice sunny hillsides here would produce good crops under the thrifty hand of enterprise. They are already cleared for the plow. Where grain-like grasses grow and mature well, it seems fair to infer that oats and barley would thrive, provided they were fall-sown, like the native grasses. This is abundantly verified by reference to the collections. Several of these grasses had already (September) matured and cast their seed before we arrived, showing sufficient length of season. Indeed no grain will yield more than half a crop of poor quality (on the Pacific slope), when spring-sown, whether north or south.

"The Russians affirm, with confirmation by later visitors, that potatoes are cultivated in almost every Aleutian village ; and Veniaminof states that at the village in Isanotsky Strait they have raised them and preserved the seed for planting since the begining of this century.

"Wild pease grow in great luxuriance near Unalaska Bay, and as far north as latitude sixty-four degrees."

There is no trouble about wintering cattle and sheep in Alaska. Old traders have declared to me that the

musk-ox exists in considerable numbers in the northern
part of the territory, especially near the British boundary
line, on the other side of which, in the vicinity of
the Mackenzie River, Northwest Territory, they are quite
numerous ; and although some naturalists strenuously in-
sist that it does not, and never did, exist in Alaska, there
seems no reason why the Rocky Mountain range should
constitute an insuperable obstacle to their transit. There
are several fine specimens of the musk-ox in the United
States National Museum, all of which were obtained
in the Mackenzie River country, but there are none
from Alaska; so that bodily proof is wanting. On
the other hand we read in Lieutenant Schwatka's
article printed in the *Century Magazine* in 1883, that
the range of the musk-ox is from latitude 60 degrees
to 79 degrees, and from the Rocky Mountain divide, westward, almost to the Behring Sea. The native
mountain sheep and goats of Alaska weather through the
inclement winters without sheds or cotes, or any shelter but
the dense undergrowth which chokes every gully and ravine.
Domestic utensils and ornaments are made by the natives
from the horns of each, and the latter animals are in such
abundance as to furnish wool for quite an extensive manufacture of blankets and clothing. Wool-growing should become an important industry in Alaska, as it is in Oregon ;
and better, for the atmosphere there is not so damp. Last
summer a single train of twenty cars loaded with 438,000
pounds of wool was made up at Portland for Philadelphia,
and this was only a fraction of the product of the State. So
fine is the texture of the fleece of the Alaskan Mountain
goat, that the meanest homespun Chilkoot blanket fetches
twenty dollars. There is not the shadow of a doubt that
these animals can be easily domesticated, and the wool
product made immensely profitable. The very fact of their
preference of location by the wild goats and sheep show
that there is no portion of America more favorable for ovi-
culture than the ridges of Alaska, while the numerous herds
of cariboo, moose, and deer, away up on the plateau of the
Yukon, testify with equal favor of the moors and moss-
barrens of the interior. What subsists one class of animals
should subsist its kin.

In addition to the farming and herding, large supplementary revenues should be derived from the dairy, the
poultry-yard and hog-pen. Indeed, butter, eggs, beef, pork
and poultry should be always staples. A pork-packing establishment might become an indispensable institution of

the coast, if one could only guarantee the flavor—as the hogs feed greedily on the sea-castings, growing enormously fat.   Silk culture might be prosecuted, and also the culture of sugar beets.   Alaska ought to manufacture her own sugar.   A current newspaper paragraph states that the factory at Alvarado, California, made 1250 tons of refined beet sugar last season.   The Alvarado factory has been in operation six years, and its profits are computed at $104,-000 on an investment of $125,000.   The growers get $4.50 a ton for beets, and the yield is said to average twenty tons to the acre.   The factory pays out about $90,000 a year for beets.

Here are some Sitka market prices for the summer of 1885 : Venison 5 and 10 cents per pound ; a six pound salmon 10 cents ; grouse, per pair, 50 cents ; sugar 18 cents ; medium butter 75 cents the roll of less than two pounds ; eggs 50 cents per dozen ; a cabbage-head 25 cents ; new potatoes one dollar per bushel.   Some goats are kept for milk.   There is not only good land all along the coast, but plenty of it fit for cultivation of all the produce that there is likely to be a market for during many years to come.   The present population of Southwestern Alaska, according to the report of Gov. Swineford, is, whites, 1,900 ; natives, 7,000.   For the whole Territory the most reliable estimate is 30,000.

The timber forests of Alaska are a standing testimony to the value of the "Seward Purchase," which   even the most obstreperous objectors could not deny.   The visible wealth of Alaska lies in her forests.   Alaska is the great timber reserve of the continent.   Trees of such size and commercial value exist nowhere else on the globe in such numbers and extensive areas of growth.   There is a supply here of five thousand seven hundred million feet at a low estimate, a very large part of which is at once accessible for shipment, as saw-mills and vessels can lie right alongside the timber at tide-water, all the way up the coast as far as it extends.   Saw-mills at two or more prominent points on the coast ought to pay well, for lumber is very high. If prices were less, the Indians alone would purchase large quantities.   The first sawmill ever set up in South America was by a citizen of the Unitrd States, who went to Ancud, Chili, in 1828, and it laid the foundation of his great wealth, accumulated there.   The example might be followed here. We are approaching a time when the resources of the Union will be overtaxed, and timber will be scarce; but when all the states are drained of their product, there will remain in Alaska a virgin reserve of more than 300,000,000 acres of the noblest timber in the world—a source of wealth upon which the people may draw for generations to come. All the islands are clothed with it; the mountains of the adjacent main-land are covered with it; great areas of the interior plateau, which reaches to the verge of the Arctic sea, are untracked wildernesses of spruce. Only when people who are now strangers to the land and listeners to the story come to see the magnitude of these forests, and the stupendous individuality of their giant trees, will they be able to realize the truth of what is told them. The lumber-men of the old states, whose lives have been passed in logging camps, would stand appalled at the majesty of the Douglas pines, which tower heavenward, and whose diameter is nine feet at the base; or the famous red cedars, out of which the Indians make their dug-out canoes, some of them sixty feet in length with eight feet beam!

Alongside of some logs which one finds prone, the choicest cull of the Wisconsin and Minnesota drives, would look like fence posts. Beside standing trees, the tallest rampikes of the Maine forests resemble saplings. Here the alders grow to a diameter of sixteen inches, and an ordinary maple leaf has thirteen inches span. Rankness characterizes all the growth. But the trees are not all gigantic, or the forests all unscathed. The bulk of the forest trees are of ordinary height, say seventy feet or so, and the giants are distributed throughout at neighborly intervals, occupying the low-lands between the shoulders of the mountains; but many of the angular hill-sides along the coast fairly bristle with the skeletons of dead spruces, which have died from dearth of nourishment among the rocks; the survivors meanwhile drawing life from their decaying remains. As in all known forests frequented by man, fires have here run through vast areas of the wilderness, starting from carelessness of hunters and trappers, causing conflagrations whose smoke obscures the sun for months together. It is sad to contemplate the great destruction; yet some of the forests of Alaska are over-populous. Time was, I ween, when the only smokes seen in the distant view were the signals of the tribes who wished to communicate with each other; some for the purpose of barter, some to intimate the presence of intruders; some to indicate the direction to be taken, or a point of rendezvous. Sometimes the signal was a big smoke, at others only a thin spiral; again there were two or three adjacent, some large, others small, with many variations adapted to the information to be conveyed. These

Indian signals were almost as perfect as the crude symbols of our army at the beginning of the war, before they were formulated into a fixed code.

Commercially considered, the trees of Alaska rank as follows : Yellow cedar, spruce, hemlock, alder and a species of fir or black pine. The Douglas pine, which is so abundant in British Columbia and possesses the chief commercial value there, is replaced in great part in Southern Alaska by the white cedar, a splendid finishing wood, out of which the Indians carve their totem poles or heraldic columns. The red cedar grows in special abundance on the lower coasts, and extends inland to the Rocky Mountains. It is in great demand because of its durability. Of it the Indians make their canoes, roofing their houses with the bark and weaving the fiber into blankets. The cypress or yellow cedar is found in southern Alaska. It is susceptible of taking a very fine polish, and considered valuable for boat-building and finishing purposes. It sells for $80 per thousand in San Francisco. It possesses a delightful odor, which like camphor wood it retains for a long time ; and, manufactured into boxes and chests, is very valuable for packing furs and other goods, as it is said to be a moth preventive. It is also extremely tough, and proof against the teredo sea-worm, and for this reason is in demand for piling and all submarine purposes. Samuel's *West Shore Magazine* supplies the following list of the principal trees of British Columbia, nearly all of which I believe are common to some portion of Alaska, but not all of equal perfection in the higher latitude : —

" Juniper, or pencil cedar, found on the east coast of Vancouver Island, and on the shores of lakes in the interior. The Weymouth, or white pine, (*Pinus strobus*) found on the Lower Fraser, where it attains great size and beauty. The balsam pine attains a vigorous growth, but is of little value as timber. Yellow pine, (*Pinus ponderosa*) flourishes in the interior. The wood is close-grained and durable, though very heavy. Scotch fir, (*Pinus Bankskiana*) is found in the interior ; also on Vancouver Island, though of a smaller growth. Throughout the lower coast the hemlock, (*Abies sitkensis*) grows to large proportions, its bark being exceedingly valuable for tanning purposes. The western larch, (*Larix occidentalis*) grows to immense size in the bottoms along the international line. The yew, (*Taxus brevi-folia*) is found on the coast and as far up the Fraser as Yale. It does not attain the size of English yew. The natives utilize it for bows. Oak, (*Q Garryana*) grows abundantly on Vancouver Islands. It is tough and service-able. Alder grows along the streams of the coast, and attains great size. It is useful for furniture. Maple is abundant on the islands and coast up to latitude 55 degrees. The wood is very useful for cabinet making. Vine maple, a very strong white wood, is confined to the coast. Crab-apple grows along the coast. Dogwood is found on Van-couver Island and opposite coast. The aspen poplar is found throughout the interior. Another variety of poplar abounds along the water courses near the coast, and is the kind so much in demand on Puget Sound for barrel staves. Two other kinds of poplar—all known as "cottonwood,"—as well as the mountain ash, are found in the interior valleys."

The white spruce is the most widely distributed of Alaska trees, covering the country inland to the Rocky Mountains and up to the very shores of the Arctic Ocean on the north. The white birch is also abundant in the interior, and is used for canoes by some tribes. The cottonwood is found on the upper Yukon, where it is used for navigating its rough waters. Manifestly, there is in Alaska a great variety of merchantable woods which are available for new uses, and new woods which may be substituted for others nearly used up commercially. I am fully convinced of the great value of what is there unrecognized and unappreciated, but which we can not afford to ignore or overlook any longer.

Some of the mosses of Alaska are of special economic value. They have long been utilized by the natives in various ways. Within twenty years the tree-mosses of Florida, Texas, and Louisiana have become important articles of commerce, chiefly as substitutes for curled horse hair in the manufacture of mattresses, cushions, etc., and the mosses of Alaska are equally desirable and available for like purposes. The supply is practically inexhaustible, and when it is contiguous to the coast it may be gathered without great labor.

The impenetrable jungle of the Alaskan forest, with its windfalls of timber and profusion of wild fruit and succu-lent mosses, constitutes an incomparable nursery and pro-tection for its fauna, while the open ridges above the timber line are no less secure from man's intrusion by the natural obstacles interposed. Assuredly, there is no place on the continent where wild animals enjoy such perfect immunity from harm. It remains by its natural gifts the only great game and fur preserve left in the western world, and stands ready and wide open for the operations of intrepid hunters and trappers at the very time when other sources of supply

have been drained, and denizens of cold countries are looking about them for substitutes for buffalo robes and the
more costly furs which have now at last become priceless or
extinct. American furs are becoming scarcer every year as
civilization pushes into the wilds. Oregon, which within
the memory of men not old, was one of the finest of hunting
grounds, has practically ceased to yield any thing of the
kind. Washington Territory is only productive in its wilder
portions, and the same may be said of British Columbia.
Alaska, however, remains almost intact, and not only the
lucrative seal isles of Prybilov, but all the fastnesses of the
coast range, the "barren grounds" of the great plateau, and
the banks of the great rivers flowing into the Arctic Ocean,
still make it worth the absorbing attention of the fur trader,
and the trapper. The stock of good merchantable fur is
neither abundant nor cheap in Alaska; but squirrel robes
containing six or seven dozen skins neatly sewed together
may often be bought cheap at the Indian "ranches." They
make excellent cloak and coat linings. A red fox skin
costs two dollars; mountain goat fifty cents; black bear
from ten to twenty-five dollars unmounted. Hair and fur
seals range in price, undressed from three to ten dollars;
sea otter from ninety to two-hundred dollars—the most
expensive of all American fur and the most desirable.
Land otter is very pretty, and at one of the Sitka stores a
shoulder cape and muff made up in San Francisco was offered
at twenty-five dollars. The Russian occupation, which was
founded on the fur trade and enriched itself for a century
on its profits, withdrew from the field before the lead was
half worked out, nay, scarcely opened! The Hudson Bay
Company was long ago attracted to the country by its
inducements, and attempted to secure a foothold in it by
establishing trading posts on the upper Yukon as far back
as 1850, crossing the Rocky mountain divide from the head
waters of the Mackenzie; but they were soon driven out by
the Chilkoot Indians, the most energetic and business-like
of the coast tribes, who had been for generations the self-
constituted middle-men between the seaboard and the interior; and the interior of Alaska has since remained an
unoccupied field for the pursuit of an industry, which for a
century enriched a masterful corporation and made it almost
a sovereign power. If the brave spirits who started the
Northwest Fur Company of years ago, and whose survivors
are now few and hoary, could renew their youth and energy,
they would ask no better opportunity for business than
the one now so opportunely presented, with transportation

made easy and bases of supplies convenient, the natives not
only friendly but earnestly disposed, the cost of outfit cheap,
and a market more remunerative than was ever offered
before.   It is true that an enterprising company—now
known as the Northwest Fur Company—has within a comparatively short time, established trading posts at Chilkat,
Sitka, Wrangell, and other points along the coast; its
methods are business-like and progressive, and its policy
liberal; but it will take an army of traders to fully occupy
the field; and so I repeat, it practically remains unoccupied.   The successes of the Hudson Bay Company, through
the protracted period of its sovereignty, are an earnest of
the resources which are held in reserve in the Alaskan fur
lands; and inasmuch as its earnings reached millions annually, who dare say that the " Seward Purchase " is not
as good as gold? How long before our government will
awake to realize the truth?

With regard to the mineral resources of Alaska whose
richness is rapidly coming to view with their development,
I have chosen to devote a separate chapter.   I will merely
pause to mention that the total out-put of Alaska mines for
the year 1885, is officially placed at $251,000.   This amount
is 3½ per-cent on the purchase price of the territory.

The most lucrative and best known industry of Alaska, is
the seal " fishery," so called, though the animals are usually
driven upon the land and knocked on the head with clubs.
For the exclusive privilege of catching seals, not to exceed
100,000 in number per annum, the Alaska Company of San
Francisco, pays to the goverment the stipulated price of
$317,000, every year.   When the lease expires in 1890, it
will have paid into the United States Treasury $6,340,000, a
sum equal to six-sevenths of the original purchase money.

With regard to the possibilities of the Alaska Commercial
fisheries, they may be regarded as simply illimitable. Fish are
so abundant everywhere, that a dime will at any time procure
from a native all the fish that ten men can eat.   Halibut
banks, cod-fish banks, and rock-cod bottoms, occur at intervals all along the coast.   Salmon jam the rivers and tidal
estuaries so that they can not move, in masses many yards
wide and as deep as the normal rise of the tide (18 feet)
from the surface to the bottom.   In their spawning season
candle-fish, or caplin—beautiful fish some seven inches
long, like smelts—line the beaches at each flood-tide in
windrows a yard wide and several inches deep, all
alive and kicking, each incoming wave stranding a host
of them.   Herring swarm in all the estuaries and channels.

All the inlets abound in fish of a hundred known and unknown kinds, good for food and good for oil and fertilizers. Whales and blackfish are plentiful off the coast and in the estuaries. There is wealth here for all who will spread their nets or cast the hook. Devastating storms and periodical dearth of fish do not make the fishing business too hazardous to undertake. Starvation never threatens. Our Cape Anners and Gloucester fishermen who breast the hardships of the Atlantic, will here find a more congenial climate ; spring opening with fulsome benefi- cence in early March ; fish swarming into every estuary and congregating on every outlying bank in ample season for Lenten market ; herring, cod and halibut enough to sat- isfy an eternity of Fridays. There labor stands already provided—men, native Indians accustomed for many gener- ations to the perils, intricacies and abounding munificence of the sea coast ; men, intelligent and industrious, waiting with open arms to welcome any enterprise which will give them congenial and profitable employment ; men of dusky hue, and strong sinews to breast the waves and haul the seine and heave the ponderous halibut and rock cod from their sequestered depths, who have *already*, of their own motion and energy, established canneries and oil factories along their sea-girt home ! Here on this boundless Pacific coast, where Yankee and Kanuck have each a thousand miles of scope, no questions of jurisdiction or marine pre- rogatives need arise ; whispers of awards and claims will be lost in the sounding surf ; dissensions and jealousy will be drowned in the overwhelming flood of fortune ; and no one will have to wait on the flow of tide. All the vessels of the coast-guard will be impressed for holiday jaunts among the clustering islands, and moods and tenses of men and tempests will remain symbolically " pacific." Should the attachments of home be too strong for the sturdy New Englanders to cut their latch-strings loose altogether and deter them from migrating for permanent establishment on new cruising grounds, the annihilation of time and distance by modern facilities of transcontinental transportation will make each trip and periodical sojourn little more than an annual holiday excursion. Compared with the precarious ventures of their progenitors who flocked to the North Atlantic fishing grounds before the early days of colonial settlement, their new departure would be a bagatelle—a mere reflection of personal hazard and commercial risk.

Out in Alaska every thing which is required for this stu- pendous industry grows spontaneously—an abundance of bait without cost ; all materials for building and cooperage; ice for packing, salt for curing, if it can be evaporated profitably, and twine for nets and seines, which is supplied by the gigantic kelp, a hundred feet in length, whose fiber is too tough to break. At no distant day ice from her glaciers will be harvested for consumption in lower latitudes, just as it is now gathered in San Rafael Bay, in South America, for refrigerating uses in Chili and equatorial towns. Some enterprising company will establish a set of piers or breakers in the bays where the glacier streams debouch, with flumes and machinery for squaring the ice for stowage in cargo ; and among the ice, packed in galvanized iron cases inclosed by wooden crates, fresh fish will be dispatched on ten-knot steamers to lower ports, and thence perchance to eastern cities where Pacific salmon have long been the precursors of the coming traffic. Thus a combined industry may secure a two-fold return from the capital employed. The rapid drift of time will see all these things accomplished, for men will not be content to grub when they can possess bonanzas for the gathering. Glut of labor will return no more " like a dog to its vomit," nauseating the whole industrial system ; but the surcharge will flow into the open channels of our new possession, and, with the relief that must follow, the present pressure will measurably cease to aggravate distress. Capital will prefer to invest where it is least liable to disturbance, and in Alaska the field is broad, the laborers few, and the branches of industry new and almost untried. But, while we are listless, the citizens of British Columbia seem fully awake to the opportunities which lie before them, and appreciate the importance of their undeveloped resources, so very like our own in kind and quantity. Already they have steamers running to all essential points up the rivers and along the coast to the international boundary line. They have established numerous industries, thrown open public lands to settlement, civilized the Indians and instituted schools for them and sumptuary laws. We have no need to try a single economic or political experiment. All this they have done for us, and we have only to profit by the outcome. Even the Indian problem, so difficult in the east, has been most satisfactorily demonstrated, as may be attested by their well-regulated and self-governed native communities, and by the public commercial records which show that the majority of fishermen, especially in the northern canneries, are Indians,* who are expert and reliable

---

* Chiefly the Hydahs and Shimpsheans.

and are preferred to any other kind of labor. On the steamers they are employed almost exclusively for roustabouts, and are paid higher wages than white men, because they can do more work and are more reliable and steady.

What a blessed word of encouragement this is to our home philanthropists! In this very department of fisheries, the authorities have taken advanced steps to attract that class of immigrants which, if the movement should become popular, must transfer a large share of the fishing interests of the Maritime Provinces to the Pacific coast. The laws of British Columbia are very liberal to those engaging in the fisheries, for they accord to all persons the right to use any vacant public property for the purpose of landing and curing fish. The Dominion Government, too, has promised valuable assistance to immigrants, and it is stated that a very considerable number of Lower Province fishermen will this year avail themselves of the inducements offered. If our neighbors now forestall us, the blame will be our own, for sagacious men of far-reaching perspicuity have been constantly pointing out our golden opportunities and instructing us how to improve them. In the matter of public lands, the Canadian law provides that any surveyed or unsurveyed crown lands not already occupied or recorded, may be entered, either as a pre-emption or homestead, by any head of a family, widow, or single man over eighteen years of age, who is a British subject, or an alien who has declared his intention to become such. An alien can transact business and hold real estate. The price of land is $1.00 per acre.

Side by side with this progressive policy, and as between two countries lying side by side and equally endowed by nature, we find that in Alaska there is no way provided by which a home may be procured. The territory having been ceded to us by treaty is not subject to pre-emption, and Congress has been most dilatory in providing means to remove the disability, or in enacting remedial laws. There has been an unwarrantable neglect of Alaska ever since its purchase in 1867, and the only wonder is that there has been any development at all. Not until the autumn of 1884—seventeen years after its purchase—was it represented by a Territorial governor ; and up to date of the present incumbency, which took place in September, 1885, no fruitful or serious endeavor was known to have been made by the territorial administration to use the large discretionary powers conferred on it for the advancement of the people, or the improvement of the country's natural capabilities. To the enterprise of large private companies is due the prosecution of the seal fisheries, and the gold mines, to which of late considerable attention has been directed. For the application of individual capital and labor there is as yet but small encouragement. Nevertheless, two negro men of nerve (praise to the race!) under stress of local pressure, have instituted a very creditable barber shop at Juneau.

Bancroft's "History of Alaska" has summarized the general situation in a nutshell : "A country where there is no commerce, where there are few industries, where there are no schools except those supported by charity, where no title can as yet be gained to land, where there are no representative institutions and no settled administration, does not hold out any very strong inducements to emigrants. Although in name a civil and judicial district, Alaska is still, in practice, at this time—almost nineteen years after its cession—little more than a customs district."

However, within the past twelve months, a good deal has been accomplished toward providing for the educational interests of the Territory, and under an act, or acts, of Congress which appropriated some forty thousand dollars for the purpose, common schools have been established at seven or eight points, as well as an industrial school at Sitka ; other schools have been authorized to be established at as many more points.* The present governor, too, upon taking possession of the not too stable seat of government last fall, at once undertook the establishment of a weekly paper there, through whose columns have been periodically disseminated truthful statements respecting the country and its needs and prospects, whereby the public mind is being prepared for the wholesome change which is anticipated in the not distant future. In his first official message to Congress he earnestly pressed upon their attention the importance of immediately instituting an efficient police system and water patrol, of opening trails or roads from the coast to the headwaters of the Yukon River, of fixing the boundary lines beyond dispute, and increasing the mail facilities. He also recommended high license as the best device for correcting and checking the evils of a defiant and unwarrantable liquor traffic. And he sent a commissioner in the winter to New Orleans, with native exhibits for the Exposition, the collection embracing, according to the catalogue, specimens of gold-bearing quartz, coal, iron, and mica ; logs of spruce, yellow cedar, pine, alder, and fir, together

---

* The Sitka public school has fifty pupils, boys and girls.

with polished boards and cubes of the same woods ; salmon,
cod, rock cod, sea trout, sea bass, arctic trout, etc., preserved in alcohol ; wheat, oats, timothy, clover, red-top,
blue-joint ; potatoes, turnips, cabbages, cauliflowers, etc.,
together with wild fruits and berries in hermetically-sealed
glass jars, articles showing the handicraft of the native
Alaskans, and interesting curios.   Subsequently, in May
just past, he appeared in person before the Territorial Com-
mittee of Congress, at Washington, to urge all that he had
previously suggested and prayed for.   The governor is
obviously a live man, and enthusiastic, and well qualified to
promote and guard the interests of his official charge.   His
principal appeal is for the privilege of local legislation ; and
it ought to be a sufficient assurance and encouragement to
us to know from our Canadian neighbors that " under wise
local legislation the Province of British Columbia has pros-
pered greatly, despite the neglect which it [also] long suffered at the hands of the home government, which could
neither appreciate the value nor understand the needs of
that far-distant dependency."   So admitted the Earl Duf-
ferin.   And as our territorial neighbor has done, so may our
new possession.

The southwestern portion of Alaska, in particular, is a
region so desirable that efforts have been repeatedly made
within the past half century by the British or Canadian gov-
ernments to acquire it by absorption or purchase.   During
the Crimean war schemes were afoot to wrest it from Russia, and as late as 1878, in the Dominion Parliament, while
the question of the boundary between Alaska and British
Columbia was under consideration at Ottawa, the Hon. Mr.
Bunster said :   " Honorable gentlemen might laugh, but
looking at the matter from a national point of view, he fully
meant what he said from his knowledge of the country, that
the Territory of Alaska possessed a more genial climate
than Ottawa, notwithstanding its latitude, while its natural
resources and capabilities were more valuable than people
had any idea of.   When honorable members of this house
sneered at Alaska, he had a right to speak from his own
personal knowledge and tell them they were mistaken ;
and the day was not far distant when, from the geographical position of this country, they would see the force of his
remarks on this subject.   The lease of Alaska was more
than enough to pay one million dollars annually. It was the
best investment the United States had ever made."

At present there are scarcely a score of people who are
aware what a revenue it brings, and what far greater income

is likely to accrue, and those who read or listen to the governor's testimony smile with incredulity! But it will hardly take "a generation," as Secretary Seward believed it might, for the people to learn the truth. Lots of excursionists and "*che-chah-cos*" (new comers intending to settle) will visit there this year. Every steamer's complement will be filled, from June to September.* Among the most observing and sagacious are to be Chief Justice Waite, of the U. S. Supreme Court, and Associate Justice Gray, and these we may be sure will judge correctly and report honestly. Whatever prejudiced or incompetent persons may say to the contrary, Caleb and Joshua will be believed.

* The May steamer to Sitka took three hundred prospectors to Sitka and Chilkoot.

STONE TOTEM-POLE (HAIDAH)

AN INTERIOR VIEW.

Alaska is an *ultima thule* only to those who live far from it. This is no more paradoxical than the fact that proximity always makes objects seem near. Alaska is a friendly and familiar neighbor to all the dwellers of the North Pacific, and the people of Port Townsend and Victoria think no more of the bi-monthly run to the Alaskan boundary than New Yorkers do of a trip to Boston. The departure of the bi-monthly mail for Sitka attracts less attention than the sailing of a Cunarder for Great Britain. Vancouver passed this way and northward a full century ago. Up to 1793 the Spaniards disputed with the English for the possession of the coast. The shores of British Columbia have been settled for half a century at least; fur-traders and miners have long kept it in a state of constant activity. So also Alaska is not a new discovery; neither is its interior a *terra incognita.* It has been known to the Russians throughout its length and breadth for nearly a century, and to the Hudson Bay Company for forty years or more. Voyagers, trappers and hunters have traversed it in every direction, but geographical explorers have known but little about it. There are Indians who have grown gray in the business of freighting goods across the mountains into the interior, over the very trails selected by the government parties who have been exploring the Yukon within the past three years. As much as eight tons of merchandise have been packed over tne Chilcat trail alone in a single season, and there were some eighty men in the brigade. There are lots of old residents, American-born, who are competent to speak of the resources of the entire country from personal acquaintance with it. There is Alex. Choquette, of Wrangell, a French Canadian trader, who has dwelt in Alaska for twenty-eight years, and speaks all current languages, and the dialects of all the tribes, having mingled constantly with them. King Lear, a native of Ohio, also living at Wrangell, has been a sojourner in the territory for nearly as long, and so has Capt. George, formerly of Massachusetts, who married a sister of the Russian priest at Sitka, and now serves as coast pilot for the regular steamers ; and so has Dick Willoughby, of Juneau, once of Virginia and now famous as a proprietor and mining expert. He has tramped the interior all through for hundreds of miles back, and knows every quarry, ledge, and stringer of quartz from the coast to the "Stewart." Tom Haley, of Sitka, an old soldier, has been prospecting since 1872, and has located a dozen gold "finds" during the interval, to which I shall refer at length. From such hardy men as these, weather-stained and self-informed, some of them settlers before the civil war, authentic and comprehensive information could be obtained at trifling expense in lieu of fitting out costly government expeditions, whose best use is to verify current reports and establish facts upon official data.

The United States Fishery Commission has of late years stimulated investigation of marine objects by enlisting the co-operation of sailors and fishermen at large, with the result that not less than 60,000 specimens have been collected by them, and thirty new varieties added to the list of North American marine fauna. Their interest and activity has been stimulated by honorable mention and an occasional intrinsic token of merit. By like methods, equally simple and inexpensive, the government might enlist the aid of all miners, traders, voyageurs and Indians penetrating to the interior of Alaska. It should have an agent at all outfitting points to give instructions, present inducements and furnish maps and diaries for entering each day's observations—meteorological phenomena, the contour of the land, the quality of soil, the streams and their courses, and all plants, trees, animals, birds, fish, rocks and minerals should be scrupulously noted and the dates given. The Northwest Trading Company, who are the successors of the Russians, but whose views and policy are liberal and progressive, have warehouses at all principal points, which would constitute efficient bases of future operations under some such method as has been outlined. The establishment should be in charge of some officer of the signal service to be stationed at Sitka, who would also furnish tabulated statements of daily meteorological reports. Such weather statistics would be invaluable in determining the capabilities of the country whatever they are, and define the precise limit and duration of the seasons.

However, the value of authorized expeditions should in nowise be belittled. The public will build with confidence upon official guaranty. Lieutenant Schwatka's exploration of the Great Yukon Valley from its headwaters to its

mouth, an intrepid voyage with no visible base of supplies or succor in the last emergencies ; the arduous journey of Lieutenant Henry T. Allen, across the " Alaskan
Range," in the 145th Meridian, from the headwaters of Copper river to the sources of the Tenana, a great tributary of
the Yukon, 500 miles in length ; the winter residence and
researches of Lieutenant G. M. Stoney, in the Northern district of Alaska, along the rivers which empty into the
Arctic Ocean ; and the indefatigable investigations of
the Hon. James G. Swan, whose remarkable collections
enrich the United States National Museum ; all these, covering such an extensive area, attest the heroism of modern
science and the economic benefit therefrom derived, immediate and deferred. The published results of these investigations have as yet appeared only in part ; the total
will give final proof of their collective value. Newspaper
writers who visit Alaska fall into the habit of repeating
what some careless scribblers have placed on record, so that
erroneous opinions hastily formed upon insufficient data
soon become a popular impression. Transient visitors to
the coast, who observe the snow peaks and the glaciers,
delight to fancy themselves in regions hyperborean, and invest them with a romance of the most frigid character ;
hence misapprehension. Says one writer : " Flood the
cañons, gorges and plains of Colorado and you have Alaska."
This might satisfy a view of the Archipelago from the apex
of Mt. Edgecumb, but it will hardly apply to the great
Yukon plateau, which is as broad as the Dakota plains from
the Mississippi River to the Black Hills.

It is in no respect remarkable that knowledge of the interior has never come to the exterior light until now. It
was not for a long time in the interest of the Russian Fur
Company, until necessity subsequently modified their policy,
to encourage prospectors and miners, nor immigration and
settlement, because the Russian government reserved the
right to take away from it the control of any land in which
mineral deposits were found. Wherefore maps and facts
were kept secluded from vulgar curiosity, specimens of ore
were kept locked up in iron chests tighter than they had
ever been in the rock-ribbed pockets of the earth. At the
same time the Chilcat and Chilkoot Indians, who maintained
a monopoly of trade between the coast and that part of the
interior drained by the upper Yukon, were not only jealous of
white intrusion, but protested to Captain Beardslee, of the
United States navy, that " the white men demoralized the
Indians by selling or giving them liquor and debauching

their women." They naturally discouraged all investigation and took pains to represent the interior as " kultus "
—worthless, sterile and unprofitable. They were not only
reticent, but evasive, and when closely questioned were very
clever always in devising a substitute for the truth. And all
this time the Yukon River, which is the great water-way and
thoroughfare of the interior, traversing its entire breadth,
was lined with Russian trading posts and native villages as
far up as the Tenana River, a thousand miles or more from
its mouth ! There was a British trading post as far up as
Stewart River, five hundred miles higher, in the year 1851,
notwithstanding a current newspaper paragraph declares
that an Indian tribe has been found there recently who never
before saw or heard of white people ; and miners had
pioneered the way in search of gold for a considerable distance down that portion of the river which lies still higher
up and nearer its source.

Following Lieutenant Schwatka in his voyage over this last
mentioned section of the Yukon, which comprises a stretch of
500 miles, and referring to his record, we find one log-house
located in the lake country which feeds the mighty stream,
and from whence a trail only thirty-five miles long leads
over the intervening coast range to the sea. Thence to Fort
Selkirk, which marks the terminus of the first fluvial division, two native villages were found, one at Nordenskjold,
and the other at Kittahgon. In the next interval from Fort
Selkirk to Fort Yukon, five hundred miles more, he enume-
rates the following settlements :—

1. A populous Ayan village, situated a little below Selkirk, whose people were conspicuous for their " Hebrew
cast of countenance," and were " respectably neat and clean
compared with Indians in general." They use birch bark
canoes, and in summer occupy brush houses constructed
with a ridge pole—in winter moose-skin tepees or lodges.
They cure large quantities of salmon which have run up
the river to spawn.

2. On the opposite bank of the river another village
called Kowsk-hou.

3. At the mouth of Stewart River the ruins of an old
Hudson Bay Company's post.

4. An Indian camp of a tribe called Tahk-ong.

5. Old Fort Reliance, abandoned.

6. The Indian village of Nuclaco. These people had
many guns.

6. An Indian village of six log-houses with gable ends,
called Klot-ol-kin, or " Johnny's Village." These people

used canoes of birch bark and cured their salmon on scaffolds of spruce poles.

8. Charley's Village, the counterpart of Johnny's, with the same number of houses.

9. Fort Yukon ; a collection of tolerably well built houses, with stockade and block-houses. " For two hundred miles above and two hundred miles below Fort Yukon," Lieutenant Schwatka says, " the river flows through a region so flat that it seems like the floor of an empty lake. This area is densely timbered with spruce." The pale blue outline of the Romantzoff mountains are seen in the dim distance, far to the northward. The outlying spurs of the Alaskan range are seen to the south. The lower Yukon, a thousand miles in length, extends from this point to its delta in Bering Straits ; its banks all occupied by people.

10. An Indian village, a short distance below Fort Yukon.

11. An Indian burial-ground indicating the vicinity of a village.

12. Indian village above the " Lower Ramparts." This part of the river was picturesque and not unlike the Hudson at West Point.

13. Old town above Lower Ramparts.

14. Another town below Lower Ramparts.

15. Trading post of Nuklakayet, eighteen miles below Tenana River. A ten-ton schooner was found here.

16. From this point down enumeration becomes tiresome. There is a continuous succession of Indian villages, and small trading stations all the way, day after day, with chaloupes and fishing craft. Fish weirs are spread all over the river, which has become very wide, and shallow near the shores. A steam tug plies between places.

17. Town of Kaltag, near the ancient mouth of the Yukon, "the south bank being a simple flat plateau, though the north bank is high and even mountainous for a distance of more than four hundred miles further on."

18. The picturesque trading post of Anvic.

Just beyond Anvic, the last Indian village is passed, and about forty miles below it the Esquimaux Villages begin, of which there are many. Yet further down is a Russian Mission with a Greek church ; still lower the town of Andreavsky, near the head of the delta of the Yukon.

Koatlik lies at the river's mouth.

Two days' journey by steamer along the coast, northeast, is the picturesque seaport of St. Michael.

To sum up, the whole country covered by Schwatka's

interesting journey, and especially the lower river, is far more populous than most persons had any idea of. The estimate of the interior population is 2,000 all told, of which the Ayans, the Tahk-heesh, the Tahk-ongs, and the Tenanas are the principal Indian tribes, and chief fur collectors of the unsurveyed wilderness. These constitute the nucleus of a commercial strength and a potent factor of production which should not be disregarded by political economists. They do not require civilizing at an inordinate cost to the public treasury, after the foolish old method now happily becoming obsolete, but merely to be shaped and directed. They are not indolent, abject, and apathetic, but merely unemployed sufferers by a temporary commercial depression. Since Russia withdrew her fostering care they have patiently been awaiting the revival of business. If so much merchandise went into the upper river country in the days of the Muscovite regime, to be distributed all over the contiguous districts, what an increased traffic would result from the impulse of a new successful deal, with Yankee enterprise at the front and the stimulus of inevitable success constantly before it like a pillar of fire?

The territory of Alaska, is naturally divided into two immense districts, insular and continental; and the latter, owing to its vast area and mountainous interruptions is again subdivided into three districts with more or less distinctly defined boundaries and characteristics. The northern district, bordering the Arctic Ocean, and comprising a third, is principally a series of spruce timber flats and moss barrens, or "tundras;" the eastern division, lying between the coast range of mountains and the Rockies, is occupied by the broken and diversified country which is drained by the upper Yukon, presenting every contour of mountain, valley and plain. The southwestern portion, not including the Alaska peninsula, and the Aleutian Islands, is in large part a spruce timbered flat, but the "Alaskan range" of mountains, 500 miles or more in length, occupies its southern portion. The delta of the Yukon on the west coast, is an alluvial flat. The Yukon, itself, nearly as long as the Mississippi, almost bisects the territory. It lies midway between the Arctic and Pacific Oceans, flowing in a general east and west direction, but with a tremendous curvilinear sweep conformable to the outline of the coast, which carries it up through seven degrees of latitude into the very verge of the Arctic Zone. With its twenty or thirty great tributaries, it constitutes a vast fluvial system which drains almost the entire territory. Besides this, there are several large rivers like the Stickeen, the Taku, Suchitno, and Copper Rivers, which find their way to the sea through great gaps in the mountains, and others which drain the glaciers and the melted snows of the peaks. On the north shore are several large rivers flowing into the Arctic. The prevailing level of the great interior plateau is interrupted only by a few isolated mountains and mountain ranges, which lie principally in the southwest. It is a co-ordinate and extension of the plateau of the Columbia and the country south of it, between the same meridians, except that the arid sage and prickly pear of the latter are replaced in Alaska by boundless grass prairies and the so-called "tundras," on which the moss grows knee-deep, nurtured into rank exuberance by the constant melting under the fervid heat of midsummer of the omnipresent stratum of ice, which underlies it. In like manner the grain of Manitoba and the Northwest Territory is stimulated into a marvelous yield by the very instrumentality which wiseacres in the early period of investigation declared would kill it. And the interior of Alaska is much milder than the region which lies east of the Rockies in the same latitude, as every body knows. The conditions of prolific growth in high latitudes are continuous moisture, and a temperature sufficiently high and evenly maintained to constitute an equivalent for the longer seasons of lower latitudes where rainfall is insufficient. Maturity can be secured by a forcing process in half the time that is reached by natural operations where the temperature and irrigation are uneven. In the long days of an Alaskan midsummer the sun dips but little below the horizon, and Venus, the brightest star that shines, alone is visible at midnight. Between sunset and sunrise the warmed earth suffers no temporary chill, even though perpetual ice lies not two feet beneath. Cole's new system of subsoil irrigation, which is attracting such general attention, and shows such prodigious results, is merely an artificial application of the natural process in operation under the shadows of the north pole. It counteracts solar evaporation, supplying moisture to the growing plants as they need it, and becomes, as it were, the measure of the fertility of the soil. It is not unusual to find the ground frozen eight feet deep in northern Minnesota; and if it freezes a hundred feet deep in Alaska, what does it signify, more or less?

When the future requirements of settlement shall test the capabilities of the interior climate, it will undoubtedly be found as fruitful as Minnesota for all crops not requiring a long period of ripening.

TOTEM-POLES.

Lieutenant Schwatka says that luxuriant moss fields and great timber flats, densely covered with spruce, extend to the very verge of the Arctic Ocean. In his admirable report, which is more tropical than boreal in its coloring, he refers to these frequently, and to the great bands of caribou or reindeer which find pasturage on the tundra. He writes of grass-covered bluffs along the rivers ; of foot-hills, with an impenetrable underbrush of deciduous vegetation ; of vast expanses of treeless prairie, of thick black loamy soil ; of rank dead grass, which remains over until June from the previous year, looking like fields of yellow stubble. He speaks of thunder storms, of broods of young grouse early in June, of flowers on all sides, of cloudless skies and blistering sun, of wild hops and onions and berries in profusion, of myriads of great mosquitoes, which drive the game to the mountain slopes above the timber line, and other like phenomena altogether at variance with commonly conceived opinions of the territory. Up to the very headwaters of the Yukon and its lateral tributaries, the noble salmon run ; the adjacent lakes are filled with salmon trout, which reach ten pounds in weight, and all the brooklets teem with mountain trout like those of Montana ; in the long reaches of the Yukon itself, as well as in its fluvial feeders, grayling which weigh a pound may be caught in great abundance ; and if one will pass through the country in mid-summer, as Schwatka did, he will find brush camps and canvas tents lining the river banks at frequent intervals, where the Indians are curing fish for their winter supply ; and should he for any reason penetrate beyond into those vast tracts which white men have seldom trod, he will discover other Indians with stores of hides and pelts stripped from the scores of cariboo and moose which they have captured among the willow copses of the far-reaching " tundras," or perchance the skins of a few black or grizzly bears picked up accidentally beside some river bank or shore of lake—for the Indians fear to hunt in the tangles of the forest where the multitude of bears and the difficulties of the jungle make it unsafe to look even for small game ; and so they resort only to runways there, and the methods of the " still hunt." There is no use for hounds in the coverts of Alaska ; they might as well try to run through an osage hedge. The Indians use the reindeer or cariboo hide for clothing, dog-harness, and covering of tepees, or lodges ; and the very fact that so slight a habitation is a sufficient protection against the extremest rigors of the climate is evidence of its compara-

tive mildness; albeit the Indians of the lower river have
greater need of more substantial houses, which they build
like those of white folks, with boards riven from the helm-
lock and smoothed with adzes, thatching them with the bark
of cedar.   The tundras or moss barrens where they hunt
professionally, and except for daily supply, are similar to
the " muskegs " of northern Minnesota, and the adjacent
country—not wholly a growth of yielding moss, knee deep,
but interjected with thickets of willows and mingled with
rank, coarse grass which grows breast high ; sometimes they
are interspersed with cranberry bogs and patches of wild
roses, with here and there a slough or pocket of water, dyed
wine-color with the steepings of the dead leaves and mosses.
Walking over a tundra is like promenading a feather-bed.
This thick undergrowth of moss is found in all the forests
and above the timber line as well ; and a lady correspondent
of the *American Register*, of Paris, France, who is a botanist
and an impulsive student of the woodlands, has written :
     " The Alaskan forests are the finest, in a picturesque way,
in the United States.   Trees grow upright from prostrate
and dead trees, from the tops of stumps, and they are draped
with black and white moss, dry, fine, and crinkly, like hair,
which produce a most weird and Druidical effect.   Mosses
grow to a depth of from six to ten inches, and on the
top of stumps, dead branches, and every dead thing is
cushioned deep with moss and draped with vines.   Par-
ticularly does the *Cornus Canadensis* enwreath logs and
stumps in the most charming way."   All of which I hope
will corroborate what others say of the exuberance of
Alaska ; yet I think the tree mosses there can in nowise
compare with those of Florida or Louisiana.
     The upper portion of the Yukon valley, or rather the
entire region which the upper river drains, is spoken of as
almost a perfected Eden.   Flowers bloom, beneficent plants
yield their berries and fruits ; majestic trees spread their
umbrageous fronds, and song birds make the branches
vocal.   The water of the streams is pure and pellucid ;
the blue of the rippled lakes is like Geneva's ; their banks
resplendent with verdure, and with grass and shining peb-
bles.   Wherever the rocks lift up their crags they are
cushioned with luxurious moss.   Nature is enjoying a
grateful surcease from labor.   Lower down, in the middle
country, the creation is quite unfinished.   One can perceive that the processes of the glacial forces are still in
operation.   All the fluvial waters are white or milky with
the glacial mud washed down from the sluices of the out-

lying chains of mountains, where the Titanic pulverizers of
their rocky flanks are yet industriously grinding. Like the
muddy Missouri into the limpid Mississippi, pours the
impetuous White River into the Yukon, with a current so
swift that it sends its discolored waters, chalky with the
debris of the glaciers nearly across the other streams,
changing its sparkling blue into an element which even the
fish avoid. A few miles below the White another river of
the same size and character comes in, called the Stewart ;
and others still, at frequent intervals—at least a dozen of
them—as far down as the majestic Porcupine near Fort
Yukon, five hundred miles or more. All such lakes as are
widenings of the river beds are bordered with deep deposits
of the same mud, which are gradually filling them up, preparing a richness of alluvial land which in the course of a
brief span of geological time will constitute the most fertile
fields of all the hyperborean world. And a thousand miles
further down, the outflow of the Yukon delta is building
out land in the Bering Sea, just as has been going on for
centuries at the mouths of the Mississippi, forming shoals,
dangerous to approach from the outboard, which every
storm lashes into a muddy froth. The delta of the Yukon
is a labyrinth of channels and islands whose upper ends are
piled yards high with driftwood brought down by the current, and all the levels are fringed and interspersed with
low willows which have replaced the poplars and spruces of
the upper country. This is the land of the Esquimaux ; and
hereaway, not only up stream, but along the coast, one can
study their native habits and peculiarities, not so primitive
and boreal as in the Kane country and Greeley land, yet
still suggestive of sealskin, blubber, and whalebone.
Though their houses are modern and within the civilizing
influence of the Greek missions around which they have
clustered for two generations, one will see their kayaks and
bidarkas (sealskin canoes) and their toupiks (or summer
tents of sealskin) scattered along the shore ; and if he
should search behind the permanent winter dwellings he
would find a cometik, or sled, convenient for winter use
early in September, with sharp-eared dogs at hand to draw
them at the proper time, though now listless in their summer
indolence, lazily snapping at flies congregated in the tena-
cious atmosphere of stale fish. On pegs inside hang
hairless sealskin boots well tanned and preserved by their
natural oil, waterproof jackets made of walrus intestines,
which find a ready sale to the tribes far southward, nets
made of the prepared fibers of the sea-kelp, queer fish-

hooks of wood and bone, and many an ornament or utensil into whose ingenious composition are fabricated portions of the skeletons and integuments of walrus, seal and whale.

Such are the varied features of our interior domain, not less foreign because our flag floats over them, but concerning us the more on that account, and well worth our investigation, not merely as hunters of curios, but as speculators and shrewd men of business. Undoubtedly portions of Alaska are very charming at certain seasons of the year, but the sophisticated explorer will incline to avoid them in fly-time. The romance of natural history is not confined exclusively to the tropics. The mosquitoes of Alaska are unquestionably bigger than the southern bred, and the higher up the Arctic pole we climb, the bigger and more insatiate they become. "In fact," says Schwatka, "our greatest inconvenience within the Arctic circle was the tropical heat (July 29th) and the dense swarms of gnats and mosquitoes that met us everywhere when we approached the land. That night none of the party could sleep notwithstanding the mosquito bars over us." But our summer saunterers along the coast will have none of these excruciating experiences. There are no pestiferous insects to be dreaded, for every blessed breath which blows from the south will waft them inland, over the hills and far away. Seated in his comfortable easy chair on deck, while the steamer steadily pursues her weaving way through the clustering islands, each happy tourist who languidly follows these closing lines will be content to take for granted the truth of what they say, and scarcely incline at present to push the matter to a personal inquiry.

SEAL-SKIN BIDARKA.

HOME OF THE SIWASH.

From the broad blue waters of Puget Sound to Bering Strait, beyond the Aleutian Isles, the high-prowed gondolas of the natives are ever present. Crossing some wind-swept sound with bellying sails, gliding under the shadow of bold shores or drawn high and dry among the rocks before some temporary camp, they animate a solitude whose vast loneliness would otherwise be wearisome, despite the exquisite charms of the natural scenery. Whenever a steamer comes to an anchor, no matter in however so sequestered a cove or fiord, a half dozen canoes appear as if by magic, where none were visible before, and surround the vessel, eager to dispose of curios to the passengers. *"Sitkum tolla* (half a dollar), *sitkum tolla !"* pipes the shrill treble of the klootchmen, using the common Chinook vernacular, as they hold up to view their baskets, mats, miniature canoes, and carved spoons made from the horn of the mountain goat. *"Sitkum tolla !"* chimes in the deeper voice of the stolid Siwash, who steadies the cranky craft with his paddle. And one of the smart Alecks among the passengers, who under-stands human nature better than Chinook, yells back : "Sixteen dollars be hanged, I'll give you $2.50." And so the trade is eagerly made, but the market is spoiled for the rest of the passengers, and Aleck enjoys a short-lived tri-umph until he learns true wisdom by experience.

As ponies are to the plains Indians, so are canoes to the shore dwellers of the Pacific. They are the universal vehicles of locomotion and livelihood. In all Alaska there are but three horses, and one of these is said to be a mule. Be-yond the limits of compact populations there are no roads, excepting foot trails over the mountains, only the intermin-able waterways through archipelagoes and long rivers which penetrate far into the land ; and the Indian who wishes to haul freight or travel, instead of hitching up his team, simply launches his canoe. These craft are of several different patterns, but the distinctive type is quite like a batteau in outline, high and sharp at both ends, with a broad flare and an inordinate prolongation of prow, which is often ornamented with grotesque carvings of nondescript creatures, animals, birds or fishes. One model has a projecting prow or beak below the water-line, precisely like that of the old triremes of the Romans and the modern ram of our war ships. There is another pattern similar to the common Indian birch canoe. Their old-fashioned war canoes were formidable craft, carrying a hundred men, and Alaskan history relates how a fleet of ten of these made an expedition of 1,000 miles down the coast to one of the Hudson Bay posts, in the early days, to capture a man against whom they had a grievance. The magnitude of their naval demonstration is sufficient evidence of their inherent nerve and determination.

Indian trails are found all along the coast, which lead up to bodies of fine timber where canoes have been built, and the valuable wood otherwise utilized for totem poles and for carving and building purposes. Upon some of these trails much labor has been expended in bridging ravines, corduroying marshy places, and cutting through trunks of fallen trees no less than six feet in diameter. Across the mountain ranges, in the interior, white birch grows to great size, and there its bark is substituted for the cedar. Dugouts of cottonwood are also used in broken water. There are no skin canoes used in Alaska south of Bering Sea. The largest wooden canoes are more than fifty feet long, capable of carrying sixty men, hewn from great cedar logs with much labor, being dug out with axes, and then thinned with adzes to the required thickness. They are next steamed by filling the cavities or holes with water heated by hot stones, so as to give them their graceful curves, after which they are spread to the desired width and braced. They have often as much as eight feet beam. Usually they are painted black outside, but when new they often show quaint decorations, in bright colors, which, however, are very soon lost by weathering. The Indians take as great care of their canoes as the Arabs do of their horses. When not in use they are drawn up on sloping beaches in front of their villages or camps, and carefully covered with brush, mats or sails to protect them from the weather. A native will take off his own coat to wrap around the ornamental prow of his boat, which is as much as he would do for his "klootch." The best of the canoes, of course, cost a high figure, and great pains is frequently employed in clearing away bowlders and rocks to provide a snug berth for them upon the beach. They are weatherly craft in a sea way, and the fact that none

of them are decked, speaks with high testimony of the
habitually quiet moods of the Pacific, to say nothing of
skillful seamanship. The native Alaskan is seldom wrecked
or drowned. In tempestuous weather he propitiates the
spirit of the storm by tossing a few wads of tobacco into the
rock caves alongshore, and in calm he leisurely stuffs the
same into his pipe and smokes serenely. By the way, these
people smoke less than any others I have ever met, which is
a fact phenomenal. One seldom sees a native with a pipe in
his mouth.

In the dry and sunny days of summer, when the salmon
are running, and the climate is uniform perfection, the temperature scarcely varying ten degrees from sun to sun and
month to month, the Siwash locks his winter cabin and
takes his "klootch" and fishing outfit to some choice location where he can catch and cure a supply of fish for
winter's use; and as the natives incline to be gregarious and
combine for mutual help in hauling nets and hunting, he
usually has plenty of company. Very picturesque are their
aggregations of canvas tents and shanties of bark and
boards which skirt the shore of some landlocked cove under
the shelter of some circumjacent forest and overshadowing
mountain, with busy canoes plying to and fro with the seines,
and the klootchmen spreading out the ruddy salmon on the
adjacent rocks to dry. "Klootch," or klootchman, is
synonym for woman in the Chinook lingo, who may be wife,
concubine, mistress, or actual slave, for partnership attachments are not always fixed by formulas of marriage in that
lone country ; and every sojourner has his "klootch" in
wedlock or otherwise, who acts as constant housekeeper or
handmaiden. In the same vernacular her liege is known as
"Siwash," which is a corruption of the French word *sauvage*,
and is applied to the male sex generally.

A queer jargon is this Chinook. Once upon a time,
when very many nations were represented by a very few people in that vast region dominated by the fur companies, embracing Oregon and Washington Territories and all the
country lying to the northward (the French perhaps being
numerically the strongest), a sort of congress of national
representatives formulated this universal language to
facilitate intercourse. The words in most common use
were adopted, a few of them purely native dialect, but
a very large proportion bastard French. The remainder
are simply phonetic, expressing, when pronounced, the
ideas conveyed by the sounds ; for instance, amusement
is *"he-he,"* rain *"patter-chuck,"* a crow *"caw-caw,"* a

cough "*hoh-hoh*," the heart "*tum-tum*," a handkerchief
"*hak-at-chum*," etc. There are about five hundred and
fifty words in all, and with this limited vocabulary and
the use of signs, a man can travel the whole North-west
over from Central Montana to Bering Sea. In fact,
Chinook has almost superseded the native dialects, of which
there are no less than ten upon the coast, and perhaps as
many more in the interior. The different tribes seldom
attempt to converse in each other's language. There are a
few words in which the letter "l" is substituted for "r,"
Chinese fashion, indicating possibly an ancient Asiatic connection ; for most of such words are appropriated from the
native tongues, a fact which no doubt must be gratifying
to those who claim to be able to prove that the Chinese were
the earliest discoverers of America.

In the early days when the monotony of isolation was
varied by reprisals among the tribes, slaves were habitually
made by the victors, and I have heard it stated by white
men who claim to have been residents at the time, and cog-
nizant of the circumstances, that the Shimpshean Indians,
near Dixon Channel, used to kill and eat certain parts of
their prisoners, taking bites from the fleshy portions of
the arm and breast and thigh to give them courage
"*skookum tum-tum.*" Others placed the necks of their
captives across a log, fastening the bodies to the ground by
saplings weighted with stones at the ends, and so killed
them with axes. Slaves were often killed at "house-
warmings," one being placed under each of the corner up-
rights when the frame was raised, the ceremony being
sometimes attended with the greatest cruelty. With a
house of irregular foundation lines the sacrifice of life was
great. One occasionally catches accidental glimpses of
old-time war-implements which indicate an ancient degree
of savagery out of which these people seem to have long
since passed. Slavery however continues to this day, and
a sort of traffic is constantly maintained, whose conditions
are more binding than the obligations of matrimony.
Women often, and sometimes men, are traded for a valuable consideration, or thrown into a bargain as a sort of
remplisage—white people not seldom being the purchasers ;
and I have heard that those so obtained make far more
dutiful servants than others who farm out their labor, showing conscientious fidelity in their obligatory relationship.
Some of the old settlers have women living with them
whose legal status it would be difficult to determine, but so
it is in all the wilderness domain of the fur companies, the

number of the half-breeds in the North-west being counted by tens of thousands. On the Alaskan coast the hybrid product of a native crossed with a Russian is designated a " Creole," as with the French and Spanish mixtures in the Gulf of Mexico and West Indies.

At Kasaan Bay the Indian widow of old Baronovick, the Russian smuggler, still lives, with a goodly inheritance and two buxom daughters, which, I have been informed, are at disposal for the moderate sum of $4,000—for the lot ! The girls, as I saw them, seated on their home-veranda near the savory salmon cannery, and dressed in comely black dresses of modern mode, were not bad looking. The young women of the coast are uniformly comely, but their mouths are immense, and they have an excess of adipose, which grows greasy and more flabby as they grow older. They are very partial to gaudy frocks; but the prevailing costume is a black shawl over a calico skirt, and a bright yellow kerchief over the head. Very often they blacken their faces with deer tallow and charcoal, some say to keep off mosquitoes, some to improve their complexions, and others to hide defects. The older women thrust great stone ornaments into their pendulous ears, and even some young women use a lip pin of silver, steel, or bone, which they push outward through the flesh from the inside of the lower lip. It is said this is the badge of wife-hood. But such fashions are not pretty. Like many of their discarded customs and implements, they are the relics of a barbarism which passed away fully two generations ago. The girls look much better, according to modern ideas, in their silver bracelets and earrings, and the marvel is how so great improvement has taken place in so comparatively short a time. I have seen some of the gray-headed old folks take from their capacious chests souvenirs, such as medicine-rattles, masks, dance-blankets, stone war-clubs and idols ; and I fancied they regarded them tenderly, with some lingering regrets of the old time ; but very often they will part with these readily for cash to the curio-hunters, who frequently pay most exorbitant prices. Industry is one of the virtues of the Alaskans. When the men are not engaged in fishing and hunting, or employed at the several canneries on the coast, they build canoes and houses, pack goods on their backs over the mountains to the mines, and do all sorts of manual labor. They are very powerful. The regulation pack-load is seventy-five pounds. With this on their backs they will keep ahead of the most experienced mountain climbers, and I know of one who packed

over a steep new trail, which was hardly more than
blazed and cleared, a load of 125 pounds, to-wit: two sacks
of flour, a shovel, some drills, a ten-pound salmon, and his
clothes and blankets.   They do tremendous tasks on very
short commons, but when they do get afoul of a full kettle
they never leave it while there is a mouthful left.   In camp
they are splendid attendants, drying wet clothes, cleaning
guns, cooking, building shelters, and doing all manner of
"chores."   Once I followed the trail six miles over the
mountain from Juneau into Silver Bow Basin, and was astonished at the work going on there in hydraulic and placer
mining.   Sluices were built or dug up to the very snow
line, and ten-inch iron pipes, as well as every other article
of use and construction, and contents of dwellings and stores
had been carried there upon the backs of Indians at one cent
a pound !   These men are ambitious to earn praise and
money, and are not mere eye-servants.   The women, too,
are seldom idle, and when at home are occupied with the
needle, or with braiding, weaving, basket-making and em-
broidery.   Dogs are always members of the household.
They are civil and mild-mannered, like their owners, and seldom bark.   In the winter season they also do their share
of appointed work, dragging sleds over the deep snows and
freighting goods and fuel when the water courses are frozen.
They are of the true Esquimaux type, of colors brindle, white
and tawny.

However, the Indians have their bad traits as well as their
good ones.   In trading they are very unscrupulous.   They
will take a mean advantage of every opportunity.   They
will not abide by a contract.   They will demand back what
they have already sold, and tell you that their " klootch "
objects to the trade.   Like the strikers in Belgium, they
put their women in front when they would shield their own
craven selves.   But this is policy; for they well know the
consideration with which the whites regard the fair sex.
Indeed they are themselves quite chivalrous and considerate toward their women, imposing upon them no inequit-
able burdens, but assuming upon themselves those heavier
physical tasks which eastern squaws are obliged to perform
unassisted ; even declining to excel them in the emulous
and honorable competition of a canoe race, an act which
they declare would cover them with everlasting disgrace.
But it may be that the women wield the better paddle.—
" *Klaxta kumtux* "—who knows ?   When a tribe or community becomes imbued with the elements of politeness,
which is refined humanity, there is indeed hope for them.

Nevertheless, they are arrogant and exacting when they have the upper hand, and like all subordinates must be kept in their lower places. Once the Chilkats threatened to kill some miners who wished to cross the mountains over to the Yukon, and refused to pack goods for them. The distance was seventy miles. But when they discovered that two of the miners had started for the gunboat for assistance, they wilted at once, and offered to take the party over for nothing. The moral effect of the gunboat now on the Alaska station has proved most potent on more than one occasion. It is an admirable substitute for the garrison, which was a needless expense and only made trouble.

The typical native house is a one-room affair built of upright split slabs, with a door-way in front and a square hole in the roof for the passage of smoke. Sometimes there is a small window as well. The bare earth is the floor and a goat-skin or a bear-pelt the bed. Dirt, filth and abundance are the accessories. The walls and ceilings are grimy with smoke; the pots and kettles smeared with a conglomerate of grease; nothing seems ever to have been washed. Every thing is foul and squalid, and the strips of dried meat and fish, the oil bladders and pelts hung over the low rafters, are eloquent of degradation in the midst of plenty. The most pretentious houses in the country, with three or four exceptions, are those at Wrangell, some of which are 60x30 feet in dimensions, one story high, built of logs, planked on the outside, nicely whitewashed, with gable roof and doors and windows. They never have chimneys. The fire is built in the center of the smooth earthen floor, and the smoke escapes through a flat cupola in the roof. An elaborately carved and gaudily painted totem pole usually ornaments the front. Some of these are sixty feet high. They are popularly supposed to have some religious significance, but are merely heraldic devices illustrating the family history and showing the family crest, whether it be bear, beaver, eagle, shark, whale, wolf, frog or raven. To injure one was to insult the family to which it belonged; to cut one down, an unpardonable offense, Incidentally, it may be mentioned that descent is reckoned through the female line, and it seems to prevail throughout the North American tribes, a custom which is probably of very ancient date. These totems have their counterpart in the pictured buffalo robes and coup-sticks of the Indians of the plains. To one who has never seen them before the effect is most startling. One writer says:

"Seen in the wet, gray dawn of early morning, as I first

saw them, they have a most weird and strange appearance ; for the ravens which are carved upon them, the whales and the bears, are all of huge proportions, and have a most melancholy way of glaring down upon all who stand gazing at the barbarous relics."

But the totem poles are becoming weather-beaten and time-worn. The paint is nearly off, never to be renewed, and the pride of ancestry and achievement, as manifested by visible testimony, seems to have vanished with the preceding generation. In many cases similar devices appear upon the tombs of the dead. Around the four sides of the interior of these houses is a raised platform several feet wide, the rear portion of which, opposite the entrance, is partitioned into state rooms and screened by curtains of cotton or woolen stuff. On either side of these sleeping apartments are slabs of heraldic devices fixed to the walls. The best houses have modern stoves, furniture, crockery and kitchen utensils, and are very clean and comfortable throughout. There is always a variety of traps, guns, nets, fishing implements, harpoons, spears, decoys for catching seals and all kinds of fur animals, birds and sea fowl. The families have ample supplies of oil suits, rubber boots, blankets, miscellaneous clothing, and even ornaments. No simple people were ever better " fixed " ; and, as I have stated, their capacity for improvement and adaptability to new and better methods of living and doing is very marked.

If some master of the æsthetic school could only instruct them properly, what beautiful designs they might contrive in mats and rugs and shells and carving, and how handsomely they could embellish their homes ! They have not only good taste, but a natural genius which could be cultivated to marked advantage. Their preference for the grotesque manifests itself in all their ornaments and implements, their cooking utensils and their costumes ; and there is scarcely an article of adornment, use or wear which is not elaborated with studies in natural history, some literal and others fanciful and ridiculously distorted. A good many devices are simply heraldic, corresponding to those seen on their totem poles, like the family crests paraded on the panels and dinner-service of people in a higher state of civilization. They have elaborate chests and boxes of red and yellow cedar; spoons and dishes made from the horns of the mountain goat and sheep, set with mother of pearl obtained from the shells of the abelone ; trays of wood and stone highly polished and wrought

INDIAN CHIEFS (HYAS-TYEE).

in the forms of frogs, fishes and creatures half-animal and half-human; fish-hooks, harpoons and spears of wood, bone, iron and copper, all ornamented with quaint devices; masks and head-dresses made hideous or fanciful by every conceivable complexity of adjustment and contrivance; blankets woven from the wool of goats and sheep in allegorical designs, and shirts of softest buckskin, beautifully painted and ornamented with bead-work. They are very clever in contriving pipes of old gun-barrels, and also of stone, wood and bone, inserting into the bowls of the wooden ones the brass collar of a kerosene lamp or the slide of an umbrella to serve as a lining. Formerly they made women's skirts of cedar bark and the fiber of sea-kelp. Some of their manufactures have attracted the attention of outside capital, and there are firms in New York and San Francisco who are regularly supplied with basket work and mats, which are made of the inner bark of roots and twigs of trees, shredded, dyed and plaited by hand. For dyes they extract the colors from calico, blankets, etc., and produce some brilliant hues, but they are not permanent. However, as they fade, they get to resemble more and more the India and Persian colors, and are very pleasing. A better dye of black and yellow was obtained from charcoal and a species of moss called *sekhone.* Their hats made of plaited roots and their wicker work are skillfully dyed to form pretty patterns. As silversmiths they are quite expert, making attractive bracelets from hammered coin, so attractive that the native market is kept well supplied by counterfeits shipped from San Francisco makers, which sell readily to tourists at $3.00 to $5.00 per pair. One considerable item of their handiwork is the manufacture of wooden decoys representing animals, birds, seals, etc., which they use in trapping and hunting. They cover bottles, demijohns and carboys with exquisite wicker work; they make good beds from moss, caps and tobacco-pouches of furs and skins, and water-proof bags and pouches from the intestines of animals. Their magicians' rattles are perhaps the most elaborate of all their handi-work, being made hollow, usually in the form of a strange bird covered all over with carvings of strange creatures and human deformities, emblematic of the mysteries of their profession. They will trade readily for any thing they take a fancy to, or which is novel, but as they can buy almost any thing at the trading stores, they usually require silver coin to complete a purchase.

Finally they manufacture a beastly intoxicating liquor

from molasses, called hoochinoo, the equal of which for vileness is hard to find anywhere.

Like many other people with more sense, they have an inherent passion for gambling, in the prosecution of which the popular implements are polished ivory or bone sticks about the size of a pencil, which have their respective values and uses, best known to the initiated.

INDIAN HOUSES AT WRANGELL.

GOOD INDIANS.

The cold-blooded maxim that the " only good Indians are dead Indians " does not apply to the natives of Alaska. Whatever may be truly or erroneously stated of the tribes east of the Rocky Mountains has small significance with respect to the dwellers on the west side. The "great continental divide " seems to have segregated traits and characteristics as effectually as it has separated climates and indigenous products. As a whole the Indians of Alaska, both of the coast and of the interior, as far as known, are normally peaceable, tractable, intelligent, clever, eager to learn, useful, and industrious to a degree unknown elsewhere among the aborigines of America. The general statement, however, is subject to some qualification, inasmuch as there are a good many different tribes—ten at least on the coast, and perhaps as many more in the interior—who are manifestly of divers origins, and, of course, differ variously in respect to the meritorious attributes accorded to them. Some are very slovenly and semi-barbarous, while others have attained a degree of civilization which compares favorably with the status of Caucasian communities. Vincent Colyer said : " I do not hesitate to say that if three-quarters of the natives of Alaska were landed in New York as coming from Europe, they would be selected as among the most intelligent of the many worthy emigrants who daily arrive at that port. In two years they would be admitted to citizenship, and in ten years some of their children, under the civilizing influence of our eastern public schools, would be found members of Congress." The great majority of all the people dress wholly or partially in the costume of the whites, and in the towns, where there are shops and stores, the women affect even the latest procurable fashions in frocks and headgear. In complexion, they are olive rather than red, not unlike a seafaring man or a worker on a farm ; and many of the men wear beards. The Hon. James G. Swan, correspondent of the Smithsonian Institution at Port Townsend, Wash., who has made a special study of Pacific coast ethnology, thinks the whole population up to the Arctic belt have a common origin among the Aztecs, and attempts to establish this position by demonstrating an identity of many generic words common to both languages, and by similarity of features, implements, handiwork, carvings and religious emblems and ceremonies. One strong corroborative coincidence rests on some old-time silver idols, which are quite identical in size, feature, and figure with the Chiriqui idols of the Isthmus of Panama. Capt. Beardslee, U. S. N., who has likewise carefully investigated the subject, sustains Mr. Swan, so far as respects the tribe of Hydahs, who are exclusive occupants of Queen Charlotte's Island, in latitude 51 deg., but regards all other coast tribes as of Asiatic origin. He thinks the Hydahs were driven north by Cortez during the Spanish invasion. Diametrically opposite is Mr. Newton H. Crittenden, in the *West Shore Magazine* published at Portland, Or., who infers from incidental evidences that the Hydahs are castaways from Eastern Asia, who, first reaching the islands of Southern Alaska, soon took and held possession of the Queen Charlotte group. Mr. Edward Vining, in his new book entitled " The Discovery of America ; or the Uncelebrated Columbus," inclines to a Chinese origin and reiterates the story from the original Chinese sources of the landing of Hwin Shin and a party of Buddhist monks on the coast of Mexico about the year 500 A.D. The spot marked out is about 20,000 Chinese miles east from Kamtchatka. There is also a record that the indigenous populations reached a high degree of civilization. The houses were small, and of wood ; stone dwellings were not known. The people knew how to write, and used a paper made from cotton wool. They wore garments of fine linen. There was no iron, but copper, gold, and silver existed in large quantities. Also the fact is on record of the Spaniards finding at Quivisa the wrecks of large ships which Mr. Vining feels assured were of Chinese origin. The Hurons also had a tradition that ages ago their ancestors were visited by beardless men clad in silk and wearing pigtails.

There is assuredly a strong facial resemblance between the Chinese coolies now living on the coast and some of the native Indians. They seem to affiliate naturally, and to have some few words of common derivation. It is also true that there are Alaskan words of Aztec construction, especially those having the terminal " tl " and " xtl." With regard to the Hydahs, they certainly have a remarkable physical and intellectual superiority over all the other Pacific coast Indians, while marked contrasts in the structure of their language denote a different origin from them. They are of fine stature, with exceptionally well-developed chests and arms, high foreheads, and lighter complexions than any other North American Indians. These people are engaged in the manufacture of fish-oil on a large and scientific scale, and they have a Protestant mission and trading post. It is proper to state that this tribe, with the exception of small detachments, is attached to British Columbia and not to Alaska, being situated a short distance south of the Alaska boundary ; and it is equally proper to credit their enviable condition to the wise policy pursued by the British government in cultivating friendly relations with them and educating them to employments suited to their inclination and tastes. The plan of the British government has been never to recognize the Indian title, but certain tracts of land most prized by the Indians have been appropriated to their exclusive use, while at the same time they were made to understand that they must earn their own living the same as the white men they saw around them. It is gratifying to know that this view is likely to obtain with us henceforth, and to govern our own policy hereafter. Yet it must be allowed that the Indian problem in the United States has been more difficult to manage from the outset, because the Indians were vastly more numerous, wilder, and subject to food conditions which made them constantly nomadic, instead of communal and stationary. On the Pacific coast the advent of the white man has never diminished the food supply of the natives. They have fruit and game as before 'n abundance, and more fish than they know what to do with, while the lessons in farming which have been taught them have given them a source of food supply and variety which they were previously ignorant of ; so that they have never been compelled by starvation to make reprisals, like the transmontane plains Indians, to whom the buffalo in its prime supplied houses, fuel, food, clothes and utensils all at once. To the latter the extinction of the animals was like cutting down the palm trees to the South Sea Islanders ; and the shifts to which they have been forced in consequence are what is subduing them to the methods of those who toil for bread.

In writing of the Indians of the Pacific coast, it is not easy to segregate the tribes of Alaska as distinct from most of the others, for all of them have many traits, customs, peculiarities and occupations in common, and some are intermixed by marriage. It is true, however, that the inhabitants of our new possession are much more degraded and generally demoralized than those of British Columbia, whatever they may have been under the Muscovite occupation. Dawson's book, entitled "Indian Tribes of British Columbia," gives a very correct idea of the present status of the British Indians. While the Russians held possession of Alaska they also exercised a conservative and fostering care over their wards under a similar policy and system ; but since the American succession, the Indians have been left without visible control or guidance, and their course has been miserably downward. For nineteen years their women have been the special prey of a large floating population, and both sexes suffer a great deal from resulting maladies and consumption, and many are blind. Old age is rare, and all look old at forty. The Russians established churches, mills, and trading posts along the coast, but the agents of Uncle Sam have let every thing go to decay and ruin, and at the capital itself (Sitka) the official quarters are located in buildings whose roof and gables are open to the weather, and the foundation timbers nearly undermined by rot ! No wonder the natives are laggards in the race of self-improvement.

For a long time after the American succession they maintained a hostile and often aggressive attitude. With all moral support and conserving influences withdrawn, they relapsed into partial savagery. For many years there was no civil government whatever in the territory. The " Shamans " or native magicians began to regain their ascendency over the people. The garrisons stationed at Sitka and Wrangell kept perpetually drunk on home-made hoochinoo ; they debauched the women and quarreled with the men. All industries along the coast were paralyzed. No business was done. There were none to buy the furs which the hunters had trapped and collected, and utter ruin seemed inevitable. At present, however, thanks to a combination of wise measures and ameliorating influences which have extended over the past six years, the country has settled into serenity of hope, and good order everywhere prevails. The Indians are hostile no more. They have pledged themselves to perpetual amity ; a consummation chiefly effected through the instrumentality of a *wau-wau*, or conference held with the *hyas-joint* or grand commission of 1880, at which the first condition imposed by the Indians was " teachers, so that our children may not grow up stupid like their fathers ! " In one brief hour of conviction they spontaneously abandoned the traditions of the past and never looked back to the flesh-pots of barbarism. They were willing and ready to accept the new dispensation, to live by it, and to qualify themselves to promote it. All they wanted was, to receive it undefiled. These Indians have sagaciously forecast their approaching opportunity, and are looking for the advent of commercial ventures with eager longing and open hands ready for employment. It would seem as if the red men were in advance of the philanthropists. All they want is a clean deal, and it is the fault of the government if it does not step in and occupy a field so nearly ripe for the harvest. The resources of Alaska are now known to be varied and rich enough to tempt investment. The outlook is propitious, and the natives will aid us in every way to find out all there is to know about the country.

The history of this palaver by which the entire population of the country may be said to have been conciliated at one diplomatic stroke, is interesting if not remarkable, inasmuch as the key of the situation came to hand at the very outset. It seems that a domestic quarrel was on the eve of an outbreak between the Chilkats and Chilkoots in consequence of a drunken brawl the previous summer, at which blood was shed, and which could only be expiated by a requital in kind, or its equivalent in blankets ; and as the Chilkats did not consider the dead Chilkoot worth quite one hundred blankets (say $400), the usual " potlatch " preliminary to a war was in progress at the date of the proposed " wau-wau " (Aug. 24, 1880), at which fully three thousand Indians were estimated to be present. The object of the " wau-wau," or conference, to which the contestants were peremptorily invited by the naval commandant of the Alaska station, backed by a persuasive gun-boat, was to settle the difficulty without war, and to re-establish peace. Now, nearly all of the Indians of Alaska are, according to tradition, descended from the Chilkats, and among these descendants are the Chilkoots, who have largely inter-married with them. The villages of the two tribes are about thirty miles distant from each other, situated well up the rivers, one of which, the Chilkat, flowing southeast, and the other southwest, converge to the head of a narrow peninsula which divides the upper end of Chatham Straits into two bays. There is a trail and portage across this peninsula, and at the lower Chilkat village on the west side, and at Portage Bay on the east, the two tribes meet to trade or get drunk when in harmony. At Portage Bay the post agent is in the confidence of the two. The Chilkats are the most powerful and warlike of all the tribes and as they have always dominated the trade with the interior tribes, it is obvious that a maintenance of friendship and amicable intercourse with them was all important to secure the protection of such whites as were prospecting in the far-off interior, as well as to conserve the future welfare of the entire territory. The happy result of the conference is thus related in Capt. Beardslee's own written account, addressed to the author of this book at the date of the occurrence. The vessel which did duty on the momentous occasion was the North-west Trading Company's tug-boat, "*Favorite*," with a howitzer in the bow and a gatling mounted on the upper deck. The regular naval coast detail, the "*Jamestown*," lay in Sitka harbor. I quote :

PYRAMID HARBOR, August 25.

"That you get this letter may be a sign and token to you that success has crowned our efforts. I gave in yesterday afternoon, too restless to continue my summing up, and in spite of my prudent resolution donned my shooting habiliments and started across the trail. About half way over I met in single file, first Pierre Errassan, who, with his handsome six feet of figure arrayed in red shirt, leggins, and well revolvered, would have made a capital robber in Fra Diavolo ; and behind him five Indians, the foremost of whom I at once recognized by descriptions I had had as Klotz-Klotz, the chief of the Chilkats, a tall, well-built, dignified old fellow, from whose good looks, however, a wad of cotton, stuffed into a hole in his left cheek, somewhat detracted. From this hole, caused by a gun-shot wound, one of his sobriquets, " Hole-in-the-Cheek," has been derived. With him was another veteran, almost equally powerful with himself and much older, Klotz being about sixty and Kak-na-tay about seventy or more. Both welcomed me most heartily, for in spite of my decidedly unmilitary rig, Errassan, with true shrewdness and French politeness combined, drew himself stiffly up as we neared each other, and making to me the most profound obeisance, omitted to offer me his hand, thus paying tribute to my greatness, which was his trump card with the Indians, and most gracefully and solemnly introduced me.

" The costume of Klotz and Kak was not so gorgeous as to add to my discomfiture, as both they and their attendants were arrayed in blankets and leggins ; but in a big box carried by the latter was the wardrobe, in which he had expected to astonish and impress me. The retainers were in war paint, with cotton or down on their heads, which indicated determination. Thus stripped of all external show of power, the old chief and I sat down under a great cedar tree and discussed the situation. I think that this meeting was a fortunate one, for I had with me cigars and a breech-loader, the free use of both of which I at once accorded; and the influence of a large meerschaum pipe, which some months ago I sent him as a present, had its weight. After all, if the true history of wars and diplomacy could be written, how many times such little matters have had more weight than elaborate speeches, convincing only their utterer. Free from disturbing influences, Klotz-Klotz unbosomed himself, and during that interview he admitted to me that his family was in the wrong, and that he would willingly assist in establishing peace. He claimed that the killed Chilkoot was not worth a hundred blankets, but that he would pay two hundred if no less would heal the breach.

" The post trader made Klotz & Co. comfortable for the night, and this morning about ten o'clock several large canoes, with flags flying, drums (Indian drums) beating, and propelled by about a dozen painted paddlers, each came around the point of Chilkoot Inlet and were shortly along-side. In the foremost was Danawah, the chief of the lower village, and a blind old Shaman, who is chief of the Chil-koots. They were directed to go ashore to the post trader's, to wait until the firing of a gun announced the readiness of the Tyhees to receive them. They refused to go to the trader's, because the Chilkats, their enemies, were there, but instead paddled in to the mouth of a creek, where on the beach they prepared and ate their meal and donned their pow-wow garments. At 11 the sharp bark of the howitzer summoned them to the meeting, and both parties came alongside on different sides of the boat, and avoiding all intercourse with each other. When duly seated in the cabin they presented a not undignified appearance. All wore good American clothes, of which the coats were orna-mented with more or less insignia of various ranks of American and English officers of both army and navy, white shirts and shoes and stockings. On our side of the table, epaulets and full dress undoubtedly produced good effect. The interview lasted two hours, and during it the whole difficulty was adjusted, and when we left the stifling atmosphere of the cabin—for Indians even of high rank are odorous—for the upper deck we were a party of friends all under pledges for mutual benefit. Mine to them was, in answer to the request of both parties, ' Yes; I will do my utmost to assist you in this matter,' which matter was this :

"When you go to your country please tell them to send teachers to us as well as to the Stickeens, so that our children may not grow up stupid like their fathers." (The Stickeens are the Indians at Wrangell, where the Presbyterians have established a mission school which is doing much good.) I believe that they will keep their promises to treat well all white men coming to their country, and I know I will mine, and through you I now ask of any Christians you may have among your readers—and I doubt not that such there are—to send to the missionary at Sitka, such articles as will be useful to the school which Mrs. Dickson, the wife of the post trader, has started on her own hook, and at which half a hundred children are being taught, and which is soon to be transferred to a neat frame building, which, designed for a store at Taku, has been, by Capt. Vanderbilt, given to the Indians at Portage Bay, and on each side of which building the Chilkats and Chilkoots, now re-united, promise to build villages so that their children may attend the schools.

"The Indians were entertained by a few shots fired from the howitzer, and more by several volleys from the gatling which was mounted aft, and which was made to sweep an arc of one hundred and eighty degrees, at good canoe distance.

"Then they paddled ashore in company, lit a camp fire, and began a friendly potlatch on the beach, and we, satisfied with the day's work, started at 3 P. M. for home, as we have learned to consider Sitka, and are now anchored in a snug harbor for the night.

"Yours &c.,   L. A. B."

"*Potlatch*" is a term of varying significance applied to any assemblage, for whatsoever purpose, at which good cheer is provided. Sometimes a native will invite his friends to a house-raising and give away more grub and blankets than ten such houses would cost to build. Potlatches are given at the outset of great undertakings, and in commemoration of the same. In its primary sense a potlatch is a gift. In its expression, as an economic, or social, or moral force, it amplifies the uses and applications of the customary tobacco pipe in all grave affairs of red-men. It is preliminary to weighty councils, social entertainments, business undertakings, unexpected meetings of old or new friends, family reunions, celebrations, special observances, obsequies, etc. When grave complications threaten, and diplomacy is invoked, arguments are invariably re-enforced

by a war dance, or a series of dances, in the course of which
the jarring factions who have met together to investigate
and settle their differences (peaceably, or by arms,) endeavor
to impress and intimidate each other by extravagant displays of costume, menacing attitudes, hideous noises,
uncompromising yells, consummate braggadocio, and
illustrations of prowess and muscular science in pantomime,
so that peradventure, each other's opponent may weaken
before he ventures upon hostilities, or at least be timorous
on the field of battle. The full significance of these
methods is presumably understood by the present generation of natives, though the young men do not appear to be
well posted in the formula, seeming to regard the whole
demonstration as a noisy farce ; and it is seldom nowadays
that young or old can be induced to illustrate the nearly
obsolete customs of their forefathers, an exhibition of
which is apparently regarded with some such mixed interest
as "ye old folks' concerts" of their progressive white
brethren. However, for a few dollars contributed by
inquisitive spectators or tourists they can usually be persuaded to do the proper thing, and it has got to be quite
the fashion, within the past two years, for excursionists to
drum up some recruits from the Indian "ranche" at Sitka
to give a war dance, or some other dance, on the parade
ground, although such improvisations are obviously not as
striking as the bona-fide demonstrations held at the Chilkat
potlatch in 1880. The form is to build a huge bonfire in
the center of the plaza, and after a sufficient time for suitable preparation, the maskers appear, marching in from the
Indian quarter through the gate of the old Russian stockade, in full panoply of buckskin, paint and feathers,
singing in a wild weird monotone which has a swinging
cadence or rhythm that is quite infectious, and while the
glow of the bonfire lights up their painted faces and fantastic toggery with the lurid tinge of Tophet, all the by-
standers catch the inspiration and join the chant with sway-
ing bodies and ever kindling fervor. It is much like the
regulation Indian dance which most eastern readers have
witnessed at the "Wild West Show" of Buffalo Bill in
these later days—chiefly mechanical posturing and posing,
with wild gestures and much brandishing of weapons—
only that the Alaska natives do not pass and chassez around
the fire, but dance in a single row, all on one side, like so
many jacks-in-the box. Neither their performance nor their
costumes begin to compare with what I have seen among
the Mountain Crows and Sioux. Most of them had their

faces painted red with dashes of black, chiefly on one side, and they wore preposterous head-dresses of cotton waste and goat horns, and fantastic ornaments that dangled, feathers which wabbled, and bits of metal that made a tinkling noise. Some wore their blankets, and others more meager costumes, with bodies daubed. The women bound their silver bracelets about their heads, spread wide open in crescent form, like the characters in old mythology, and the firelight glistened on their polished points like scintillations from the moon ; but a pervading odor, whose origin was familiar and unmistakable, added a substantial realism to the scene.

There are, perhaps, thirty thousand Indians in Alaska—though this estimate is based solely upon the number of tribes or bands known to the trading posts on the coast and in the interior ; and they are not only expert in their natural gifts of hunting, trapping and fishing, but they are splendid navigators and seamen. They would make good soldiers, surveyors, coast guards and policemen. They are very efficient help in the salmon canneries and oil factories, and they make good mill men, miners and agriculturists.

That Indians will become farmers when it is made worth while, is shown in an appendix to General Crook's report, whence it appears that during 1885 the White Mountain tribes of Arizona had 2,120 acres of land under cultivation, raised 80,000 pounds of barley, and 3,500,000 pounds of corn. They sold to the government 700,000 pounds of hay and thirty-two tons of barley, and had 1,000,000 pounds of hay awaiting the quartermaster's order. These Alaskans are natural-born carpenters and workers in wood. Some of their carving on wood, bone, stone and metal is exquisite, and always original and unique. Their permanent houses are one-story and occasionally two-story frame buildings, and many of them have two or more windows fitted with sash and glass. The women weave beautiful cloth and blankets from the fleece of the mountain goat ; they sew very deftly, embroider, weave hats, mats and baskets, and make fishermen's nets. They also make waterproof clothing from the intestines of the moose, bear and sea lion. There are also among them regular artificers in metals, jewelers, who manufacture the silver rings, bracelets and lip ornaments which are so common among themselves. If a dollar ever comes into their possession, it is hammered out at once into ornaments. It never goes back to the United States Treasury. Oh, that all the silver dollars could be sent to Alaska !

There are already growing settlements at Sitka, Wrangell and Juneau, with populations aggregating several hundreds, and lesser communities elsewhere, at all of which native men and women are employed in every sort of out-of-door and household capacity, so that their versatility, industry and ingenuity have been fully tested. In British Columbia the Indians derive a considerable income from their labors in various occupations, and it has been declared that but for their aid several flourishing industries would cease to exist, or, at least, labor under serious disadvantages. The inner life of the Alaskan natives is extremely interesting to the visitor. There is every encouragement to hope for their ultmate absorption into civilization.

Though temporarily under stress, they can be redeemed and rehabilitated. Careful Christian training of the healthy children among them, and a conservation of the unblemished adults from contamination, will restore their pristine manhood and usefulness. Already the Rev. Sheldon Jackson has established, within two years, an Indian mission at Sitka, whose spacious two-story buildings, and surrounding premises, with male pupils in gray cloth uniform, are very creditable to his efforts, and whose management seems equally so to an outsider, although his labors have been persistently antagonized by local officials, to whom obviously some personal indiscretion or want of tact has made him obnoxious. Mr. and Mrs. Young have charge of a mission at Wrangell, using the old buildings which served as officers' quarters and barracks when Wrangell was a "fort." The Haines mission at Chilkoot is very flourishing.

At Tongass a native couple—very nice people indeed, who were educated at the Wrangell mission—are teaching an Indian school which has an attendance of forty-five pupils, the government paying a salary of $500 for their work. A number of young Indian men attend the military school at Forest Grove, Oregon. A Mrs. Macfarland has devoted much of a sojourn of eleven years to charitable labor among the girls and young women.

It is unfortunate that any impediments should be placed in the way of this missionary work, by whomsoever done, for it must continuously be kept in mind, when considering the natives of Alaska, that they are not listless savages, untutored and wild, but that they constitute a valuable industrial force in reserve—far superior to negroes or Chinese—which is at once available for service whenever new commercial enterprises are established. Yet it is a deplorable fact that the missionaries have many adverse influences and obstacles to contend with, the chief of which I believe is the ambiguous attitude of the general government about the Indian question. If Congress would make the natives eligible to citizenship by a plan of probationary preparation, most of the difficulties which now surround their advancement would disappear. As with the schools in the East, so in Alaska, there is no provision for graduated pupils except to return them to their homes, where they speedily relapse into the degeneracy and immoralities of the old way. In the case of girls, it is easy to perceive that those who have been trained at the missions to habits of neatness, are all the more desirable. There has been not only a lack of sympathy and co-operation with missionary work on the part of the local government officials, but the Indians themselves are interested only in the immediate pecuniary gain to accrue, so that ignorant and unprincipled parents will often hire their educated daughters out for immoral purposes ; and when the women are corrupt, what chance is there for the morality of men? The best testimony that can be offered to demonstrate the disposition of the Indians to receive the lights, rights, and benefits of Christian civilization is contained in the simple appeal made by Chief Toy-a-att, at Wrangell, as long ago as 1878, to an assemblage of several hundred whites and Indians ; and that appeal has not yet been regarded ! Is philanthropy a sop to Indian credulity? Read what follows :—

"My Brothers and Friends: I come before you to-day to talk a little, and I hope that you will listen to what I say, and not laugh at me because I am an Indian. I am getting old and have not many summers yet to live on this earth. I want to speak a little of the past history of us Sitka Indians and of our present wants. In ages past, before white men came among us, the Indians of Alaska were barbarous, with brutish instincts. Tribal wars were continual, bloodshed and murder of daily occurrence, and superstition controlled our whole movements and our hearts. The white man's God we knew not of. Nature showed to us that there was a first great cause ; beyond that all was blank. Our god was created by us ; that is, we selected animals and birds, the images of which we revered as gods.

"Natural instincts taught us to supply our wants from that which we beheld around us. If we wanted food, the waters gave us fish ; and if we wanted raiment, the wild animals of the woods gave us skins, which we converted to use. Implements of warfare and tools to work with we constructed rudely from stone and wood. [Here the speaker showed specimens of stone, axes, and weapons of warfare.]

"These," said he, holding them up to view, " we used in the place of the saws, axes, hammers, guns and knives of the present time. Fire we discovered by friction. [Here he demonstrated how they produced fire.]

" In the course of time a change came over the spirit of our dreams. We became aware of the fact that we were not the only beings in the shape of man that inhabited this earth. White men appeared before us on the surface of the great waters in large ships which we called canoes. Where they came from we knew not, but supposed that they dropped from the clouds. The ship's sails we took for wings, and concluded that, like the birds of the air, they could fly as well as swim. As time advanced, the white men who visited our country introduced among us every thing that is produced by nature and the arts of man. They also told us of a God, a superior being, who created all things, even us the Indians. They told us that this God was in the heavens above, and that all mankind were His children. These things were told to us, but we could not understand them.

" At the present time we are not the same people that we were a hundred years ago. Contact and association with the white man have created a change in our habits and customs. We have seen and heard of the wonderful works of the white man. His ingenuity and skill have produced steamships, railroads, telegraphs, and thousands of other things. His mind is far-reaching ; whatever he desires he produces. His wonderful sciences enable him to understand nature and her laws. Whatever she produces he improves upon and makes useful.

" Each day the white man becomes more perfect in the arts and sciences, while the Indian is at a stand-still. Why is this ? Is it because the God you have told us of is a white God, and that you, being of His color, have been favored by Him ?

" Why, brothers, look at our skin ; we are dark, we are not of your color, hence you call us Indians. Is this the reason that we are ignorant ; is this the cause of our not knowing our Creator ?

" My brothers, a change is coming. We have seen and heard of the wonderful things of this world, and we desire to understand what we see and what we hear. We desire light. We want our eyes to become open. We have been in the dark too long, and we appeal to you, my brothers, to help us.

"But how can this be done? Listen to me. Although I have been a bad Indian, I can see the right road and I desire to follow it. I have changed for the better. I have done away with all Indian superstitious habits. I am in my old age becoming civilized. I have learned to know Jesus and I desire to know more of Him. I desire education, in order that I may be able to read the Holy Bible.

"Look at Fort Simpson and at Metlahkahtla, British Columbia. See the Indians there. In years gone by they were the worst Indians on this coast, the most brutal, barbarous, and bloodthirsty. They were our sworn enemies and were continually at war with us. How are they now? Instead of our enemies, they are our friends. They have become partially educated and civilized. They can understand what they see and what they hear; they can read and write and are learning to become Christians. These Indians, my brothers, at the places just spoken of, are British Indians, and it must have been the wish of the British queen that her Indians should be educated. We have been told that the British government is a powerful one, and we have also been told that the American government is a more powerful one. We have been told that the President of the United States has control over all the people, both whites and Indians. We have been told how he came to be our great chief. He purchased this country from Russia, and in purchasing it he purchased us. We had no choice or say in change of masters. The change has been made and we are content. All we ask is justice.

"We ask of our father at Washington that we be recognized as a people, inasmuch as he recognizes all other Indians in other portions of the United States.

"We ask that we be civilized, Christianized and educated. Give us a chance, and we will show to the world that we can become peaceable citizens and good Christians. An effort has already been made to better our condition, and may God bless them in their work. A school has been established here which, notwithstanding strong opposition by bad white men and by Indians, has done a good and great work among us.

"This is not sufficient. We want our chief at Washington to help us. We want him to use his influence toward having us a church built and in having a good man sent to us

METLAH-KAHTLA.

who will teach us to read the Bible and learn all about Jesus. And now, my brothers, to you I appeal. Help us in our efforts to do right. If you don't want to come to our church don't laugh and make fun of us because we sing and pray.

"Many of you have Indian women living with you. I ask you to send them to school and church, where they will learn to become good women. Don't, my brothers, let them go to the dance-houses, for there they will learn to be bad and learn to drink whisky.

"Now that I see you are getting tired of listening to me, I will finish by asking you again to help us in trying to do right. If one of us should be led astray from the right path, point out to us our error and assist us in trying to reform. If you will all assist us in doing good and quit selling whisky, we will soon make Fort Wrangell a quiet place, and the Stickeen Indians will become a happy people. I now thank you all for your kind attention. Good-by."

While cruising in the Alaskan archipelago the voyager often discovers, on some lone islet or low-lying point projecting from a headland, what appears to be a miniature house, half hidden by a luxurious undergrowth. Sometimes it is whitewashed and sometimes it is painted in gaudy colors. Occasionally it has a little window in the side. As a rule it is remote from settlement of any kind, and affords the only suggestion of human occupation which is seen for miles. Only towering mountain peaks, pine-clad and snow-capped, and tortuous water channels intervene, and there is usually such an absence of animal life, owing to the physical formation of angular heights and fathomless depths, that even the scream of a gull seldom disturbs the solitude.

The stranger wonders at the apparent preference for isolation for any purpose whatsoever ; but, after having been duly informed, he learns to take it for granted whenever he sees them, that each of these diminutive tenements is the mortuary abode of some "Shaman" or Indian magician, whose supposed supernatural powers have not availed to avert the inevitable grip. Having completed the mortal period of his allotment for good or evil, whichever suits his individual caprice, he has been summarily shelved, as it were, by those who care to have nothing more to do with him or his occult dealings. They have swathed his poor body in cerements of sail-cloth and mats, covered it with a dance blanket, and laid it away like a discarded bundle whose usefulness is done. There it will dry into a mummy, or molder into decay. Nevertheless, he has been scrupulously provided for by his credulous subjects, who have carefully placed beside him, within his wooden domicile, all the properties and appurtenances of his craft—his magic charms, hideous masks, grotesque wooden rattles, fantastic toggery, and nameless implements, which it is believed will serve him in some new embodiment which he is expected to assume. Formerly these relics were held in superstitious awe by the natives, and even the burial site was shunned.

But in these days of modern civilization and vandalism the graves are plundered of their contents, not only by ethnological students and visitors in search of curios, but by the natives themselves, whose cupidity has overcome the scruples of bygone days of abject barbarism.

The Shaman,* or medicine man, is an omnipresent living conundrum to his unsophisticated people. He is a mystery which they can not comprehend, and a terror always, for while he is a handy sort of a personage to have in a community, and is supposed to have power to heal the sick, he is, nevertheless, believed to be in league with the devil. The malign influence of his spells is a constant menace, and no one can tell when or upon whom it may fall. This is a hard reputation to have, but the Shaman promotes it. He is a self constituted bugaboo, having duly qualified himself for the role by a course of trying ordeals by fire, water, famine and direst torture. It is probably his attested ability to survive inflictions which in ordinary course would cause death, rather than absolute immunity from any physical injury, which inspires his people with a superstitious fear. At the same time he is himself in constant apprehension of some clandestine influence at work to counteract his own. If his incantations and mummeries fail of success, he charges the failure and its blame to whomever he chooses. Many an innocent life has expiated an alleged interference in days gone by. Happily, his supremacy is now at an end. His sway was incontinently cut short by Capt. Beardslee, in 1879, when he interposed to prevent the murder of a woman who had been accused by a vengeful medicine man of being a witch. A witch used to have no more show in Alaska, than she did in the days of our disreputable Pilgrim forefathers.

It is the professional business of the Shaman to scare people and to keep them scared. It pays. Whenever he wants money, instead of "holding a man up," he shakes his rattle at him. One shake will impoverish an ordinary Siwash, two will clean him out. It is the same with bodily ailments. As a medical practitioner he despises the use of nostrums, and discards all physic. His method is to frighten disease away. When summoned in a case of sickness he rigs himself out in a garb that would scare a hobgoblin and increase the pallor of a ghost. An invalid must be in great extremity indeed when he will consent to send for a doctor.

" Shaman " is the name applied to the sorcerer or magician among the Kalmuks and other tribes of Northern Asia, and the word, therefore, adds another evidence to confirm the belief that the Pacific coast tribes have an Asiatic origin.

An appointment with a nightmare would not require half the nerve. The patient knows just what to expect. He has prepared himself to be frightened by a long course of mental enervation, and he feels that it is merely a toss-up which shall stand the infernal racket the longer himself or the ailment. In fact if he should fail to be frightened at all, the enchantment is *kultus*—no good—and the doctor with-draws, a mortified and disgruntled Shaman.

Such dilemma is alarming, but the medicine man is pre-pared to wrestle with it. He at once dons a frightful head-gear of mountain-goat horns, with a mask of hideous device; and down his naked spine a row of horns, jet black and polished, extends in abnormal development to the very base. Long pendants made of dried skunk-skins and as-sorted intestines dangle from his head, armlets and anklets equally repulsive encircle his shriveled limbs, and his whole body glows with ocher of green, yellow and red. Armed with a huge wooden rattle, fash-ioned in the form of a stork, with a demon carved on its back pulling out a man's tongue with its teeth, or some other collateral symbol still more repulsive, and carrying a long mystic rod or wand in his hand, he advances into the room with a series of postures and jerks, which impressively emphasize his aggressiveness, overpowering the patient and leaving him limp and paralyzed with terror. If, however, the disease should prove recalcitrant, the Shaman seats him-self on the earth in the center of the room with his back to the fire, and proceeds to beat the ground with his stick, shaking his rattle and singing with all his might. He seems in dead earnest, and, if there is any thing in the logic of sympathy, the patient ought to get well instanter. But death too often plays the stronger hand, carrying off the victim and the malady together, much to the disgust of the doctor, who is very apt to make some outsider the scapegoat of his bad luck. Quite likely he marvels that men should die at all, and it must be even a greater surprise to him when he is called to shuffle off his own mortal coil ; for a magician so capable to heal, and to forefend death, would be likely to suppose himself exempt from the common fate. But the inevitable end comes, and, in view of his peculiar relation-ship as middleman between mortality and the devil, it is little wonder that he is buried apart from his people, and that the site of his grave is shunned. In something of the strain sung of an abdicated monarch,

> He sleeps his last sleep, he has sprung his last rattle,
> No call can awake him to mischief again.

On the Alaska coast the reputable dead are usually cremated, and the bones collected into a box and preserved. The calcined remains are carefully placed in miniature houses like the Shaman's; but, instead of being isolated from each other, the houses are grouped in a common cemetery, as in civilized communities. The sites are chosen with respect to picturesque attraction on grassy islands, shapely ridges of land, and curves of the shore. On a burial island near Metlahkahtla the Indians have fashioned a number of fir trees into very artistic patterns. At Sitka there is a long ridge lined with several score of these mortuary receptacles painted in gaudy colors and arranged in parallel rows, interspersed with fanciful totem poles in quaint devices, on the apex of each one of which is a bear, a raven, or an eagle, denoting the clan to which the deceased belonged. These houses are seldom more than five or six feet cube, with a pyramidal roof, sometimes surmounted by a carved image, and are very creditable bits of architecture, considering that the boards have been split with an ax and smoothed with an adze. There are cemeteries elsewhere which are inclosed with neat whitewashed palings, and you often see small jackstaffs with pennants of white and colored cotton cloth standing by the graves. This is where the method of interment has been adopted from the whites, the bodies being placed in the earth and carved slabs set up in lieu of headstones. There are no less than four other modes of sepulture in Alaska, namely, burial in tents and in canoes raised on staddles out of reach of animals, burial in trees, aquatic burial beneath the waves, and in canoes turned adrift.

Tree-burial is more in vogue in the interior than on the coast, a dry goods box, shoe box, or even a cask obtained from some trader, being a good enough coffin for the defunct remains. One of these improvised burial caskets, which I saw in the forks of a tree, retained the original manufacturer's mark [D W] in the customary place of the coffin plate, an inscription which might have been appropriately translated to mean "dead weight."

With so many various methods in vogue in the same region, one hesitates to lay as much stress as some ethnologists do upon the assumed significance of mortuary rites and burial as indicating the religious belief of those who practice them. It depends much upon circumstances and present convenience, as well as the liability to subsequent disturbance, how Indians, or any other people, bury their dead. However, it may be said with regard to cremation, which has long been the popular form in Alaska, that the natives believe that the souls of those who are cremated turn into ravens. The raven is consequently a sacred bird all over the country, and is never molested. He is known as "tillikum" (friend), and it is considered a good omen when one of the dismal creatures is in attendance at a cremation.

In Sitka, ravens are as numerous as buzzards are in some Southern cities, so that the natives have no lack of family associations. One would think they were dead heroes, sure enough, or "*hyas-tyees*," from the way in which they strut about the place, and the independent airs they assume ; yet it is not obvious at first thought what especial advantage there may be to the evicted spirits in securing the embodiment of this ill-favored bird. What becomes of the souls of those who are *not* cremated does not appear. Doubtless they abide in that intangible middle ground which only a few mortals have ever been permitted to explore. Two years ago the Indian "ranche" at Sitka was in a chronic state of disquietude because of a ghost with teeth three inches long, which was said to have been seen along the Indian river, and many were willing to offer a hundred blankets to anyone who would capture this terrible ghost, which was believed to be that of an Indian lately drowned there, who belonged to another tribe, and whose body was not cremated but buried. A dead slave is not considered worthy of any ceremony whatever, the corpse often being thrown into the sea. There was a death and obsequies when I was in Sitka, and I walked one morning down to the end of the Indian "ranche," as it is called, which constitutes the outskirts of every white settlement on the coast, to examine the remains of the funeral pile where the cremation had taken place. I found nothing but a small quantity of charred coals. The unconsumed brands had all been carefully carried away, while the bones of the corpse had been picked out and wrapped in a mat and laid away in a dead-house. Some of these houses have compartments, and are the receptacles of as many as a dozen separate bundles of bones.

There is very little ceremony now at a cremation, but in earlier times a bereaved widow was subjected to a good deal of cruelty, being repeatedly thrown upon the pyre by sympathizing friends or demonstrative mourners, and seldom escaping without serious burns. Very few had courage to inflict the sacrificial torture upon themselves. Other near relatives displayed their sincerity of grief by various barbarous mutilations.

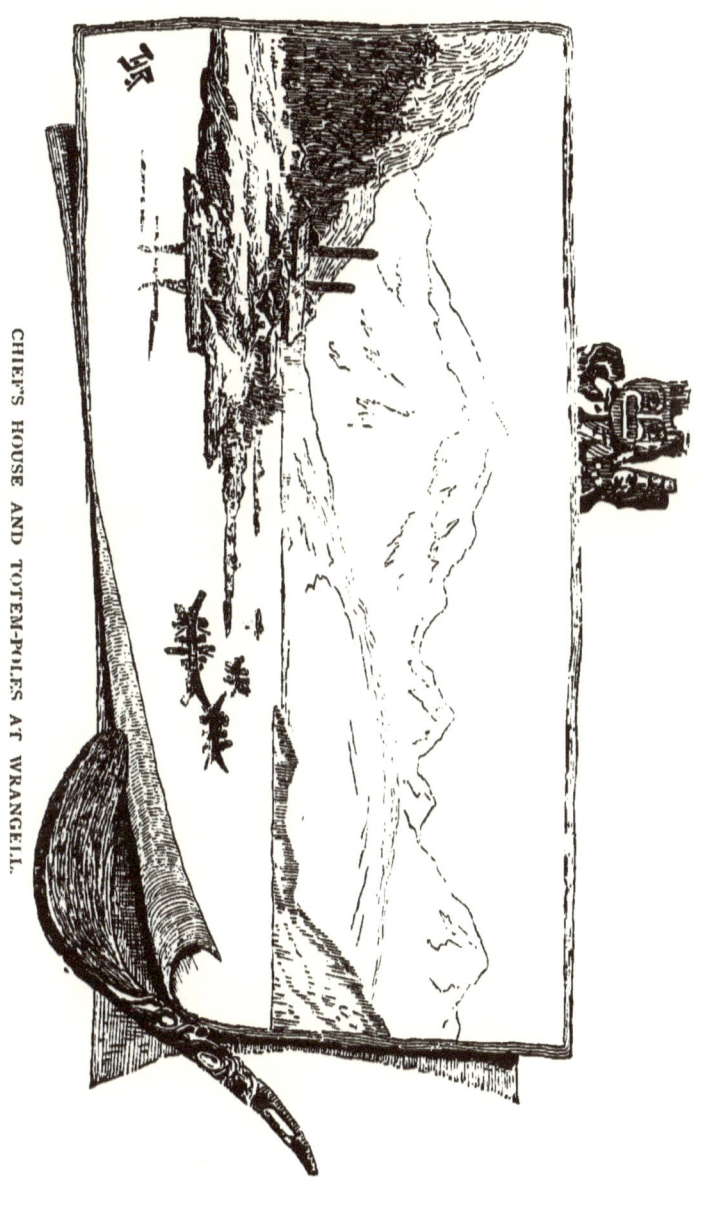

CHIEF'S HOUSE AND TOTEM-POLES AT WRANGELL.

Previous to the cremation there is a good deal of formality at the house of mourning. In.Alaskan houses a dais or plat-form runs around the four sides of the interior, which is a single compartment or reception room, opening into small staterooms on the side opposite the entrance. A brick or flagged hearth occupies the center of the quadrangle, the smoke from the fire escaping through a flat cupola in the roof, there being no chimneys. Four totem poles of fantas-tic carving, and color, showing the genealogy of the de-ceased and the clan to which he belonged, are set up at the four corners of the court. They are kept covered while the body sits in state, for the dead Indian is not laid out on a bier, but is set up on the dais opposite the entrance, with his face painted red, a fanciful crown on his head, and a blanket over his shoulders, as if living. The wall behind him is appropriately draped and sometimes festooned with small American flags.

On the evening of the day before the funeral the totem poles are uncovered and the wailing begins. The whole space between the dais and the central fire is crowded with mourners of both sexes, clad in their best blankets, who beat the ground with sticks in time with a doleful chant. This lugubrious singing and shaking of rattles and beating of the floor with long staffs is kept up all night. When the hour of cremation comes the body is hoisted out through the roof and carried to the funeral pile. A corpse is never taken out of the door of a house. It would be " bad medicine," and defile the temple. Some tribes of Indians burn the bark or skin lodge whose inmate dies therein, or they set up the lodge apart from habitations and place the dead body in it, occupying it no more as a dwelling. But this practice would be expensive where the houses are substantial and hard to build, as is the case with most of the winter resi-dences in Alaska. As a matter of belief a house in which an Indian dies is defiled, and this notion is as old as the Mosaic Law, for proof of which see Old Testament, book of Numbers, Chap. XIX., verse 14.

The funeral pile is made of resinous spruce poles of the proper length, built up in cob-house fashion, with fat pine sticks placed inside of the crib, on which the body is laid wrapped in its blanket. Logs are then added above the body, crossing other logs at the corners, and then the whole is set on fire. An intense heat and conflagration results, and a few of the Indians remain to keep the fire alive with their long poles, while a bevy of sad women contemplate the ghastly procedure from their seats on the grass not far away. When every thing is consumed the relations will cull out the whitened bones and level the ashes decorously. There is no odor, and every thing is done silently, decently, and in order.

It is customary to place the dead man's property beside the bundle of bones, which represents all that he was corporeally, and occasionally his canoe is drawn up beside the tomb, allegorically to continue the voyage of life, but in fact to remain until it falls to decay. Of late years inquisitive visitors, as well as avaricious vandals, have robbed the dead houses of all their contents, and even despoiled them of their bones. The canoes have been cut up or stolen, and the sepulchers otherwise shamefully desecrated. Grass and weeds have grown up inside to their very roofs, and if a chance stranger attempts to explore the violated precincts, he finds a satisfactory inspection prevented by an almost impenetrable jungle of undergrowth. And all this neglect and disorder is done and suffered at the capital of the territory, and there seems to be no official authority to interdict or protest.

Some writers on Alaska topics who aim to be sensational, are very fond of printing in their books engravings of totem poles and idols, and obsolete things which the young natives of the present generation regard with much the same interest that we do the calashes and warming pans of our grandmothers, or the "one horse shay," and credulous readers are apt to infer therefrom that the religious condition of the people is but one remove from heathenism, whereas it is not impossible to find Christianity in some localities nurtured and propagated exclusively by native efforts. We who took umbrage at the travesties of Charles Dickens ought not to underrate or misrepresent the poor Siwash. For myself, I prefer to write in behalf of an "improved order of red men," quite content to leave the archæology and mythology of Alaska to the antiquarians. Doubtless there is a sort of morbid interest in tracing out the hieroglyphs upon a T'linket dance-blanket, and an enthusiast may even fancy that he has unraveled some pious analogies from their mystic woof, but he who is accustomed to read the heroics of the red men of the plains as they are pictured on the rocks and sketched with pigments on their robes, and shields, and tepees, will find in the T'linket blanket but a simple analogue and repetition of the oft-told story of vaunted prowess ; or perhaps a shadowy suggestion of some familiar thoughts or objects or practices like those we see on the bronzes, fans, and screens of Japan and China. But there is not enough dust of antiquity between the blanket-folds to blind the ingenuous searcher after knowledge. Doubtless some progressive savage in these modern days has traced *our* spiritual lineage in the patterns of our Wedgewood ware, and discovered revelations of deepest human import in our Holland delf. Students of composite zoology may amuse themselves by the day, or month, in deciphering the intricacies of the emblazoned totem poles ; and some of the most pedantic will point out to you the " all seeing eye," the " thunder-bird," identical with the Aztec " bird of the sun," and the " lightning-fish," which simple natives, it is said, believe to be the authors of those profound phenomena of the air. Yet is it more absurd to attribute the noise of thunder to the cleaving wings of a supposititious bird, or the lightning-flash to the darting fish which stirs the phosphorescence of the sea, than it is to explain the sound of thunder as being caused by the swif· passage of the electrical bolt ? Verily, the sublimity of ignorance is as profound as the depth of wisdom. To the untutored savage mind the structural idea of swiftness, courage, strength, and brain, and all the mental and physical attributes of man and divinity, are best expressed and comprehended through external objects which he makes symbolical. Their modes of thought, and the notions they have respecting departed spirits, are illustrated in their rude way. The natives of Alaska have thought that the crows control the eruptions of volcanoes, and that they have power over the Spirit of Evil which incites them. They believe in transmigration, and in the supernatural powers of the bear and raven, which are prominent on all their insignia. Probably the essence of their religious belief is outlined in the following legend connected with Mt. Edgecumbe, once an active volcano, which is told by Lieutenant C. E. S. Wood, in one of the back issues of the *Century Magazine.* The story runs : " A long time ago the earth sank beneath the water, and the water rose and covered the highest places, so that no man could live. It rained so hard that it was as if the sea fell from the sky. All was black, and it became so dark, that no man knew another. Then a few people ran here and there and made a raft of cedar logs ; but nothing could stand against the white waves, and the raft was broken in two.

" On one part floated the ancestors of the T'linkits ; on the other, the parents of all other nations. The waters tore them apart, and they never saw each other again. Now their children are all different, and do not understand each

other. In the black tempest, Chethl was torn from his
sister Ah-gish-áhn-ahkon [The-woman-who-supports-the-
earth]. Chethl [symbolized in the osprey] called aloud to
her, 'You will never see me again ; but you will hear my
voice forever !' Then he became an enormous bird, and
flew to southwest, till no eye could follow him. Ah-gish-
áhn-ahkon climbed above the waters, and reached the summit of Edgecumbe. The mountain opened, and received
her into the bosom of the earth. That hole [the crater] is
where she went down. Ever since that time she has held
the earth above the water. The earth is shaped like the
back of a turtle, and rests on a pillar ; Ah-gish-áhn-ahkon
holds the pillar. Evil spirits that wish to destroy mankind
seek to overthrow her and drive her away. The terrible
battles are long and fierce in the lower darkness. Often the
pillar rocks and sways in the struggle, and the earth trembles and seems like to fall ; but Ah-gish-áhn-ahkon is good
and strong, so the earth is safe.

" Chethl lives in the bird Kunna-Káht-eth ; his nest is in
the top of the mountain, in the hole through which his sister disappeared.

" He carries whales in his claws to this eyrie, and there
devours them. He swoops from his hiding-place, and rides
on the edge of the coming storm. The roaring of the
tempest is his voice calling to his sister. He claps his wings
in the peals of thunder, and its rumbling is the rustling of
his pinions. The lightning is the flashing of his eyes."

Even the whites have acquired some of the Indian super-
stitions. There are credulous people who believe that croc-
odiles once inhabited Alaska because a wooden nondescript
exists which somewhat resembles one. So also because the
snake is a favorite pattern for bracelets, they believe that
snakes once existed in the land, when, forsooth, the first
design was furnished by a chance visitor to a native silver-
smith who began to manufacture them ; and when a San
Francisco sharp discovered how great the demand was for
them he sent seventy dozen pairs of California workman-
ship to a trusty Siwash at Sitka on commission. Verily,
when science overleaps itself, the tumble is precipitate. I
do not take much stock in the mythological significance of
the multifarious devices which are inseparable from Alaskan
handiwork. Some of them are obviously the crude expres-
sions of their primitive theology, but for the rest, they are
the mere outcroppings of a genius of deformity, fable and
incongruity, which is their inherent propensity. These
natives are born caricaturists, manifesting their broad

humor in every thing they do, or make, or say, so that all their domestic utensils, their ornaments and interior decorations, their boats and paddles, toys, dolls, masks, attire, and even their family escutcheons, are often of the most grotesque character. The images which they make are not all idols, nor worshipful. As for their religious zeal as Christian proselytes, it is related that some wicked wags induced the converted Indians of Sitka to demand a "potlatch" of 100 blankets from two Hebrew traders because, it had been told them, they had killed their "tillikum," the Christ!

INDIAN GRAVE.

ALASKA'S MINERAL WEALTH.

I suppose that mining in Alaska is much like mining any-where else ; processes are similar and familiar. The most interesting part of the business is that it is an established fact. The mines and the miners are there ; and while the incredulous are questioning even their existence, the indus-trious and hopeful are busily engaged in taking out the gold. There is no doubt that in the early days of discovery and prospecting there was more swindling to the square inch than in any other known location, but swindling was made easy because the " stuff " was there, the indications were there, and pay-dirt and bonanza-quartz were there. Officers of the army and navy who were on the station were the principal investors and chief sufferers, because nobody else had any ready cash. These confiding and intelligent gentlemen, who were on the spot and took the pains to examine for themselves, making interminable tramps through the wilderness to visit quartz ledges and placer diggings, eagerly " blew in " all they could spare each pay day, on the faith of their own investigations. I know one officer who has no less than $2,500 so placed, and I believe it is well invested, inasmuch as it is judiciously distributed. Want of capital and mechanical appliances have made investments unremunerative, but not worthless. As soon as ever capital was forthcoming the mines were developed with profits more than remunerative. The largest stamp-mill in the world has now been in active operation there for nearly a year. It is located on Douglas Island, opposite Juneau, and carries one hundred and twenty stamps, working the whole year round. It is owned by San Fran-cisco parties. The ore comes right out of the side of the mountain (which rises abruptly from the ocean) and is shot down an inclined plane to the stamp-mill, where it is treated ; and vessels drawing twenty feet of water can lie right along-side the rocks of the natural shore and receive their freight not a hundred yards from the mill. The primitive forest clothes the slopes of the mountain from base to summit, and fuel is all around in intimate proximity. No plant of such value was ever erected or operated at so cheap a cost. It is said the outlay was half a million dollars, and that $16,000,000 have been refused for the property. It is a low-grade ore, yielding $5 to $100 per ton of quartz. No stock is for sale. The first gold-brick came out in July, 1885, and weighed 297 ounces. In August the output was equal to $60,000, and the mill is now reported to be running up to $100,000 per month, with improving prospects. It is said that Senator Jones of Nevada, who is one of its principal stockholders, is adding $250,000 a year to his income from its output. Right alongside of this mine, in continuation of the same ledge or formation, is the Treadwell claim, also owned largely by San Francisco parties, which is found to be equally rich in ore. Its shares are at a very high premium, although the mine is not developed. This year machinery will probably be set up by its owners on a scale equal to the Douglas plant. Other new and valuable dis-coveries have been made on Douglas Island the past winter. At Willoughby Island in Cross Sound, at the "North Star" ledge near Juneau, and at Kilisnoo, there are said to be rich deposits of ore, and many shares have been put on the market. These insulated properties so far pan out the best.

On the mainland, just across the channel from Douglas Island, and six miles back from the shore, in the heart of the mountains, is "Silver Bow Basin," where there are stores, blacksmith shops, boarding houses and tenements for a large community engaged in placer mining, who turn out $20,000 bullion every month from May to October. The estimated yield for 1884 was $120,000. I am not aware that it was greater for 1885. The altitude of the basin, which is just above timber line, is so high that the winters are very long. The lower mountains, however, are ordinarily clear enough of snow for prospect-ing in April. Here are scores of sluices, expensive viaducts and hydraulic apparatus, "rasters," hose, pans, and iron conduits ten inches in diameter, in place, all over the basin and up the sides of the inclosing mountains to the very snow line. Several tunnels have been driven into the quartz ledges, which yield a fair supply of gold. Claims have been staked out everywhere. Lead of the richest kind is found in big nuggets, as well as gold. I have myself broken open large chunks of quartz which seemed to promise nothing, and been surprised at the richness of their revelations.

An *arastra* is a queer cheap machine for treating ore which can be used to great advantage when the quartz is decomposed and soft. It is a sort of circular tub twenty

feet in diameter and four feet high, with a hard stone floor
and an upright shaft in the center, which carries four arms,
like a clothes drier. At the ends of these arms heavy flat
blocks of stone are attached by chains, and as the arms
swing round they drag the stones over the bottom of the
tub and pulverize the quartz, which is fed into it with a due
proportion of quicksilver and such chemicals as the nature
of the ore may require. The machine is driven by a simple
water wheel attached to the same shaft ; a sluice placed a
few inches above the floor lets off the waste water, the precious metal uniting with the quicksilver and settling to the
bottom of the tub. There are two of these contrivances in
the Silver Bow Basin.

These mines have made Juneau quite the center of business in South-eastern Alaska. There are possibly three
hundred white people in the town, which is most romanti-
cally situated at the base of a mountain just in front of the
entrance of a cañon through which a beautiful stream flows
in a series of cascades and perpendicular leaps to the sea.
The store of the North-west Trading Company is conspicuous among others, but there are good restaurants, two drug
stores and several general stores, a beer brewery, two barber
shops with hot and cold baths, a jeweler's shop, blacksmith
shops, post-office and some very snug dwellings, nearly all
of which are painted and look neat. Some houses have
little gardens inclosed. A display of flags from three or
four tall staffs shows prettily against the somber background
of evergreens, and makes the place look gay. There is a
commodious wharf and warehouse for the steamer, and
usually two or three small sailing craft and numberless
canoes enliven the little bight within whose curve the town
is principally built. But there is besides a picturesque promontory at one point of the arc, with cottages climbing the
slope among the trees. A ferryboat runs hourly to Douglas
Island. Two Indian villages flank the town on either end,
with a combined population of twelve hundred or more in
the winter time ; in summer their men are chiefly employed
at the mines, but there is always a goodly number of them on
hand to handle freight when the steamer arrives. Many of
them earn $2.50 per day at the mines, and, although there are
a few Chinese at work in the basin, these are preferred, being
generally larger and much stronger and better able to
handle heavy tools and big loads. Tradesmen earn from
$4 to $10 per day, but continuous employment is uncertain.
There is a beaten trail over the mountain, made at a considerable cost, and the Indians have carried over it on their

backs every thing whatsoever that has gone to the mines. This service they perform at the uniform rate of one cent per pound.

The first attorney's fees ever paid in Alaska were to District Attorney Haskett, in gold dust, from this "basin." Last year I went up to the mines in company with him and his chief partner, Mr. Powers, who had large claims there, and now by strange fatalities both are dead.

About sixty miles from Juneau is the Chilkat country, which Captain Beardslee succeeded in opening to miners in 1880 through the instrumentality of a prominent chief named "Sitka Jack," whom he sent into the interior as plenipotentiary, arrayed in all the self-sufficiency and authority of a blue frock-coat, brass buttons, a colonel's stripes, a navy cap with gold band and device, and, I believe, a sword. He remained all winter dispensing good cheer liberally from village to village, and when he returned in the spring, the up-country natives said it was "all right ; the white people might come ;" whereupon, in 1881, a schooner immediately outfitted at Sitka to start for Chilkat. Jack lives at Sitka in one of the best houses in the "ranche," white-painted, with windows, green blinds, porch and veranda, and it is said he is worth $10,000. He is industrious and shrewd, and besides working in the canneries, picks up a good deal of money in "little odd jobs." One summer he made $300 in the cannery alone. From Lynn Channel and Chilkoot Inlet, 120 miles northeast of Sitka, there are four passes over the mountains to a chain of lakes 150 miles long, which form the head waters of the Yukon ; the best of which passes, 25 miles in length, was selected by Lieutenant Schwatka for his exploring tour, already referred to in this volume. Valuable mineral discoveries have been made on the banks of the river, and I have reliable information that one miner has staked out a claim on a vein of gold-bearing quartz six hundred feet wide. In his report, Lieutenant Schwatka says:

"The d'Abbadie, [a tributary river of the upper Yukon] is important in an economical sense as marking the point at which gold in placer deposits commences. From here on, nearly to the mouth or mouths of the great Yukon, a panful of dirt taken from almost any bar or bank with any discretion, will give several 'colors,' in miners' parlance."

This gold has been ground out of the far away mountains by the rasping glaciers, and deposited with the gray glacier mud which is brought down by the streams from the ice fields. It is probable that all the environment of the mountains which inclose the great central plateau of the Yukon is rich in minerals. Schwatka mentions having discovered a party of American miners already at work on the Stewart River, where they had found good prospects ; and since the spring of 1886 opened several hundred miners and prospectors have found their way across the Chilkat trail to the diggings, which seem to grow richer the more they are developed.

The mines about Sitka, valuable and innumerable as they are, have remained unproductive until the present year, but now the richest gold claims yet discovered are being systematically developed by a company competent in all respects, which was incorporated in November, 1885, under the laws of Wisconsin. It is called the "Lake Mountain Mining Company," and its president is C. A. Swineford, brother of the present governor of Alaska. B. K. Bowles, of Baraboo, is secretary, and M. C. Clarke, cashier of the First National Bank of Madison, treasurer. Nicolas Haley, the old pioneer prospector of Alaska, is a large stockholder.* The company has abundant capital, and began work early last February with all requisite tools for engineering, mining, assaying, etc. In May they had begun working the placers, and had erected wharves and warehouses at the head of Silver Bay, some four miles distant from Sitka, on Baronoff Island. They had also driven a tunnel into the quartz ledge with a view to the early erection of a stamp-mill, to be operated at the earliest day possible. The property of the company comprises several of the most valuable of the Haley claims, from one of which this indefatigable miner obtained an ounce of gold daily for a long period, by simply crushing the decomposed quartz in a mortar, treating it with mercury. These claims are respectively known as the Lucky Chance, Porphyry, Cleveland and Nickel lodes, and the Haley & Sons Placer.

---

* "Nicholas Haley, a practical miner, has been about the best slandered man in this vicinity. He had up-hill work to obtain credence to his tales as to the richness of Alaska in gold. It was, I remember, fully explained to me in San Francisco, that Haley was a fraud ; that ore from other regions was brought up here and mines salted, so as to make a rush which would benefit the ring of which Haley was ringleader, and with a fortune at his control. The man has struggled on in poverty, persevering, and at last his upward turn has come. Within a month he has sold to San Francisco parties, who at last came up to examine, over seventy thousand dollars worth of ledges, and still owns enough to keep him rich. If, as I believe they will, the mineralogical resources of Alaska bring her into prosperity again, its citizens should always do honor to this miner to whom they will owe it."—[*Capt. L. A. Beardslee in Forest and Stream.*

INDIAN VILLAGE—SITKA.

Official assays of specimens of quartz taken at random therefrom show from $147.60 to $1,840 per ton.

Captain Beardslee, U. S. N., who was on the Alaska station during the years 1879-'82, has given a complete history of mining operations in the vicinity of Sitka during the Russian occupation, and up to the year 1880. Its publication was commenced in the *Forest and Stream* in 1879, while I was its editor, and continued throughout the year following.

It seems that reports of mineral and marble discoveries were long ago brought in from time to time by the Indian fur hunters, but very little attention was paid to them until the year 1855, when the Russian government sent an engineer officer to examine and investigate into the mineral resources of the country. Although he was ostensibly engaged in this duty for a period of two years, the report is current that he put in the best part of his time at Sitka in "potlatch" and dancing; and as he never visited the range of mountains on which are situated nearly all of the ledges which have since been discovered, his report was unfavorable; and from that date until the transfer of the territory to the United States, nothing was done. In fact, the Russians were after fur, and not gold. The fur company itself was especially lukewarm toward prospectors and explorers; because, by the terms of their contract, the government had a right to take away from them the control of any lands in which mineral deposits were found.

The first discovery of gold in the vicinity of Sitka was made by a soldier named Doyle, in 1871. In 1872 stringers of quartz were found at Indian River, one mile from town, and in the mountains, back of Silver Bay, ten miles from town, and the "Haley & Milletich ledge," the "Bear ledge," and the "Upper ledge" successively came to light. On December 9 of that year, the first blast ever made in Alaska quartz was exploded, and from the rock thrown out and broken up by it, about sixty dollars worth of free gold was obtained. On Christmas day the "Stewart ledge" was discovered. The next year, in 1873, two mining companies were formed of army officers and citizens of Sitka. In 1877 the "Lower ledge" passed into the hands of San Francisco people, who organized the Baronoff Island Gold and Silver Mining Company. Sitka is situated on Baronoff Island. This company watered the stock so that outsiders declined to invest, although a shaft, which is down sixty feet, is in good ore all the way. In 1876 the Stewart passed into the hands of Portland men, under the name of the Alaska Gold and Silver Mining Company. This mine has been mismanaged. Nevertheless, it possesses a steam ten-stamp mill, shops, cabins, and full outfit. A tunnel is in over 160 feet, in good ore all the way. Another, 100 feet above it, is in eighty-four feet, and another was about being started in the month of February, 1880, at which date the output of eleven days' work was about $1,800 worth of bullion, with over fourteen pounds of amalgam produced from free gold alone, ready for shipment. These statements I gather from Captain Beardslee's report of 1880, and I am not aware that any thing has been done in that vicinity since then. Other ledges discovered at sundry times on the same range, are known as the " Haley & Francis," " Wicket Fall," and " Great Eastern; " and there are more still, further east. Assays of the " Great Eastern," by Selby & Co. of San Francisco, yielded $175 gold and $5.20 silver per ton in 1879. These specimens came from the surface, and showed no free gold whatever. Haley claims are found all over the country, one of which is said to have yielded him $20,000 in five years "arastra" work ; but there are lots of ."holes" said to be valuable, which are utterly worthless, and always were.

In the enumeration of mining enterprises, I should add that the Mexican Gold and Silver Mining Company, and the Admiralty Gold and Silver Mining Company each with $10,000,000 capital stock, and each with J. D. Fry, T. J. Hay, James Treadwell and C. F. Stone as directors, were recently organized at San Francisco ; the former for the development of valuable claims in the great gold belt of Douglas Island, the latter for ledges on Admiralty Island. These companies are preparing to get to work this summer.

Time was, in the days of the Frazer River gold fever, when miners fitted out at Wrangell and followed up the Stickeen River, through a defile of the Alaska mountains into the British territory beyond, where the diggings were. Wrangell had a population of three thousand people then, and could not accommodate them all. So, when the houses were filled, old hulks of vessels were converted into hotels and lodgings, and these still remain, high and dry on the shelving shore, but gradually falling to decay, like a majority of the houses in this at present almost deserted town. Perhaps in some not distant day the mines will once more pan out rich and general business revive, though, of course, there is a quantity of quartz holes scattered all over the country which are, in the native vernacular, "kultus" (no good). To conclude: Alaska is a fascinating field for prospectors. One can find there a "show" of every thing he wants—gold, silver, iron, cinnabar, copper, marble, coal, and great red garnets as big as hickory nuts ; but the results do not always realize the promise, and the reason presumably is a lack of capital necessary to develop them. Marble crops out all over the country through which the coastwise steamer regularly passes. Alex. Choquette, of Wrangell, has some very fine specimens of mottled white and blue marble from a quarry quite convenient to tide-water ; a good quality of white marble is found on Lynn Canal. Valuable coal discoveries have been made near Kilisnoo, and Mr. C. C. Bartlett, a leading merchant of Port Townsend, Washington Territory, has found excellent coal on Admiralty Island. Capt. Nichols, of the U. S. steamer Pinta, claims to have found a valuable mine of bituminous coal. There is no discouragement in the outlook. Time will prove it. After the mineral discoveries at Vermillion Lake in Minnesota, it took twenty years to convince people that the ore would pay for working, but when a certain iron company found nerve to quietly undertake the business it cleared up 63,000 tons the first year and 226,000 the next. All that is needed in Alaska is capital.

Coal mining is an industry which in nine years has undergone a wonderful development in British Columbia. Coal has been found widely distributed over the mainland and islands on Vancouver and Queen Charlotte Islands well to the north, at which last named place the only vein of anthracite yet discovered on the Pacific coast has been found. As the geological structure of Alaska is similar to that of the country adjacent, why may not like deposits exist in each ! The gold mines of Alaska are far richer than those of Cariboo and Cassiar, in British Columbia, of which the output of Douglas Island is a full assurance. At present the mining laws are satisfactory. (See Organic Act, in Appendix.) Captain Beardslee speaks with high approval of the good behavior of the miners of Alaska, even in the idle days of winter. "They not only conducted themselves in the most respectable manner, but have given their willing co-operation in carrying out such simple laws as we have found it advisable to establish from time to time." This testimony applied to the days before there was any civil government. I certainly found the Silver Bow miners a most orderly community, among whom no stronger beverage was current than the wholesome beer of the country, manufactured at Juneau.

COMMERCIAL FISHERIES.

It has been my good fortune to enjoy unusual opportunities to investigate the inland and salt water fishes of Alaska, having coasted along a thousand miles of the shore line and visited nearly all of its fishing stations in company with professional fishermen, familiar with the Pacific coast. Knowledge of the habitat of deep-sea fish can only be obtained by feeling the bottom with repeated and laborious soundings, aided by that intuition which enables an experienced person to determine where they are by the color of the water and the configuration of the land. Codfish and some other species can be traced in part by following the bait fish upon which they feed and which appear upon the surface and in the bays and estuaries at certain seasons. Seafowls, seals and humpbacked whales are of great assistance to the investigator—indicating by their own presence the presence of the fish. Humpbacked whales and porpoises are often seen in large numbers in the land-locked waters of the Alaskan archipelago, sporting and spouting in basins so small that they seem hardly more than lakelets; and it is proper at once to remind the reader that the entire mainland of our new possession is flanked by an outlying chain of islands, chiefly mountainous, with shores which drop abruptly into deep water; and that there are few open-water reaches for a distance of fifteen hundred miles that are exposed to the full force of the ocean swell and the breakers.

From all indications I am convinced that some day in the near future the fisheries of Alaska will occupy as important a commercial place as those of Norway and the Hebrides and the North Atlantic. Already the canning of salmon has become an industry of considerable importance, and establishments have been located at all the principal points as far north as Sitka and considerably beyond, the proprietors preferring the services of the native Indians to those of the irrepressible Chinese—the favorable difference between the two races compensating for the many obvious inconveniences of a location so remote from a market.

An evidence of the value to which these fisheries have

attained even now in their infancy is shown in the statistical statement that in 1884 the territory shipped 10,101 cases of four dozen 1-lb. cans, and 1,527 barrels of salted salmon, each barrel containing thirty fish. The cannery near Sitka put up 700 barrels. There were also shipped large quantities of halibut, herring, cod, rock cod and herring oil, and the year 1885 would have shown still better results but for a depression in prices which made the labor unprofitable. Notable among other establishments is the Chilkat cannery, situated in 59 deg. 13 min. north latitude, which is well up toward the frigid zone, but warmed like the rest of the Alaskan coast by the Japan current, or Kuro-Siwo, which corresponds to the gulf stream of the Atlantic. I dare say that no commercial company in the world ever found its way to a nook of earth so ineffably romantic ; for the grandeur of the surrounding scenery is supreme. Parallel ranges of snow-capped mountains of majestic height inclose a narrow strait, whose waters are deep and green, and seldom disturbed by the storms which beat the outer wall. High up in the bluest empyrean the glittering peaks flash to each other the reflections of the noonday sun, and where the silvery summer clouds rest upon the summits the eye can scarcely distinguish the fleecy vapor from the spectral snow. Below the timber line their sides are clothed with fir and hemlock, and in the dark waters under the shadow of their confronting buttresses the salmon are continually tossing the spray, so that the surface fairly boils. Through one of the clefts of the mountains the sparkling Chilkat River leaps over the obstructing rocks in a succession of pools and rapids, and upon the point of rocks at its mouth the cannery stands. Perched upon a ledge so narrow that the wharves and fishing stages can scarcely keep a foothold above the tide, it looks out toward a long vista of headlands, whose clear-cut outlines are set against the sky in graduated shades of blue, as they recede and overlap each other. And out of another great rift the famous Davidson glacier presses toward the sea, filling a valley four miles wide ; and the masses of ice, which are successively pushed to the front and break off, float away with the recurring tides, and *chassez* up and down the landlocked channel until they finally melt away or drift out into the ocean. On a beach near by is a village of Indian employés, with the usual adjuncts of half-dried salmon spread on the rocks, rueful dogs, and log canoes drawn up on shore and carefully protected from the weather by boughs and blankets when not

in use. Gray and white gulls fill the upper air, or sit on
the drifting icebergs and scream, while large wisps of sandpeeps flit constantly from point to point, feeding on the
land-wash. In hours of toil the foreground is active with the
movements of the canoes and boats hauling seines. This
location is also known as " Pyramid Harbor."

Captain Beardslee writes in his vivacious colloquial way :
" One day I jumped in with Tom McCawley, one of the
most experienced salmon seiners, and got him to show me
how it was done. Our boat, rowed by four untiring
Indians, had already a ton at least of fish just taken, but there
was room for another, and McCawley wanted it. We rowed
slowly around the various islands for an hour with no success ; the tide was high, the day too bright ; none were
jumping. We pulled into a quiet, pleasant, little cove and
lunched ; the Indians preparing for us a good pot of coffee,
of which they are very fond, when well sweetened. With
plenty of it, hard bread and smoked salmon, they can work
forever. As we lay on the grass with our pipes, an Indian
called out ' Fish! ' and pointed to a spot in the channel but a
short way off. Soon another leaped, and in a moment we
were in and off. I saw the fish jump, and, after a little
time, another, or, as it seemed to me, the same one. I
didn't think much of that school ; but when I said so, the
Indians answered ' *Tshugatahen* ' (plenty), and Tom said :
' When one jumps, there's a hundred under him that
don't ; ' and that was news to me, for I expected to see the
whole school at once, as one does porpoises. Pulling for
the shore, fifty yards to the left of them, one end of the
seine was landed and held by the crew of one of the boats
(there were two), while the other rapidly pulled around the
apparently deserted spot ; the hundred yards were soon
placed, and ' Haul in ! ' was the order. I tended boat, our
crew having also landed, and made fast to the outer row of
corks, and was drawn in with them, peering anxiously into
the diminishing circle. Soon I saw bright streaks darting
rapidly to and fro, and then a dozen in the air glistening
in the sunshine. The pool diminished, and a solid mass of
plunging fish became visible ; not one leaped over the corks ;
they dove as they approached the wall of net, rising in
the center for convulsive leaps. In a few moments two
tons of salmon, weighing five to twenty pounds each, were
huddled together in a six-foot circle, and into this the
Indians who were not holding net, dashed blow after blow
of short, stout gaff hooks, jerking out with every dash a
salmon—they simply ' fired at the flock,' and never missed.

A jerk over the gunwales, and the noble fish lay heaped up, gasping and struggling. This was in July ; nearly all of the fish were good, and, according to McCawley, there were five varieties in the catch. A few which had begun to 'dog' were cast into the canoe of an old Indian who accompanied us, and who had gleaned quite a canoe load of such as are considered unsuitable for canning."

Heavily laden canoes bring the still struggling fish to the lift which hoists them to the cleaning table, where women dexterously sever the heads, cut off the fins and tails and draw the entrails, and then divide the bright red flesh into pieces of a proper size to fit the cans. Boys solder the tins, which are then put into boilers with their contents, and afterward resoldered, labeled and packed. Thus whole families are employed, the labor being divided among them according to their ability to perform. For their own use the Indians dry the salmon on the rocks in the sun, no salt being used. Their store-houses are often placed in the branches of trees, sometimes forty or fifty feet above the ground, it is said, with a view to keep them from the ravages of blow-flies and other pests. Many of these houses will hold several tons, and are used by a number of families in common; they are reached by notched poles, which are admirable substitutes for ladders. Some persons assert that the custom of placing the boxes high is to keep them from dogs and wild animals, but the Indians assign only the one reason given. I have seen the same method employed elsewhere, by both Indians and white men. A spent salmon—a 'dog' salmon, as it is termed—after spawning, is a sight to see ! I found one in shoal water some two feet long, as thin as a slab, feebly struggling as though he were trying to push himself ashore. I picked him up and landed him on the grass. A sicker fish never continued to wag its tail. His skin was yellow, picked out with green and blue spots (such as a good recoiler will leave on your arm after an all-day shoot). Spots from the size of a bit to that of a dollar, and one about an inch wide and six long on his side, were raw as if gnawed out by mice. One eye was gone, one gill cover eaten through, and every fin and his tail were but ragged bristles, all integument between the rays having disappeared. No wonder the legend arose that all California salmon die immediately after spawning. The Creoles and Indians catch daily great numbers of these sick fish with their gaffs, and they consider that they are better eating when dried than the healthy fish.

The quantities of salmon found in Alaska are simply

enormous. I have watched the movements of Eastern salmon in the most prolific rivers of Canada during their spawning season, but have·nowhere found them in such compacted masses as they appear in Pacific waters. Only where dams or natural falls obstructed their free passage were they sufficiently crowded, in those Canadian rivers, to interfere at all with each other, or with the comfortable ascent to the upper streams ; they had always elbow-room for acrobatic leaps and somersaults. On the Pacific coast their numbers are incalculably greater—perhaps a hundred fold. During the period of their annual mid-summer "runs" they swim in schools ten feet deep or more, with ranks closed up solid. Only those of our Eastern fishermen who are familiar with the swarming of mossbunkers, herring and bluefish can have any conception of their multitudes.

Of course we are all accustomed to the current stories of their innumerable hosts out West, yet I will deliberately strain the credulity of the reader by over-reaching statements far more marvelous and declare that in Alaska the salmon jam the estuaries and inlets so that they can not move at all ! I have seen the outlet of Lake Loring, which is a rivulet two miles long and two rods wide, connecting the salt water with the fresh, so choked with living salmon that if a plank were laid across their protruding backs a man could walk across dry shod. It is so with other similar localities. On the southwestern coast the mountains rise from the ocean quite abruptly, so that there are but two rivers of any considerable length which cut their way through the granite ridges from the interior ; but the melting of the snows upon the peaks fills all the valleys and pockets bordering upon the coast, forming picturesque lakes whose outlets reach the ocean through short rugged channels worn deeply into the rocks. The tide there rises some eighteen feet, and when it is low the outflow of the lakes makes its romantic journey to the brine by a series of rapids and tempting pools, where brook trout of two varieties can be caught with a bait of salmon roe, or even with a fly, affording good sport to the angler. But whenever the tide begins to make, the whole vicinity of the outlet at once swarms with impatient salmon, and as the channel gradually fills with the growing flood the schools press inward and upward from outside, until, finally, when the tide is full, the stream becomes a slack-water channel reaching from the salt water to the very border of the lakes, of which every cubic foot is choked with fish wedged tightly. No theater lobby on a benefit night, nor sheep van on a transportation line, was ever packed more solid. In such extremity the helpless salmon become an easy prey to animals and men. One can lift them out with his hands until he is tired. It is almost impossible to thrust a spear or boat-hook into the mass, and of course a fish must come out whenever it is withdrawn. Bears take their opportunity to scoop them out with their great paws, and when they have regaled themselves to satiety they retire to the adjacent thickets for a dessert of berries which grow there in great abundance and variety. Of course a great many salmon get into the lakes at every tide, but after each recession multitudes are stranded, of which the lustiest flop back into the ocean, while the maimed and hapless remain dead and stranded on the denuded rocks.

It is said that salmon were exceptionally numerous on the Alaska coast in the two years just past, but there seems to be no doubt that they are always more abundant there than in the more southern latitudes of British Columbia and Oregon ; and they swarm clear across the Behring Strait to the coast of Siberia and down to Japan, filling all the waters with their incalculable numbers. In the vicinity of such hosts the problem of bait disappears. Salmon enough can be bought there for a dime to furnish bait for five thousand pounds of halibut or cod, and if some enterprising Yankee will only turn his attention to the opportunity which the Alaskan waters offer, he can supply every Atlantic fisherman with bait and freeze out the Kanucks so that they will never seize any more fishing vessels for violation of their obnoxious laws.

The halibut of Alaska are bound to be a source of large revenue, although at present the fishery is in its infancy. Great numbers are taken from the numerous banks along the coast ; they grow to an enormous size, sometimes reaching five hundred pounds in weight. Captain Morrissey, of San Francisco, in the year 1880, filled up the schooner *General Miller* in less than a month on the banks off Sitka, taking one hundred tons of halibut at the rate of 7,000 pounds per day. There can be no question but that this business will be some day followed up with profit, especially in view of the remarkable depletion of the Atlantic fisheries, which, in 1885, were reduced to one-fourth their former proportions ; of which Prof. Goode, of the Smithsonian Institution, has written as follows :

" At the beginning of the present century these fish were exceedingly abundant in Massachusetts Bay. From 1830 to 1850, and even later, they were extremely abundant on

George's banks ; since 1850 they have partially disappeared from this region ; the fishermen have recently been following them to other banks, and, since 1874, out into deeper and deeper water, and the fisheries are now carried on almost exclusively in the gullies between the off-shore banks and on the outer edges of the banks in water 100 to 350 fathoms in depth. The species has, in like manner, been driven from the shallow fishing grounds on the coast of Europe ; there is, however, little reason to doubt that they still are present in immense numbers within easy access off the British and Scandinavian coasts, and that a good fishery will yet grow up when the fishermen of those countries shall have become more enterprising. In the year 1879 there were forty vessels, of 3,168 tons, from Gloucester, Mass., employed exclusively in the fresh halibut fishery. The total catch of halibut on the New England coast for 1879 is estimated at 14,637,000 pounds.

" In 1885, the halibut fleet of Gloucester is reduced to one-fourth of its former size, and the total catch is estimated at from three to five million pounds. It is evident that within a few years the American off-shore halibut grounds will be so depleted that the fresh halibut fishery on our coasts will be abandoned. We shall then derive our chief supply from the waters of Greenland and Iceland, where several vessels go each year to bring back cargoes of salt 'flitches.' Halibut will come into our markets only in a smoked condition, and the species will be as unfamiliar in our fish markets as it is in those of the old world."

But why go to the British and Scandinavian coasts, or to the waters of Greenland and Iceland, when Alaska is so convenient, the cost of bait almost nothing, the transit across the continent so rapid, and refrigerators so complete ? If we have fresh Pacific salmon in our eastern markets, why not fresh halibut as well, that the species may remain "familiar ?" If salt fish are required, or halibut fins, salt can perhaps be manufactured on the coast from sea water by evaporation, as it now is at places on the California sea-board ; or the halibut can be sun-dried or smoked. Salmon are used for bait. The Indians are adepts at taking these great fish. They do not fish from the canoes, but set lines which are attached to floats—generally bladders—to which are fastened little flags on staffs. Among a group of them the fisherman watches, and when the hooked fish has exhausted itself towing the float, he is secured. It is very exhilarating to the novice to see the floats, when a fish is on, go diving and darting through the water at the rate of ten knots an hour. The hook is a native contrivance, which is far more efficient than any shop-rig, made usually of two pieces of tough wood, each about eleven inches long, beveled at the ends, so that when joined and seized with twine or sinew, they form a <, or angle, with an opening five inches wide; an iron spike passes through the lower jaw, inclining inwardly, the upper jaw of the hook serving as a guide to the jaw of the fish, which can not be withdrawn without catching on the point of the spike. A fish which once takes hold, seldom gets away.

In 1884 Captain Exon, of Portland, Oregon, equipped a vessel for deep sea-fishing, with the prosecution of which he was familiar, but had hardly demonstrated the value of this method, and the abundance of fish where sought, before he was unfortunately drowned. Other practical men are now investigating the subject with the purpose of prosecuting the business to a profitable result if they find the conditions as favorable as they believe them to be. There are also a few San Francisco fishermen who visit the Alaska coast for cod, of which they salt some 2,000 tons annually.

Another newly introduced industry is the manufacture of fish oil for dressing leather and preparing jute for market. The first factory of the kind was established at Kilsinoo, last spring, by the Northwest Trading Company, and a shipment of 20,000 barrels was made in September last, of which 12,000 barrels went the long distance to New York ; but it will not be long before there will be many oil factories on the Alaska coast, for all the bays and estuaries swarm with oil-producing fish, and the product is limited only by the capacity of the works and the supply of casks. This company expects to manufacture 300,000 gallons this season—equal to a hundred car-loads. At Skidegate, on the British Columbian coast, there is a factory for extracting oil from the livers of dogfish, whose output this year is 50,000 gallons. This oil is admitted to be superior to any other kind as a lubricant. It is shipped chiefly to the United States, where it pays a duty of 25 per cent., though small quantities are consumed in the Province, or sent to Honolulu and China. In another year or so this industry will probably establish itself on the Alaska coast as well, and thereby save the duty.

The foregoing summary refers to the meager fishing industries of Alaska already existing, but I will show, in the statements that follow, what enormous possibilities of lucrative employment and revenue lie in the immediate future. Certainly the waters of the Pacific are far more prolific of

fish and other marine forms than the Atlantic, or even the
Gulf of Mexico. For not only do we find the sea lion, the
fur seal, the sea otter, and other exceptional forms of marine
life in vast numbers, but we find the cod, the tom-cod, the
halibut, the herring, the flounder, the salmon, the sea-trout
of the same or closely related species, common to the
Atlantic coast ; and we find them differing in size, many
larger and frequently more abundant, but dissimilar in
color and flavor—and, beside these, a great many varieties
unknown to Atlantic waters, and of especial economic
value. Principal among the latter are the sculpins, the
scorpænids, sebastichthydæ, and the embiotocoid or viviparous fishes, which comprise a great number of species.
At the same time it may be borne in mind that there are
many Atlantic fishes, like the blackfish, cunner, striped bass,
porgy, sheepshead, bluefish, etc., which have no analogues
on the Pacific. The viviparous fish may be said to be somewhat intermediate in external appearance, as they are in
structure, between the labrids and the sparids, but they are
readily recognizable and distinguished from all others by
ichthyologists.   In reproduction they develop a uterus-like
envelope, which incloses the young fish to the number of
from seven or eight to forty, and these are hatched out at
maturity just like a litter of kittens or mice.   The family is
characteristic of the western coast, only two or three species
being known to ocean beyond the limits of the Pacific coast
of temperate North America, and these few only on the
opposite coast of the Pacific in the northern temperate
region, and possibly in the opposite hemisphere in the temperate seas of New Zealand and Australia.   The numerous
varieties of sebastichthys are locally known as " rock-cod,"
but they have not the remotest relation to the family
Gadidæ.   There are no less than twenty-eight of them on
the Pacific coast, of which six are found in Alaskan waters.
Several of them are highly colored and very beautiful—
bright scarlet, banded yellow and black, pink-spotted, etc.
Indeed, the fish of the Pacific are more highly colored as a
rule than their congeners of the Atlantic, a characteristic
equally true of most of the marine forms—animals, mollusks,
crustaceans, plants, etc., as well as of the land flora and
fauna, the fruits, vegetables, shrubs, trees, and flowers.
One of the rockfish just referred to very closely resembles
the Florida red snapper in color and general appearance,
though the structural differences are quite apparent when
specimens of each are examined side by side.   As a class
they are good edible fish.   Most of them are caught in deep

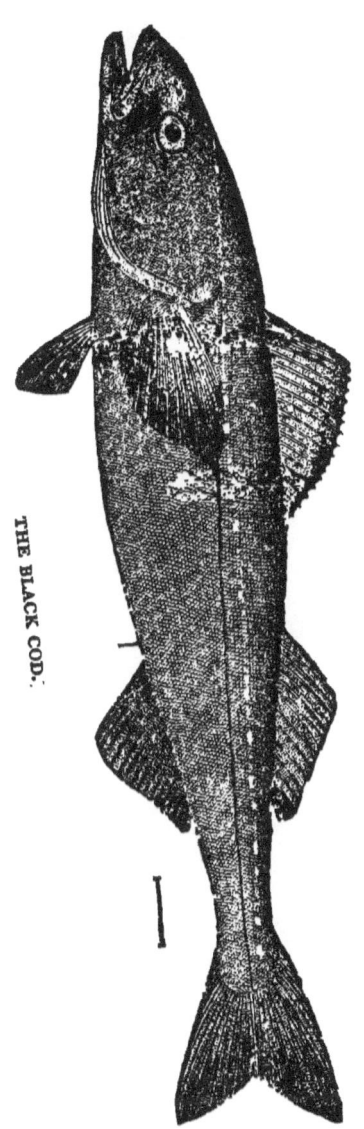

THE BLACK COD.

water on rocky ledges, a half mile or so from shore, often in thirty fathoms, with hard clams, crabs or fresh meat for bait, and it is very easy to determine whenever the fisherman swings off from a ledge, for the fish stop biting, a fact which shows how important it is to ascertain and keep the exact location of their feeding grounds. Besides these there are many kinds of fishes not at all related to this family, or to each other, which are called rock-cod. One such, which is familiarly known in Alaska as the black-cod, rock-cod, and coal-fish, is likely to form a valuable addition to our list of economic fishes, and may well fill the place of substitute for some other kinds which may have become or may become scarce. No one has labored half so hard to secure the introduction of this estimable fish into our markets as the Hon. James G. Swan, who is the Hawaiian consul at Port Townsend, Washington Territory, and a veteran correspondent of the Smithsonian Institution ; and I regard it fortunate for the integrity of this chapter of my volume that I find available for republication here an admirable report of the habits, habitat, and quality of the black-cod from the Bulletin of the United States Fisheries Commission, and from which I cull the following extracts. [Scientifically the fish is known as *Anoplopoma fimbria.*]

The report says :

"The *Anoplopoma fimbria* is known in California as the candle-fish, Spanish mackerel, grease-fish, etc.; among the Makah Indians of Cape Flattery, Wash., as 'beshow,' and by the white residents of the cape as 'black-cod.' On Queen Charlotte's Islands, British Columbia, it is called 'coal-fish ' by white settlers, and by the Haidah Indians, who reside on those Islands, it is called 'skil.' At Knight's Inlet, British Columbia, it is called 'kwakewlth.' Each tribe or locality where it is taken has a local name for it, but it is generally known as black cod. The scientific name, *anoplopoma fimbria*, has been adopted by Gill, Jordan and Gilbert, and most other writers, although a specimen taken off Mount Saint Elias, Alaska, was named by Pallas *Gadus fimbria* (Proc. U. S. Nat. Museum, 1881, vol. 4, p. 254), thus showing that its resemblance to the cod was observed by that naturalist. The term 'cod ' is applied by fishermen and fish-dealers on the North Pacific coast to a variety of fish which are not related to the genus *Gadus,* and are not found in Atlantic waters. The *Ophidon elongatus* is called in San Francisco, buffalo cod, Green cod, blue cod, etc. At Cape Flattery the Makah Indians call it 'tooshkow.' The whites call it 'kultus ' cod, or inferior to true cod. The different

varieties of *Sebastichthys* are known in the Victoria and San
Francisco markets as rock-cod, but do not resemble the
rock-cod of New England in any manner, being more like
the perch, having a remarkable development of sharp bony
spines and prickles.   The popular name of black-cod, applied to the *Anoplopoma fimbria* does not seem any more of
a misnomer than to call the *Ophidon elongatus* blue or green
cod.   In general appearance the black-cod resembles a pol-
lock, but when fully grown they have the rounded form of
a true cod, but are not so marked.   In color they are a
dark olive brown or sepia on the back, with grayish sides
and belly; the flesh is white and very fat, like mackerel, and
they have been sold in San Francisco under the name of
Spanish mackerel when of small size.   Professor Jordan
says: 'The young ones are taken off the wharves at
Seattle, but are not much thought of as a food-fish. It attains
its greatest perfection in very deep water, where it attains
a size of 40 inches, and a weight of 15 pounds. Instances are
not uncommon of black-cod being taken measuring 50
inches and weighing 30 pounds, but the average is much
less than this last.   But it is an admitted rule that the
deeper the water the larger the fish.'

  "Although I have the credit of first introducing this fish
in a marketable shape to the public, yet it has been known
to the officers and employés of the Hudson's Bay Company
for many years, but was seldom seen on their tables ; the
enormous quantities of salmon, eulachon, herring, cod,
halibut and other fish, easily and plentifully taken, made it
unnecessary to incur the trouble of fishing in the deep
water for the black-cod.   The first I saw of them was at Neah
Bay, Wash. Terr., at the entrance of Fuca Strait, in 1859.
An old Indian caught a few when fishing for halibut. I
procured one, which I broiled, and found it equal to a No. 1
mackerel.   I have occasionally seen the 'beshow' every
summer that I have been at Neah Bay since 1859, but I
have never had an opportunity to get any quantity of them
till in September, 1883, while at Skidegate, Queen Charlotte's
Islands, which I visited under instructions from Professor
Spencer F. Baird.   I succeeded in procuring about 100 of
them.   The Haidah Indians take them in considerable
quantities on the west coast of the group of islands,
in the deep waters of the inlets and harbors, for the purpose
of extracting the oil or grease, which is used as food by the
natives, and is similar in appearance to the eulachon grease,
which is of the color and consistency of soft lard.   From
Montèry to the Arctic ocean the *Anoplopoma* is found.   It

feeds on crustaceans, worms and small fish. Hitherto it has not been introduced among the whites as a food-fish, owing to the superstitious prejudice of some tribes against fishing for them to sell.

" A lot I took to Victoria dry-salted in boxes were the first ever seen in a merchantable condition in that city, and the four boxes I sent to the United States Fish Commission are the first ever exported from the Province of British Columbia, a fact to which special reference was made by the collector of customs of Victoria in his quarterly report to the Minister of Finances in Ottawa.

" As the Haidah Indians seem to be the only ones who make a business of taking the black-cod or 'skil,' I will confine myself to a description of a method adopted by them. The fish lines used in the capture of the black-cod are made of kelp, in a manner similar to that of the Makahs, of Cape Flattery, and other tribes on the northwest coast. This giant kelp the *Nereocystis* (Harvey) is of the order *Laminariaceæ*, and is of much larger dimensions than the *Fucaceæ*, the fronds being measured by fathoms, not feet. Some of these plants, it is said, when fully grown, have a stem measuring 300 feet in length. These grow where the water is rapid, and have to extend to a great length before their buoyancy will permit them to reach the surface. For about two-thirds of this length from the root up, the stem is about the size of a halibut line. It then expands till at the extremity it assumes a pear-shaped hollow head, capable of holding a quart, and from which extends a tuft of upward of fifty leaves, lanceolate in form, each of which is from 40 to 50 feet long. The slender stem is of prodigious strength, and is prepared by the natives for use as follows : The stems being cut off a uniform length, generally 15 or 25 fathoms each, are placed in running fresh water till they become bleached and all the salt is extracted. They are then stretched and partially dried in the open air, then coiled up and hung in the smoke of a lodge for a short time. Then they are wet and stretched again and knotted together. This process is continued at regular intervals till the kelp stems become tough and as strong as the best hemp line of the same size. After using, it is always coiled up, but as it gets brittle if allowed to dry too much it is invariably soaked in salt water before being used. The hooks used are of a peculiar shape, unlike any fish-hook I have ever seen; they are made of the knots or butts of limbs of the hemlock, cut out from old decayed logs. These knots are split into splints of proper size, then roughly shaped with a knife, and then steamed and bent into shape, which shape they retain when cold. This form is adopted, so the Indian informed me, because the bottom on the west coast is very foul with stones and coral formations and incrustations ; steel hooks get fast, and lines are subject to being lost ; but this style of hook does not get fast.

" When the hook is to be used the bait is tied on with the string which is used to bring the two ends of the hook together and keep them in position when not baited. After the bait is well secured a piece of stick is inserted to press the ends of the hook apart. When the fish bites the bait it knocks out the stick, which floats to the surface, the two ends of the hook, springing together, close on the fish's head and hold it fast. It is usual to tie from seventy-five to one hundred hooks to the line, at a distance of about two feet apart, and the fish are so plentiful that not unfrequently every hook will have a fish. The sticks which float to the surface, when knocked out of the hook by the fish, serve to indicate to the Indian the sort of luck he is having at the bottom. But although the fish may be abundant, the Indian is not always sure of securing what he has caught. His greatest annoyance is the ground-sharks or nurse-fish, as the sailors call them, which will often eat the bodies of the black-cod, leaving only the heads attached to the hooks. Another annoyance is from a small fish called by the Haidah Indians ' nee-kaio-kaiung,' the *Blepsias cirrhosus* (Pallas) Gün., one of the family *Cottidœ*, which steals the bait and often gets hooked ; as soon as the Indian discovers this pest he quits fishing and goes to another place. As the depth of the water varies in different places it is usual to have a lot of spare lines in the canoe which can instantly be knotted together and form a line as long as required ; sometimes two hundred fathoms will be used, as the line when fully supplied with hooks becomes a trawl. A most ingenious contrivance is the sinker used by the Haidahs in this deep-water fishing. This is a stone, from ten to twenty pounds in weight. A small kelp line is wound round this stone and held by a bight tucked under the turns, and the end made fast to the end of the larger line, which large line is wound round this stone, and a smaller stone which serves to bind it fast and as a sort of tripping stone. The large line is secured in a similar manner as the small line, by a loop or bight tucked under the turns. The stone is then lowered to the bottom and the line paid out. As soon as the fisherman sees enough pegs floating to warrant his pulling in the line he gathers in the slack till he feels the weight of the stone, when he gives a sudden jerk, which pulls out the bight and loosens the tripping stone, which falls out and loosens the big stone, which in turn becomes detached from the line, which is then pulled in relieved of the weight of the sinker.

" On my arrival at Skidegate, in the last of August, 1883, I arranged with Mr. Andrew McGregor, one of the partners in the Skidegate, to send some Indians to the west coast to procure some black-cod. He sent four Indians, Scanayune, Ske-at-lung, Ingow and Skatsgai, who all belong to the Gold Harbor band on the west coast. I sent a sack of salt with the Indians, with instructions to take out the gills, remove the viscera without splitting the fish, and then fill the cavity with salt, which was done, and the fish were received in prime condition. On the 2d of September Scanayune returned with twenty fine fish. A council was now called to decide the best way to split them. There were a number of eastern fishermen present, who were the crew of the little steamer *Skidegate*, engaged in dog-fishing for the oil works. Some were of the opinion that the fish should be split in the back, like a salmon ; but I objected, as I thought people would say they were the white-flesh dog-salmon and be prejudiced, so I had them split and dressed like cod, and well salted in a vat. But now my trouble commenced. I was of the opinion, as were all the others, that the fish should be barreled like salmon ; but we had no barrels or coopers, and the question was how to get them to Victoria without rusting, for we all thought that so fat a fish would rust like a mackerel or salmon. At last I recollected how I had seen halibut treated when it was to be smoked, and I decided on that plan. After the fish had been in salt two weeks I rinsed them in the pickle they had made, and piled them skin side up, put planks and heavy stones on them, and so pressed out the pickle. After they had been four days under this pressure I found them hard and firm, and beautifully white. I then packed them in boxes, which I made for the purpose, putting twenty fish in each box and filling up with dry salt. My intention was to repack them in Victoria and put them in barrels, but on examining the boxes on my arrival I found the fish in such fine condition that I was advised by experts of the Hudson's Bay Company to send the fish forward just as they were ; and so well satisfied were the officers of the company with the plan I had adopted through necessity, that the chief factor, William Charles, Esq., instructed the company's agent at Massett, Mr. McKenzie, to procure all the black-cod he could get from the Indians, to cure them in every respect as I had done, and to pack them in similar packages, as it was thought they would take better in the London market.

"I tested the fresh fish in every manner I could think of. I had the livers and we fried and found them delicious. The females were full of eggs, which I found very small, about the size of herring spawn. This was the first of September, but I had no opportunity of ascertaining the spawning season or their spawning ground. I tried the tongues, but did not like them as well as cod-fish tongues, as they were quite small. The fish does not make a good chowder, as it is too fat ; the heads, however, after having been salted, we found made excellent chowder. The best way in which the fresh fish can be cooked is to broil it like fresh mackerel, or roast it before the open fire like planked shad. After it has been salted, as I salted those I put up, it should be cooked by first soaking till the salt is well out, then simply boiled and served with plain boiled potatoes. Made into fish-balls it excels any fish I have eaten. On the 6th day of October, 1883, I gave George Vienna, the fish dealer on Government street, Victoria, one of the black-cod, which he hung up in his stall for every one to examine. On the 18th day of December I examined the same fish, which had been exposed to the weather in the stall all the time, and it was perfectly sweet. Mr. Vienna said it never would rust ; it was too well salted. A gentleman of Victoria, who had eaten of the black-cod heartily on several occasions, told me that he is unable to eat either salt salmon or mackerel, as the oil of these fish does not agree with his digestion, but he experienced no such effect from eating the fat black-cod, and mentioned the fact as something to be noticed.

"Now that the experiment of my method of dry-salting the black-cod has proved a success by the encomiums passed upon the excellence of that fish as tested by the experts of the Boston Fish Bureau, who are undoubtedly some of the best critics and judges of fish in the United States, I wish to call attention to the economy of my method for the poor settlers on our northwest coasts of Washington Territory and Alaska. All that is required for outlay is the cost of the salt for curing the fish, and the nails for making boxes, which can be made from the white spruce which abounds on the coast, from the Columbia River to Western Alaska. This wood splits as easily as cedar, is perfectly sweet and free from resin, as all the gum is contained in the thin ring of sap-wood and bark. The inside is free from resin. This will make the cheapest and best of boxes and save the expense of coopers and barrels, and the fish being of full size is better adapted for smoking than the same fish cut and barreled.

" *The Fishery for the Black-Cod.*—A very important question to be answered is : Will the black-cod be taken in sufficient quantities to supply the demand which is likely to spring up wherever their rare excellence is known ? I think that at present the supply will be limited, as there are no fishermen on the North Pacific coast who have the appliances or the experience in deep sea fishing as practiced at present on the Atlantic coast. Our coast fisheries are exclusively confined to salmon, which are taken in the rivers with nets and seines. The very few cod and halibut brought to our markets are taken with hand-lines and old-fashioned trawls, but it is rare to find any fishermen working in more than thirty fathoms of water. Our waters teem with fish, but as yet, with the exception of salmon, no organized plan has been tried for taking quantities of fish *What we want are Eastern fishermen with Eastern capital and Eastern methods of taking fish.* If such men would come out here they can find plenty of black-cod, but they will be found in deep, swift water, where at times it is pretty rough. But to a ' Grand Banker ' or a ' George's Banker ' our most turbulent waters would be but a plaything. In order to develop the fisheries of Puget Sound and the Alaskan ˙waters there should be some regular wholesale fish dealers established, who would take every thing the fishermen would bring, and find markets themselves. Our fishermen are too poor to send their fish to a distant market ; but let a wholesale dealer with capital establish himself, and he would find that fish would be brought from all quarters, white men and Indians working with a will to catch fish which would bring them ready money.

" The best season of the year for taking black-cod is in the spring, when the eulachon run up the inlets and streams where they spawn ; the black-cod follow them, and can be taken in quantities ; but I am informed by both Haidah and Makah Indians that the black-cod can be taken in the deep water at any season of the year when the weather will permit fishing. There are undoubtedly certain seasons which are better than others for taking this fish, but as yet no one has made a study of their habits."

Herring swarm in the bays and inlets of Alaska during the spawning season in the spring, but are not at that time of as good quality as when taken in nets from their permanent banks and feeding grounds. The Indians catch great quantities with poles and boards, armed with sharp nails at an angle. These are thrust under the schools, which swim about two feet deep, and the fish are gaffed out. The herring spawn in salt water, and their favorite places are the quiet bays along the shores, and there every kind of kelp and seaweed is crusted with the spawn, and as the tide goes down and one walks along the beach, every step crushes myriads. I can not discover that they enter the fresh water streams at all. The most careful investigation has failed to discover their spawn attached to plants beyond the reach of tide. The Indians do not collect the eggs deposited on the seaweed, but plant at half-tide marks rows of branches of cedar and balsam, which, in a tide or two, become covered with spawn ; these are replaced by others, and hung up to dry. The spawn is eaten dried, raw and cooked in various ways, and is very palatable in either. These, however, are somewhat smaller than those of Europe, though fully equal in quality when taken in their prime. There is a factory on Burrard inlet, near the Canadian Pacific railway terminus, where herring oil is pressed out and fertilizers made from the scraps. The success of the menhaden fishing in the East should encourage herring fishing in the West.

Comparing my personal observations made at sundry times and places, I find the range of the true cod, halibut, salmon, sea trout and some other fish to be the same on both sides of the continent. The cod range between the fiftieth and sixtieth parallels of latitude. In the East the principal food of the shore-cod is the caplin, and the fishermen not only use caplin chiefly for bait, but they follow their movements to ascertain the whereabouts of the cod. On the west side (the Pacific) the oolachan, or the candle-fish, is the correspondent of the caplin, and is almost identical with it. It is smoked, salted and dried on the rocks in the same way, and is largely used for food by the Indians, being very delicious, but it is much more oily and will burn like a candle. Oolachan oil is considered superior to cod liver oil or any other fish oil known. It is of a whitish tint, about the consistency of thin lard, and is a staple article of barter between the coast Indians and the interior tribes. The fish begin running about the first of March, and swarm into the rivers and estuaries by the million for several weeks, the waves of each flood tide stranding them upon the beach in windrows a yard wide and several inches deep. This period should be the cod-fishing season, which is three months earlier than in Labrador. They are caught in purse nets by the canoe load.

In the province of British Columbia, where the manufacture of the oil is prosecuted to some extent, the fish are boiled in water about four hours in five-barrel wooden tanks with iron bottoms, and then strained through baskets, made from willow roots, into red cedar boxes of about fifteen gallons capacity each. When the run of fish is good, each tribe will put up about twenty boxes of oil.

Sturgeon are said to exist in the interior, and if such be the fact, which I can not vouch for of my own personal knowledge, here is another opportunity for lucrative profit to energetic operators, who can employ the Indians to capture them. Wherever sturgeon are found in Canada or the United States, the catching of them is prosecuted with great pecuniary advantage, for there is no part of this extraordinary fish that can not be utilized, and in bulk they often reach 150 pounds avoirdupois. Sturgeon have a wide distribution, extending from the Atlantic to the Pacific, and through many degrees of north and south latitude. They are abundant in Fraser River, British Columbia, and in the Peace River country much further north, whose waters head in the same great divide or watershed which separates the north-eastern tributaries of the Yukon ; and there seems to be no physical reason why they should not exist in the interior of Alaska. Indeed, I have an impression that Lieutenant Schwatka mentions their being there. The strongest evidence to the contrary is the fact that the Russians, who make such an extensive commodity of the sturgeon and its products elsewhere, did not prosecute this industry in Alaska. However, and whether or no, the methods of catching sturgeon are so unique and the economic value of the fish so great, that I dare say a description of them here will prove interesting to the reader, even though the subject be not strictly Alaskan. In the first place, sturgeon are caught in seines, pound-nets, and drift-nets, during both winter and summer, and by hook and line. In winter gill-nets are set by an ingenious system of holes cut through the ice at equi-distant intervals, through which they are thrust and located by means of long poles with boat-hooks attached. The "pounds" used are the common trap-net with lead, heart and pocket. When drift-nets are used, they are handled from large flat-boats, and fishing is done only at night. In the morning the fish are hauled to a floating platform on the shore, where the heads, tails, entrails, backbone, and skin are removed, and the two sides are packed in ice in large boxes for shipment, to be sold for consumption while fresh, or for smoking elsewhere. Many fishermen inclose a space on the lake or river shore in three or four feet depth of water, by making a pen of piles or heavy stakes driven in the bottom. Here they are kept after being caught and fed until wanted for market. Numerous pens of this kind may be seen along the Detroit River and Lakes St. Clair and Huron. The *American Angler*, in describing the entire adaptability of the whole body of this most economical fish says :—" The meat of this fish is extremely nutritious, and when fat and properly employed is nearly equal to veal in its sustaining principles. When eaten from the young fish it highly savors, and partakes chiefly of that enticing flavor so much praised in the shad. Every part of the fish is utilized. The meat is often labeled salmon, and is often mistaken for the meat of that fish. The cartilaginous bones make a highly valued isinglass, and the stomach gives a most perfect, clear, and adhesive glue. The residue is used as manure, and by the farmers is considered equal to that of sheep. The process of smoking is quite simple. After being cleaned the meat, which has no bones, like other fish, is cut into strips from one-half pound to two and three pounds weight, put into brine ten or twelve hours for curing, hung up a short time to dry and then finished with the smoke of hickory or some hard wood for ten or twelve hours, when it is ready for boxing and shipment. The next largest industry connected with the sturgeon is the manufacture and exportation of " caviar." This is nothing else than the roe or eggs of the female which, it is said, sometimes equal one-third the weight of the fish. Generally the yield of the lake sturgeon is one and two gallons. These are taken in hand by experts, who manipulate them by several washings through sieves, with water strongly impregnated with the purest salt, obtained usually from Russia or Germany, until every shred and vestige of flesh and impurity is removed. The " caviar" is then treated to a certain seasoning of ingredients, known only to the initiated and carefully guarded from public ken, and put up in water-tight casks holding from 115 to 125 lbs., well headed to exclude the air. It is then ready for market and bears an average of twelve cents per pound, wholesale. In retail shops it sells at twenty-five and thirty cents, and is put up in small cans, one-half to two and three pounds in size. It would be difficult to give the tonnage of " caviar" that is prepared on the lakes and finds its way largely to New York and Boston, and probably in still larger amounts to Europe, and principally Russia and Germany. One dealer gives his annual trade at 400 kegs, say 60,000 lbs.; 4,000 kegs of caviar were received at the single port of Hamburg, Germany, from the middle of June, 1885, to the middle of November, from the United States. The eggs are quite small and dark colored, entirely salty in taste, and without a superior as an appetizer. For table use caviar is seasoned with onions, pepper, and such condiments as are palatable to the eater, and spread in its raw state upon bread and eaten with it, much as butter is. It is a highly popular dish among the Russians, who make it in its perfection, and is to them what Limburger cheese is to the Dutch. But the American people are gradually bringing their taste up to the Russian delicacy, as they are also fast bringing it up to the Frenchman's frog. The taste has to be educated to enjoy its gustatory flavor. It seems to have been known in Shakespeare's time. He makes Hamlet say : ' For the play, I remember, pleased not the million. 'Twas caviar to the general,' from which it would seem not to have been a universal favorite. The value of the sturgeon is still further enhanced by its large air bladder or sound. When taken from the fish it is split open, thoroughly cleansed and prepared by men who understand the business. When dry it is the isinglass of commerce, and sells usually at $1.50 per pound. The bladders are bought by the fishermen at five and six cents each. A considerable quantity is made in Detroit yearly. The sturgeon is one of the most oily of the finny tribe, and when put through the usual process yields a large percentage of oil, which is said to make a very good lubricating oil, and is also preferred for greasing and softening harness."

The Indians who dwell along the great Sascatchewan River in the British Northwest Territory, spear sturgeon in the river pockets just below shoals, where they resort to gather up whatever floats down stream and settles, just as all the tribes of suckers do ; and for this purpose they have an ingenious harpoon whose head comes out of the shaft whenever a fish is struck and fastened, but which is prevented from being carried off or lost by a free line which attaches it to the staff or handle. In roily or turbid waters where the fish can not be seen, they use a long pole, at the end of which are fastened, loosely, several large hooks, the shanks of which are tied to the pole with sinew or strong marline. The red man feels for the fish with his pole, and knowing by long practice when he has touched a fish he gives a strong pull backward, which sinks the sharp hook through the tough skin and deep into the flesh. The fish struggles and the hooks loosen from the pole, but are held fast by the line. Then it is only a question of strength to get the lethargic fellows out of the water, with may be a hearty wrestle on the bank to keep them out.

In Alaska, flounders, anchovies, and sole are found in large numbers, but quite unlike the fishes called by the same names on the Atlantic coast. The sole is especially different from his celebrated European namesake. Dogfish and sculpins are not esteemed as edible fish, although they are very numerous and great nuisances to those who fish with hook and line. One kind of dogfish is beautifully spotted, and one of the sculpins (*Hemilepidotus tracharul*) looks very much like a rutabaga turnip covered with warts, with a slit clear across the big end for a mouth. He is so ugly that old fishermen torture him just for his ugliness.

There are two kinds of coral found on the coast, and also sponges of fine texture, not round like the recognized sponges of commerce, but palmated with digital divisions, which might be made useful for many purposes. The sea cucumber is abundant also. When cured and dried it makes the article of commerce known as the *beche de la mer*, highly prized in China for food, where it is called "trepang." A valuable industry might be built up by preparing this commodity for market. Indeed there are lots of economical natural products in this new and unprospected region which might reasonably prompt mercantile effort if attention were only called to them.

The immunity of the North Pacific ocean from the intermittent storms which devastate the Atlantic, makes most favorable comparison in its behalf as a field for commercial fisheries and a cruising ground for fishing vessels. Cyclones are seldom heard of there, while on the Labrador coast and the gulf of St. Lawrence alone, no less than three hundred vessels and twelve hundred lives have been lost in storms during the past twenty-five years. Besides this consideration, the scarcity of fish in Eastern waters within the past few years is making the fisheries a precarious business. Let the disappointed fisherman of the Atlantic coast migrate to Alaska ! The fishing seasons are different there, and not subject to interruptions of drifting ice in the spring and rough weather in the fall ; and there is no danger of starvation, even if the fisheries should fail. I see no reason why the banks and littoral waters of the Alaskan Pacific may not swarm with fleets of fishing vessels as well as those of Newfoundland and Labrador.

As regards the anadromous and inland fresh water fish of Alaska, there are the salmon and the sea trout, the lake trout, at least two kinds of brook trout, pike, grayling, and a very superior whitefish. Silver salmon begin to arrive in March, or early in April, and last until the end of June. They generally weigh from four to twenty-five pounds, but sometimes reach seventy. The second kind are caught from June to August, and are considered the finest. The average size is only five or six pounds. The third, coming in August, average seven pounds, and are an excellent fish. The humpback appears every second year, remaining from August until winter, and weighs from six to fourteen pounds. The hookbill arrives in September, and remains till winter, its weight ranging from twelve to forty-five pounds. There are several other varieties of salmon, not all strictly edible, of which the most numerous is the dog salmon, eaten only by the Indians. The rainbow trout, *S. iridea*, and the cut-throat trout, which is especially distinguished by the crimson slashes under its gills, are found in many streams and also in the lakes. A larger lake trout, of the Dolly Varden type (*S. Malma*), with red spots as large as a pea, is found in the lakes on the small islands, as well as the mainland. The sea trout, identical with the Canadian sea trout, and spotted in the same way with blue and crimson spots, much like the Eastern brook trout, makes its appearance at stated intervals like its Atlantic brothers, and ascends the rivers to spawn. All kinds of trout take bait and fly. The sea trout takes the trolling spoon readily in the bays. It is found all the way from Victoria, B. C., northward to Bering Strait, and in the Arctic seas replaces the salmon, which is not found there at all. Its north and south range on the west coast corresponds very nearly with its range on the Eastern coast. It winters in the lakes which connect with salt water, and runs down the streams in the spring. The indigenous fish of the streams are the *Salmo iridea*, but there are many streams in Alaska which are bare of all fish except in the early summer and fall, and then these self-same sea trout, migratory and anadromous, run up their channels to spawn, just as they do in the Canadian Atlantic.

For other varieties of trout than this, Indian River and Saw Mill Creek, near Sitka, the Lake Loring outlet at Naha Bay, and other streams, afford good rod-fishing. Sport with the artificial fly is by no means as satisfying as it is in the East, or even in Oregon and Washington Territory, although at certain times it is fair. It may be said that, owing to the condition of water as affected by the melting snows in spring, and the subsequent superabundance of salmon roe with which every crevice is crammed after those fish begin to spawn, even bait-fishing can hardly be enjoyed except at certain periods. No fly will tempt the trout, nothing in fact but a chunk of nasty sticky spawn, which they will approach leisurely and feed on as daintily as a full fed kitten on a bit of meat. You must sink your weighted hook to the bottom, and keep up a series of little jerks as though you were bobbing for eels, and by and by you strike one ; once hooked they are quite gamy.

The *Salmo iridea* is found here both in the lakes and streams, but there is another trout which differs much in appearance from varieties which I am familiar with. A specimen ten inches long, called "mountain trout" by the Indians, had a body covered with black spots, from one-sixteenth to one-eighth inch in diameter. These extend considerably below the medial line and cover the tail and the dorsal fins ; the second dorsal is adipose, but slightly less so than that of a fontinalis, having a slight show of membrane on which there are four spots. The ventral and anal fins are yellowish in center, bordered with red, the tail is square, the belly a dull white.

That the spawning seasons of families of fish similar to those of the Atlantic should be different on the Pacific, is easily accounted for by the warmer temperature of the water. It would seem that the laws of heat and cold have the same effect upon fish as they do upon vegetation, ordering the seasons accordingly ; and the spawning of fish, like the budding of trees, may be advanced or retarded by mild or inclement weather ; stated visitations of pelagic or anadromous fish may be postponed or even prevented by cold weather ; but the Pacific is less subject to these vicissitudes than the Atlantic.

In Alaska there are few sandy beaches or gravelly shores. The margins of the mainlands and islands drop plump into many fathoms of water, so that the tide never goes out—it merely recedes, and when it is lowest it exposes the rank yellow and green weeds which cling to the damp crags and slippery masses of rock, and the mussels and barnacles which crackle and hiss when the lapping waves recede. In some places there are little bights, a few yards wide, between the rocks, where there is a sort of beach formed entirely of comminuted shells ; and one can pick up cockles, round hard-shell clams and abelones by the peck—clams of all sizes, some large and tough, and some small and very sweet. Exceptionally there are areas of mud, where the gigantic geoduck, a soft-shell clam which sometimes weighs 8 lbs., vegetates in oozy retirement a foot beneath the surface, squirting aloft its tremendous jets, four feet high, whenever a passing foot chances to disturb its shellfish privacy, and there are also flats near the mouths of rivers which, on gala days when the festive clam luxuriates, seem to be filled with miniature fountains, squirting. As for the luscious and toothsome oyster, the abrupt conformation of the coast, with its rocky shores and almost fathomless waters, explains why there are none. I cannot learn that any person has ever seen a native Alaskan oyster ; but there are a good many beds further south, in British Columbia, and I have eaten lots of the bivalves with genuine gusto. However, along side of a regulation "Saddle-rock" they look insignificant, inasmuch as seven stewed oysters go to the teaspoonful, by actual count !

To me it is a great pleasure to see what the ebb-tide uncovers, and to watch the career of the counter currents as they surge to and fro in the narrow channels betwixt sunken rocks—visible now at low water, and eloquent with the dangers of Peril strait or Seymour rapids—which are invisible when the flood is full. At flood or slack water the surface is as placid as the moon, but whenever the tide turns and the ebb or flood begins, it is strange to observe the tide-rips in what seems to be an interior land-locked lake. If one were to unexpectedly behold a surging commotion in the placid basins of the Adirondacks, he would scarcely be more startled. It is hard to grapple with the phenomenon. Immediately on the flood, all the trash and floating trees, chunks of ice, dead fish, loose seaweed, and what not, which have been floating about on the slack, begin to set in with the tide ; giant kelps with stems 20 fathoms long and broad streamers spreading in all directions and half under water, like the hair of a drowned woman, lift their weird forms as they drift by ; jelly-fish and medusæ, almost translucent, with delicate tints of pearl, lavender, mauve, and brown, come in countless myriads, contracting and expanding like a living pulse, and with streaming filaments like threads of glass steadfastly follow the inexorable stream of fate, as if striving to overtake the lead ; schools of herring and small fish of all sorts swarm in all directions, skurrying onward and fretting the surface like flaws of wind ; and last of all, predatory and with fell intent, follow the whales and porpoises and thresher sharks, tumbling, sporting, diving and feasting with appetites never cloyed by repletion.   Here and there along the shore, where some little bight makes into the land, herds of seals bob up serenely out of the water and gaze with large and solemn eyes.   All the atmosphere is filled with the softened light of a summer haze, and the air aloft and roundabout is noisy with the scream of gulls and terns quartering the azure fields on the wings of the warm southwest winds.   This is a summer picture of Alaska.

As I stroll along the seething shore, with all the bowlders and crags slippery and rank with a pervading odor from the uncovered repository of the sea, peering into clefts and crannies, opening out rough snarls of seaweed with my crooked stick, and lifting pendulous draperies of soggy kelp, uncouth creatures with horny claws and bristling spines stare at me with glassy eyes, clinging defiantly to the place of their exposure.   If I poke at them, they rise up on edge and snap and dart and pinch the stick.   Some pettishly withdraw, spitting spiteful jets of acrimony, while others attach themselves by insidious discs or suckers which no small force or shrewd device is able to unloose.   The Spirit of Evil clings not more tenaciously to human nature.   If it had been my hand, nothing but shreds of flesh and blood would satisfy the grudge.   With their protecting element, the sea, withdrawn, they are practically *hors du combat*, yet repellant.   When the tide comes in, they will be aggressive enough.   It is not a nice place for a bath.   Here are giant crabs.   Close by, moving inexplicably over the rocks, there seems a pewter wash-basin, bottom up, dingy with use, but turn it over, and we find it filled with a tangle of legs, sprawling and kicking ; and it has a handle a foot long, three-sided like a bayonet, serrated on the edges.   It is a horseshoe crab, more horrid than hurtful.   All over the sodden premises, scattered among the party-colored kelp and seaweeds, are conchs, abelones, periwinkles, and spirals, with their protruding tenants gasping for the beneficent moisture of the tardy tide.   Touch them ever so gently, and some will pull in their heads, and some thrust them out further.   They have a bland, innocuous look, yet if one of them once shuts down its **valve on** a presumptuous hand,

the creature will hold its grip until the tide comes in and
drowns the man, for some of them are glued fast to the
rocks so that no ordinary means will pry them off. In soft
places sand-lances burrow deeply, leaving only their tails
out ; and fiddler-crabs and craw-fish have burrows into
which they dart when frightened. In some pockets of
standing water left by the ebb, we will sometimes see a clam
or scallop suddenly lift himself from the belittered bottom
and go, by little convulsive jerks, to another place a few feet
off. Yes, the object which seemed so helpless and inanimate, almost like a stone, will actually rise up and swim.
By opening and shutting his valves quickly, he inspires and
expels the water from the membrane which joins the two,
in such a way that he can propel himself through the water
clear of the ground. I suppose he knows why he wishes to
change his position, but how can he tell when and where to
go with his shell shut ? or does he take the chances, happy-
go-lucky, where he may land ?

One can not always tell for certain which are sentient living creatures, and which are inorganic and inanimate. Here,
for instance, is a cluster of tubes like hollow stalks or reeds
cut off six inches above the ground and filled with water.
Keep quiet for awhile, and blossoms of exquisite purple will
begin to protrude from every one, and finally mature into a
perfect bloom. It is like magic so to see things grow apace !
We think they are natural flowers, but they are only sense-
less and slimy mollusks, capital for fish-bait and agreeable
for the table, and the purple fringes are their gills. So also
one picks up rough substances like bits of rock, and lo ! they
are coral insects in their cases soft and juicy ; or we find on
strings of sea-weed little bulbs like berries, which perchance
are eggs of fishes. In wet caves, arched and smoothed by
churning waves, starfish of many patterns pave the bottom
like cobblestones—starfish of five, eight, ten, eighteen and
twenty-two fingers or points, and of bright crimson, green,
purple, pink, dark-red, yellow, drab and gray hues, and all
the crabs and prawns left by the ebb climb and skip over
their motionless bodies, seldom provoking them to stir the
least bit out of position. On the piles of all the wharves,
and wherever there are sunken logs or trees, anemones of
pink and purest white grow in clusters shaped like lilies,
only more mysteriously beautiful in their composite character and blending of animal and vegetable forms. And
there are many kinds of the repulsive octopus, with deca-
pods and cephalopods and all the tribes of sepia and cuttle-
fish, growing sometimes to gigantic sizes ; creatures such as

we used to think were mere fictions of gross fable, but are terrible realities, though seldom seen. And yet the little ones, only a few inches long, perhaps have all the villainous attributes of their superior kin—malicious eyes aflame, and yearning tentacles, which seem to shrink while momentarily alert to fling out their inexorable clasp upon the wrist or arm. And there are ink-fish, which in their natural element eject a liquid cloud to befog their pursuers or blind their victims—double-dyed scamps, who advance backward by jerks, and look one way when they are going the opposite. And on every landwash, when the tide is out, are stranded jelly-fish, limp and flabby, which blister where they touch the flesh, and beautiful medusæ with stings like nettles, and great black sea-spiders, ugly but harmless, and shark's eggs which look like leather wallets. How strange the marvels which the ebbing tide reveals !

Outside, along the shore, are large areas of amber-colored kelp, with intervals of open space, where there is splendid trolling with a spoon for a fish of the genus Sebastichthys (*S. melanops*) locally known as " kelp-fish " and " black sea-bass "; but they are not bass at all, although somewhat like the *Micropterus* of the East. Their play on the rod and line is not so vigorous, but upon the whole they answer very well as substitutes for the favorite game-fish of our eastern inland waters. Fishing for them after this method is better sport than hauling up their deep-sea kindred hand over hand, from hidden depths so many fathoms down that they come to the top drowned dead, with their eye-balls out of the sockets, and their air-bladders reversed and protruding from their gaping mouths. There are seven species of *Chiridæ*, the largest of which—the " kultus cod "—reaches sixty pounds' weight. Indians troll for them with a strip of halibut belly-skin wound on a single hook. In such hours of pastime, life afloat is enlivened by watching the bird-life along shore—the enormous flocks of fish-crows which hang around the islands and visit chosen places regularly to perform their ablutions and await the ebbing tide ; the solitary sand-pipers which run about the rocks, and the wisps of beach-birds which continually flit from cove to cove ; the black brant, which also have their stated feeding-places on the tidal flats, breeding here on the inshore lakes ; the bald eagles and ospreys, which sit in stately watch on the tallest firs or hover above the water spaces ; the big horned owls in the secluded shadows ; and the few little song birds which venture to lift their voices in this wilderness. Of the avifauna of Alaska the sea-fowl constitute by far the largest

proportion, breeding on the rocks along the shore in countless numbers, but other species find the coast too warm, and
so prefer the wooded districts and moss "tundras" which
lie between the Yukon and the Arctic Ocean. Of such are
the snow goose, the white fronted goose, the painted goose
or wavy, the blue brant, and a majority of the ducks found
on the coast in the seasons of their northward and southward migrations, among which may be included mergansers,
harlequins, brown ducks, widgeon, sprig-tails, surf-ducks,
canvas-backs, golden-eyes, oldwives, scoters, grebes,
shufflers, butter-balls, scaups, and lesser-scaups, all of which
remain in the vicinity of Sitka all winter, and fly north to
their nesting-places early in March. Canada geese and
mallards breed about the mountain lakes around Sitka.
Green-winged teal and blue-winged teal winter further south.
They are the first to come and the first to go in the fall.
Puffins, guilemots, coots, sea-pigeons, shags, terns, petrels,
hagden, and gulls are found in the south of Alaska, but they
all breed further north. There is a fine showing of beach
birds for variety, the list including golden-plover, upland-
plover, Wilson snipe, gray snipe, semi-palmated snipe, least
sand-piper, Baird's sand-piper, jack curlew, black-bellied
sand-piper, ring-necks, and a rare kind of four-toed plover,
some of which are found in immense congregations, so that
fifty brace to a gun is no bag to mention. The flights of
wild fowl from North Alaska follow the coast down to San
Francisco and below, where they are so numerous that
farmers pay men to shoot them off their wheat fields. Those
which tarry or remain on the Alaskan coast afford great
sport among the islands in the narrow channels where the
kelp grows upon which they feed. Landing on the side
opposite to where they are feeding, parties send the boat to
stir them up, and the gunners, who have taken position,
shoot them as they rise through the openings between the
islands.

Alaska is without doubt a fascinating field for the naturalist, as well as the fisherman, and also for summer vag-
abondizing. I venture to say that in the near future it
will become a favorite cruizing ground for steam yachts.
Perhaps the American Canoe Association will like to make
a trip to its land-locked waters next summer, and remain a
month between steamers.

If they should happen upon some of those inlets, into
which the salmon crowd, and where there is no presence of
man to disturb, they will not fail to discover the bears fishing. It is not even sport to bruin, for the fish get jammed

in so they can hardly move, and the bears have only to "scoop" them with their paws, and fill their bellies to satiety, after which, in berry time, they may take to the woods for their dessert. In some localities, close to the towns and villages, the bear-paths are plenty, and worn quite smooth, and I have been fooled more than once by following them to a terminus too abrupt to be pleasant. During the month of August the mosquitoes and flies are so blood-thirsty and persistent in the timber as to drive not only the deer, but the bears themselves to high altitudes. It is said that carcasses of dead bears have been found, that have manifestly perished by starvation, having been first blinded by the flies so that they could not forage. Once, in the province of New Brunswick, I remember to have seen a tame moose blinded in this way so that he was unable to find his way home, and only a timely rescue saved his life. In September the snow on the mountains drives the deer (black-tails) down to the water, and they swim constantly from the mainland to the islands, many of which are interspersed with grassy flats, where good grazing is found. They are then easily captured *in transitu*, often in pairs. Bears also are caught in the same way, the one on board the regular mail steamer having been picked up *en voyage*. There is fine deer-shooting about Wrangell, and some of the mission boys there once brought in forty as the result of a five days' hunt. A saddle of venison can be bought for a dollar at any time.

The impenetrable jungle of the Alaskan forest, with its windfalls of timber and profusion of berries and succulent mosses, constitutes both a nursery and a protection for its fauna. It is a veritable paradise for bears, whom neither dogs nor men can reach, except at the very season when they "hole in" for the winter. The boldest and most practiced Indian is afraid to go into the woods for game, for fear of bears. There are bears enough in Alaska—grizzly, cinnamon, and black—to furnish every man on the Pacific with a cap and overcoat, and leave breeding stock enough for next year's supply. Besides, there is a small albino bear found on the coast, which is known as the coast bear. Being white, and a good deal about the ice in winter, some have supposed it to be a variety of polar bear, but the zoologists dispute it.

Blue grouse, ruffed grouse, spruce grouse, and ptarmigan are very abundant, but hard to shoot, and difficult to gather when shot, by reason of the forest jungle. I have heard from those who are familiar with them, their descriptions of the grand scenery among the mountains, where crags and

rocky peaks were alternated with deep cañons in which were
located many beautiful lakes, fed by everlasting brooks,
which found their origin in great glaciers and immense
banks of perpetual snow; of lofty barren plateaus, where,
on the bare rocks, ptarmigan were in profusion and of
sky-parlors high above the timber line, where the mountain
goats and sheep make their aerial home; but, as I have
never reached the higher altitudes, and my own experience
in mountain-climbing has been chiefly confined to beaten
trails, I feel privileged to copy from one of Capt. Beardslee's letters the record of a characteristic trip accomplished
by himself when he had his "land tacks" in proper trim ;
and so I quote :

" Three-quarters of an hour carried us up a height of
one thousand feet and a distance of three-quarters of a
mile ; but we found, before the trip was finished, that three-
quarters of an hour was, in some cases, a very moderate
amount of time in which to advance a quarter of the distance. When at each step the perpendicular gain is twenty,
and the horizontal about three, inches, a mile is a long
journey. The trail wound its way through a dense forest
of great hemlocks and spruce trees, with a few yellow cedar.
Many of the former were of such dimensions that a spot in
the Adirondacks, so well covered, would, for its " bark " or
" counts," prove very valuable. When we reached Bald
Mountain, we had traveled three miles, and had ascended
over three thousand feet.

After the first sharp rise of a thousand feet, we had but
little ascent for a long distance, the trail leading along a
sharp ridge, or " hog-back," which, on each side, was flanked
by deep ravines, way down in whose depths we could hear
the rushing of waterfalls, and occasionally the click of the
miners' picks, for they are prospecting in all directions ; but
we could see nothing, for a dense fog filled the ravine and
hid from us the grand mountain scenery which at this part
of our journey we knew still towered above us. An
occasional momentary clearing away of a small bit of the
curtain gave us provoking and tantalizing peeps, but for an
instant. Once a glacier, not far from us, cast loose from its
moorings and went crashing down with thunderous noise.
We were far above the timber ; our trail was no trail, for
we trod on the primitive rock ; but there was no danger of
our getting off from it, for it we could see, and nothing
else. Before we had got out of the timber my siwash gave
a low whistle and stopped. As I joined him he pointed to
"chicken," and then, not forty feet away, I saw my first

ptarmigan. There were four, and they ran behind a bush of low hemlock, or ground pine. I advanced slowly, ready to take them as they rose ; but they wouldn't rise, and dodged in and around that clump like a woodpecker around a tree. So at last, satisfying the sportsman part of my conscience by resolving to aim only at their heads, I let go at a couple, who were in line, and killed them, the other falling to my friend's shot, as he rose at last. The birds were simply beautiful ; their backs and tail feathers were like those of our ruffed grouse ; their wings and breasts pure white.

There seems to be two varieties of this bird. Those found at this level are as I have described ; higher up they are nearly snow white, with black tail feathers bordered with white, and the dark feathers of the back, instead of as with those found lower down, being brown grouse-colored and predominating, are nearly black, and simply amount to spots, for each dark feather is surrounded with white. They may be the same bird, at different stages of transformation. They weigh about a pound each (six averaged fifteen and one-half ounces, the heaviest weighing eighteen), and are very delicious, especially at this season, when their food is almost altogether huckleberries ; later they feed on spruce and other bitter food, and their flavor suffers. They are very tender. No. 7 shot were very killing, and it was impossible to preserve a good specimen. The feathers came out in handsful, as they were gathered, and our dog's mouth looked as though he had the hydrophobia, so thoroughly blood-and-feathered was it. In skinning, the skin tore like wet blotting-paper, and an attempt to carry one by the leg involved a fracture of the same, if held at any angle. They are full-blooded, bleed a great deal, and, I should judge, very hot-blooded, for they spread themselves in great flocks on the surface of the snow patches, with wings extended, as hens when dusting themselves. They have a peculiar call, a grating sound, which often betrayed to us their vicinity when the fog was too dense for us to see them. As we got above the snow we could get a view of a portion of the banks nearest to us, and saw on it many birds, but we soon learned that it was mere slaughter to shoot them, or any flying over, for they would go sliding and plunging into the abyss below, and our siwashes could not be persuaded to trust themselves on to the snow, for they feared the starting of the glacier.

" We arrived at the summit of this part of the mountains at about 4:30, and it was clear enough for us to obtain a

A MOUNTAIN HUNTING PARTY.

splendid view of Bald Mountain Peak, a few hundred feet above us, and at our feet, a thousand feet below, two beautiful lakes on terraces, connected by a stream, near which we saw the cabins of the Witch miners, their arastra and their mine some hundred feet up the opposite wall of the cañon. The second day the fog had turned into rain, but we were as determined as the youth who "bore, mid snow and ice," etc., and determined to go on and up, for beyond and above us were ledges and birds well worth going for."

A recital of the remainder of the ascent would be chiefly a repetition, but clambering among the rocks is far less severe than tracking through the woods. There are those who make it a business to hunt the wild goats in these rough and almost inaccessible regions, and the number of these animals killed must be very considerable to supply the quantity of wool used in making the native blankets and the horns for the manufacture of the many utensils and ornaments in common use. Their pelts handsomely dressed, are employed as floor rugs and bedding, and of late many entire specimens as well as heads, have been stuffed and mounted for museums and private collections. Until comparatively recent years, very little accurate knowledge of the habits of the mountain goat was possessed even by well informed naturalists. It was often confounded with the bighorn sheep, or when referred to, assumed to be identical with it. At present, however, little remains to discover, and it is, moreover, believed that in Alaska there are not only one but two distinct species. The maximum of the larger variety is fully 150 pounds. Its range is from Montana to the extreme limit of the Alaskan chains, though specimens are said to have been met with as far south as northern Colorado. These goats are still in considerable numbers in Washington Territory, no less than six of them having been shot on Mt. Ranier by a single party in the summer of 1884. In British Columbia they are abundant, even in the southern portion. I have before me the photographed result, taken in camp, of a single day's shoot, on the Coast Range in the district of New Westminster, which shows six goats to three guns, besides three black bears and one grizzly. It is a long-bodied, humpbacked animal, standing fully thirty inches high, not at all like the domestic sheep in shape or fleece, with very long hair, except on the face and legs, which is underlaid by a fine, soft, thick wool, the whole coat being of a snow-white color. The chin is ornamented with a beard-like tuft of long hair, as in the common goat. The horns are six to eight inches long, awl-shaped, ringed at the base and bending slightly backward. These, like the hoofs, are shining black, like polished ebony, and for handles of spoons, forks, etc., make beautiful ornaments when skillfully carved. Notwithstanding its name, this animal is regarded as an antelope by naturalists, and not a goat at all. Its true home is among the loftiest peaks of the snow-clad mountains, above timber line, where no vegetation grows save mosses, lichens and a few alpine shrubs and grasses. I have met those who liked the flavor of its meat when young, but generally it is not esteemed. It is usually killed by a method of hunting known as stalking, and the regulation outfit of a native would be a belted shirt of squirrel-skin, a grotesque head-dress made of fur, close seal-skin bootees laced half way to the knee, old-time spears to serve as alpen-stocks, bows and arrows, raw-hide ropes and Hudson Bay rifles. Up on the ridges back of Mt. St. Elias, which constitute a favorite hunting-ground for goats, is found a bear similar to the "roach-back" or "silver-tip" of the Rockies, but of a beautiful bluish under-color, with the tips of the long hairs silvery white. The traders call it " St. Elias silver bear."

The range of the bighorn sheep extends much further south than the goats, even to the mountains of Arizona on the south, as well as to the sphagnous barrens of the north. Its habitat is by no means confined to high altitudes, much less summits, though it is restricted to rough regions. It delights in table-lands and dry mesas, not so much for the precarious pickings of their scant vegetation as for the outlook they afford against surprises from enemies. Up to six years ago it was not unusual to shoot them on the Yellowstone river-bluffs from decks of passing steamers, the land back of the bluffs being broken, but by no means mountainous. Stalking the mountain sheep is extremely delicate work, requiring much *finesse*, but as game the animal may be regarded more valuable than the goat, since it affords not only pelt and fleece, but estimable mutton and horns of much value for dishes and sundry domestic utensils. Not nearly so many of these are killed as goats in Alaska ; indeed the latter are undoubtedly far the most numerous of the two. Alaska seems to be the ultimate preserve of their breed, which it will be a pity to exterminate without an effort at domestication. The sheep is much the larger animal, reaching upward of 200 pounds in weight. It has been aptly described as having the head of a sheep and the body of a deer. The horns of the male are marvelously immense, curving backward and outward until they form a circle whose circumference may reach three feet. Such a horn would measure six inches in diameter at the base, and make a dish which, when split, steamed, spread and shaped, would measure almost a foot in width, with length to suit. The horns are often badly splintered as the result of fighting, but not from pitching headlong over precipices, according to hunters' fables. The female horn is much smaller and nearly erect, with very little backward curve, a fact which will readily account for their being confounded with mountain goats by inexperienced persons who perhaps never saw them except at a distance. The color, however, should readily distinguish the two, as the sheep in summer are a wood-brown, and often darker, while in winter they are never pure white like the goats. The legs and belly, however, and a portion of the buttocks are white. In spring the old rams are a dingy white. Outwardly the coat is stiff and wire-haired, not half the length of the goat's, but it is underlaid by a fine, thick wool. Successful hunters stalk them in the early morning when they are feeding low down, after first having climbed convenient heights to reconnoiter. When a herd is discovered, the most cautious, patient and wily hunter, who takes a judicious advantage of such inequalities of the land as favor his approaching unobserved, will bring in the most meat. At noon the sheep retire to the sky-parlors for rumination and siestas.

THE GLACIER FIELDS.

The excursion steamer which makes its monthly trips from Portland, Oregon, to Sitka and beyond, cruises along a thousand miles of Alaskan coast. No fewer than six large glaciers can be seen, including the Davidson, Sundown, Brady, Patterson, Taku, and Muir. The foot of the Brady glacier, in Taylor Bay, is estimated to be from four to six miles wide. It has not been visited much and no measurements have been made ; but on a clear day not only it and its well defined moraine, but the magnificent Fairweather group of mountains, sixteen thousand feet high, with La Perouse and Crillon, in which so many glaciers take their rise, are all in full view. A more magnificent sight is rarely seen, and those who have had opportunities in Europe say that there is nothing to compare with it there, certainly in purely glacial scenery. The Muir and Davidson glaciers are spurs or outflows of the same ice-field, which has an unbroken expanse of four hundred miles—large enough to lie over the whole domain of Switzerland. The Muir is the ultimate objective point of sight-seers, who, by the time they have become accustomed to the unfamiliar blending of Mediterranean with Alpine scenery so exclusively characteristic of the North Pacific coast, are partially prepared for the astounding revelation which presently awaits them at the head of Glacier Bay. This bay is about one hundred and twenty miles north-east of Sitka, and lies in latitude fifty-nine degrees and twenty minutes. It is, therefore, the most northern point reached on the regular trips of the excursion steamers. Sitka has yet to be visited, but that polyglot settlement lies south. It occupies a secondary place in the anticipations of those whose conceptions of a glacier have been inspired by visions or readings of the Matterhorn or Rhone. Briefly this whole region is full of glaciers, although under the fervid sun of July it would seem as if every thing in the shape of ice and snow would speedily melt.

Until a comparatively recent period, glacial dynamics have remained to a certain extent a matter of theory. The birth of an iceberg is said to be a phenomenon unknown in Europe. On that continent the glacial force is almost spent, and he who would witness the mighty outcome of its latent power must seek it on the confines of the New World. He will not find it in the fastnesses of Switzerland. There the once overwhelming accumulations of snow, which filled the mountain valleys to the level of their topmost peaks, no longer supply the glacial streams with material for bergs. The ice-fields have dwindled to insignificant areas, and their discharge is, for the most part, fluvial, though much of their bulk is dissipated by evaporation or absorption into the warm earth of the lower altitudes. But in Greenland, which has recently been investigated by Danish explorers, the ice-fields were found to cover the country like a pall for one thousand five hundred miles from Cape Farewell to the furthest discovered point, and their breadth is absolutely unknown. Out of the almost interminable waste of frigid desolation pours the great glacier Sermitsialik, with a width of from two to four miles, completely occupying the valley out of which it debouches to the depth of two thousand feet or more. It is only one of hundreds of similar frozen rivers, all of which, as far as is known, are pigmies beside the great Humboldt glacier discovered by Dr. Kane at the head of Smith Sound. This is sixty miles in width, with inclosing walls of rock a thousand feet high. Its front abuts the sea, and is washed by the waves like any other coast line.

From these Titanic sources of perpetual supply are emitted those stupendous icebergs which fill the north Atlantic from June to August to such an extent that dozens can be counted from the masthead within the scope of view. The dimensions of some of them are incredible. I have seen one off the coast of Labrador which was estimated to be two miles long and three hundred feet high ; and this great mass was sloughed off entire from the Humboldt Sea wall with one tremendous cleavage, plunge, and surge, as a great ship leaves the ways. Such mountains of ice are perpetually falling all along the line, with an intermittent crash and roar like the tumult of a tempest. The din of the great commotion can be heard for miles ; and even after they are adrift in the warmer currents of more southern latitudes where they melt and diminish by the sea's erosion, they are constantly turning over and over in the effort to keep their balance, and the noise and commotion of the heaving waters is heard for distances of miles. The Esquimaux, it is told by the Danish explorers, regard all this as the work of evil spirits, and believe that to look upon these

agonizing throes is death ; so, while they were innocently
observing their phenomena through their glasses, the timid
natives, usually circumspect enough, roughly ordered them
to turn their backs !

The glaciers of the North Pacific are much smaller in
comparison with those of Greenland, but the Muir is three
miles long, with a perpendicular face of four hundred feet,
stretching like a frozen waterfall or gigantic dam entirely
across the head of the bay. Its breast is as blue as turquoise. At a distance it looks like a fillet rent from the
azure sky and laid across the brow of the cliff. When the
full blaze of the south-western sun lights up its opalescence,
it gleams like the gates of the celestial city. I suppose that
an iceberg of no insignificant size is sloughed off from some
portion of its sea wall as often as once in five minutes,
but these detachments seldom represent more than a limited
section, and most of them break up into comparatively
small fragments before they are fairly launched on their
seaward journey. It is an axiom that mechanical forces
are best comprehended by their products ; so that no one
can begin to realize what a stupendous factor a glacier
is until he sees the measure of its infinite power thus made
supremely manifest. Visitors are told that glaciers move
at the rate of so many feet or inches daily. Ocular evidence
may be obtained by fixed landmarks, which indicate a stated
progression. From the size and frequency of the cleavages
here it would seem that the progress of the Muir must be
several rods a day, though an estimate can only be ap-
proximated, as there is no true alignment, and the center
moves faster than the sides.

Long before the steamer reaches the entrance of Glacier
Bay straggling lumps of ice appear, dazzling white, and
resting like blocks of marble on the polished sea, which is
scarcely moved by an imperceptible swell pulsating through
the Sound. The sun is warm and grateful, and the sky
without a cloud, excepting those which stretch like filmy
gauze from peak to peak, the temperature perhaps 6o degrees in the shade. Half of the passengers have never
seen an ice-cake, and they are eager with excitement to get
nearer the polar videttes which are drifting by, away off
under the land. The course of the vessel bears gradually
toward the headland at the entrance, and the lumps of ice
become more numerous. Bevies of ladies rush to the taffrail as one of them passes close under the counter. Presently a passing promontory opens out a large iceberg of
fantastic shape, and then another, tall and stately, with

MUIR GLACIER

turrets like a castle. Sea gulls, hagden and shags hover about their gleaming walls like snow-flakes in the air, or sit in solemn ranks upon the battlements. Objects change positions constantly, and countermarch across the field of view. Fancies dissolve before they are formed. Reflections from the land appear in darksome shades across the water, and from the looming icebergs in tremulous semblances, ghost-like and pallid. The scenic effects, at once so magical and duplicated everywhere, grow momentarily more weird.

Meantime, the steamer slacks her headway, slows down, and presently with a sullen thud, lies alongside a small berg, whose rounded apex peers up over the deadeyes into the head of the companionway, looking for all the world as if it was going to come aboard. All the curious ladies pipe a combination scream, and make for the door of the captain's stateroom. Then the quarter boat is swung out of the davits and lowered away; and the steward and the mate and the sailors tackle the glistening harlequin with pikes and axes, and, after much chopping and maneuvering with bights and bowlines, contrive to split off a big lump, and hoist it inboard with a sling. This supply is for the ice-chest. How pure, and cold, and beautiful, and transparent it is! How precious to passengers who have been for two days stinted, and to the steward whose meat was likely to spoil! The chunks cut off seem colorless, but the central core of the berg itself glows like a great blue eye, sentient and expressive, with that sort of poetical light termed "*spirtuelle.*" You never tire of gazing into the translucent depths of the glacier ice, whose radiance emulates the blue and green of beryl, turquoise, chrysoprase and emerald. You gaze into them as into the arcana of the empyrean, with some vague awe of their mysterious source, and the intangible causes which gave them birth. And the grand icebergs!—so cold, yet so majestic; so solid, yet so unsubstantial; so massive, yet so ethereal!—whose bastions are mighty enough to shiver an onset, and yet so volatile that the warmth of wooing spring will dissipate them into vapor. Children of the Arctic frost, conceived in the upper air, inspired by the effulgent sun, and molded in the bowels of intensest congelation: the human mind can not contemplate them without a sympathetic inspiration, for their duplex entity is so like our combination of soul and body!

Who will tell me what paints the ice-bergs, and gives the sky its blue; colors the depths of the ocean, and imparts to

Niagara its hues of intensest green? Behind an intelligible explanation lies the revelation which all men wish to know. Let us wait.

A stiff breeze was blowing as we entered Glacier Bay, and the breath came bitterly cold from off the ice field. The bay was filled with floating bergs and floes, and the temperature dropped quite rapidly to 46 degrees. The ruffled surface of the water assumed that peculiar tinge of cold steel-gray which landscapes wear in winter. The atmosphere put on a sympathetic hue and grew perceptibly denser. Snow covered all the peaks, and the *mer de glace* spread out before us like a great white apron on the lap of the mountain. It is twelve miles from the entrance to the head of the bay, and over the entire landscape nature seemed dead. Not a living thing appeared—not a gull on the wing, nor a seal in the gloomy fiords. Desolation reigned throughout, for there was nothing to sustain life. The creation was all new, and the glacier was still at work gradually preparing it for the abode of organic life. Darkness only was needed to relegate us to the primordium of chaos. But the sun was bright on the distant peaks, which inclosed the bay on all sides, and their intangible, ghostly outlines, scarcely distinguished from the fleecy clouds about them, seemed indefinitely beyond the convex line of earth. Seldom are mundane gloom and supernal glory contrasted by such startling juxtaposition.

As the steamer neared the glacier, speculations began respecting the height of its perpendicular front, but no one guessed higher than the vessel's topmast. It was only when she lay anchored in ninety fathoms of water, close under the ice, and not a quarter of a mile from shore, that spectators began to conceive the magnitude of the glacier and all its surroundings. The glacier wall overhung us with its mighty majesty, three times the height of the steamer's mast, or more, and we seemed none too far away to escape the constantly cleaving masses which dropped from its face with deafening detonations. The foam which gathered from the impetus of the plunges surged upward fully two-thirds of the height of the cliff, and the resulting swell tossed the large steamer like a toy, and rolled up in breakers of surf upon the beach. The vessel was in actual danger from the fragments of ice which occasionally thumped against her sides. Indeed, her wheels were afterward badly mashed in making her way out of the bay into open water. A paddle-wheel steamer is unfit for such navigation, and I suppose a propeller will be used hereafter.

The glacier wall is by no means smooth, but is seamed and riven in every part by clefts and fissures. It is hollowed into caverns and grottoes, hung with massive stalactites, and fashioned into pinnacles and domes. Every section and configuration has its heart of translucent blue or green, interlaced or bordered by fretted frost-work of intensest white; so that the appearance is at all times gnome-like and supernatural. No portion of the wall ever seems to pitch forward all at once in a sheer fall from top to bottom, but sections split off from the buttresses, or drop from midway, or the top. The apparent slowness of their descent is sublimity itself, because it carries with it the measure of its stupendous vastness and inappreciable height.

Impressions of magnitude and majesty, I opine, are not conveyed so much by any relative standard of comparison as by the degree with which we come within the range of their power or influence. One must realize before he can appreciate, and he can not realize fully until he becomes to a certain extent a participator. Proximity shudders and trembles at what remoteness and impunity view with dispassionate equanimity. I can not conceive how any one can sit close by and contemplate without emotion the stupendous throes which give birth to the icebergs, attended with detonations like explosions of artillery, and reverberations of thunder across the sky, and the mighty wreckage which follows each convulsion. Nevertheless, I have seen a lady loll with complaisance in her steamer chair, comfortably wrapped from the chilly air, and observe the astounding scene with the same languid contemplation that she would discuss her social fixtures and appointments. Zounds! I believe that such a human negation would calmly view the wreck of worlds, and hear the crack of doom at the final rendering, if it did not affect " her set." She could watch at a suitable distance the agonies of Christian martyrs; the carnage of great battles ; the sweep of cyclones; and diluvial submergence. Dynamite would not appall her—but to me it would be the acme of satisfaction, ineffably supreme, to startle such clods of inanition by a cry of "mouse," and electrify them into a momentary emotion. No vinaigrette would ever mitigate the shock.

I say, one can not estimate the magnitude of these glacial phenomena by contiguous objects, because they are all unfamiliar. The steamer itself, although considerable in size, seems like an atom. As for the rest, the fragments of ice which are seen stranded along the beach, looking no larger than blocks, measure twelve feet high. Those lumps drifting past yonder fiord are icebergs higher than our topmast. The other side of the bay which, we imagine, one could swim across with ease, is five miles off. The ice ledge itself is four hundred feet high. The peaks in the distance, forty miles away, are sixteen thousand feet above the level of the sea. There is the Devil's Thumb, looking no higher than the Washington Monument, a sheer monolith six thousand feet high, with faces almost perpendicular. The timber line around the feet of the distant ranges resembles a cincture of moss.

From a pinnacle of elevation overlooking the Muir ice field, which is obtained by an arduous half day's climb, although some expected to accomplish it in an hour, one can count no less than fifteen tributary glacial streams, any one of which is as large as the great Rhone glacier.

Drawn from the inexhaustible but annually diminishing accumulations of snow which fill the mountain valleys to a depth of at least 2,000 feet, these separate streams of plastic congelation unite like the strands of a rope to form the irresistible current of the Muir. The surface of the glacier is not uniformly level and smooth like a boulevard. It has its drifts and dykes, its cascades, riffs, and rapids, like any unfrozen river. In the immediate front, and extending a mile or more back, its whole surface is the most rugged formation imaginable. It is utterly impossible for any living creature to traverse it, being in fact a compacted aggregation of wedge-shaped and rounded cones of solid ice, capped by discolored and disintegrating snow. But away back in the mountain passes it is easily traversed with sledges or snow shoes. Indians cross the divide at sundry places all along the coast from the Stickeen to Copper River.

Looking afar off into the blank perspective the icy re-enforcements which pour out of the mountain fastnesses like gathering clans seem compacted into indefinable fleecy masses, while in the immediate van they pass in review in serried phalanxes of cowled and hooded monks twenty feet tall, wrapped in dirty toques and capuchins, snow powdered, and bedraggled, and pressing forward with never-ceasing march, as if all the life-long denizens of the Gothard and St. Bernard had set out at once to temper their frigid tongues in the tepid waters which are warmed by the Kuro-Siwo. In other places, where the *mer-de-glace* is level like a plain, its surface is seamed with deep crevasses and slashed with rifts and chasms whose sides and walls deep down for sixty feet are dazzling blue. Thus the incipient bergs are split and carved and chiseled and prepared for their final segregation, so that they will break off easily when they reach the front.

Meantime the sub-glacial river which is flowing underneath buoys up the ice and floats it to the sea. It is estimated, by soundings made as near as vessels dare approach, that it is fully eight hundred feet deep. The water flows beneath the glacier, just as it does under the deposit of a snow-laden roof, forming icicles at the eaves. To this mighty channel, between its flanking slopes of rock, the glacier is at last restricted. Evidences are abundant that it is continually receding. They are scored high up on the abutting rocks by the adamantine ice. They are attested by the stranded débris of the lateral moraines, and recorded in the written narratives of Vancouver, who speaks of his inability to enter this bay in 1793, which is now navigable for twelve miles inland. Once the ice-field was level with the distant mountain tops; now it has settled, with melting and thaw, until the peaks are far above the surface. The annual accumulations are dissolving and diminishing faster than they can be replenished, and centuries hence snow will no longer be perpetual in the valleys. The warm hills will throw off their useless mantle, and nothing will remain of the Muir glacier except a goodly stream and some tributary rills leaping with a musical cadence from the vernal melting among the peaks. The deep and cavernous gully which now retains the sub-glacial outflow of the ice-field will become an estuary of the ocean, and the legend of the Muir will be illustrated in parti-colored tapestry lining the verdant slopes and meadows with flowers and foliage. Perhaps some goodly village will nestle at the terminal moraine, as it now does in the Matterhorn among the Alps. Then all the soil deposited in the valleys and upon the hillsides will tell us of the wear and tear which even now is grinding down the mountains, of the denudation, pulverizing, leveling, and filling up of which the glacier has been the potent agent since the world began.

Glaciers always carry on their frozen tide great bowlders and masses of stones and rock wrenched from the mountain sides, just as rivers carry logs and drift. Whatever is not deposited along its course is carried out to sea by the ice-bergs to strew the ocean bottom, precisely as we find them on our Western plains, where they were deposited when the salt waves covered their unlimited expanse.

Some of the lateral moraines (as the dry beds of spent

glacial outlets are termed) are still underlaid by an ice stratum 200 feet thick, which became detached from the main body of the glacier many decades since. It will take a half century to melt it. Clambering over these is no child's play. Visitors should be prepared with waterproof anglers' wading trowsers and alpen-stocks and hob-nail shoes, leaving all top coats and superfluous wraps where they can be resumed after the jaunt is finished. Rubber shoes or boots are liable to be torn to shreds. There are spots, looking like solid earth, which often prove to be mud-holes of uncertain depth. Bowlders are everywhere—bowlders, ice, and slimy silt, or till, and nothing else. Bottomless crevasses head you off at every turn. To land dry-shod from the boats is not easy, on account of the surf.

Altogether, it is astonishing what a minimum of distance or altitude one can accomplish with a maximum of clambering and perspiration, even with the chill wind blowing fresh ; for every object sought is at least five times the distance guessed at, and the road is hard, indeed, to travel. Nevertheless, the ladies are generally foremost, and old Swiss explorers will distance all the rest.

It is a consolation and a comfort, when on the apex of the moraine, with the polar desolation all around, and every resource of succor or deliverance clean cut off, to look far down upon the little object which is our only hope—the steamer, which seems an atom more than ever—and know that although the bay be filled with floes, there is open water and safety and genial climate just beyond, and that no hopeless Arctic winters intervene. By some trivial accident, possible enough, a party of excursionists might be left in a situation almost as hopeless as the hapless sufferers of the Lena. The perils are precisely the same, modified only by the relative accessibility of succor, and therefore too much stress can not be laid upon the stanchness of the vessels sent into the ice.

Last winter the citizens of St. Paul instituted an ice-palace and illuminated it with electric lights, and all the heavenly planets lent their aid to make it resplendent. At night when the full moon shone upon its crystal walls and battlements, and their translucence was reflected, it looked more like an ethereal creation than one of substance. It was stately in its magnificence and overwhelming in its supernatural majesty. But what shall compare with the Muir glacier when the moonlight is upon it, and all the phosphorescence of the Pacific Ocean beats in billows of liquid flame against its toppling, crumbling walls ? When lunar rainbows are tossed in air against the mounting columns of foam that are shivered into spray by the plunging mountains of ice ? In the everlasting tumult, and whirl, and crash of explosions which seem to split the glacier itself from front to mountain source, when nothing at all takes definite shape upon the ghostly interchange of lights and shades, one can imagine only the revels of chaos and the scroll rolled back to the genesis of creation.

RUSSIA IN AMERICA.

It is a "great day" for sleepy Sitka when the steamer comes up to her wharf and makes fast. The whole town rubs its eyes and turns out.

Ever since the previous sailing day, when the last box of freight was leisurely trundled into the warehouse, it has been supremely quiet. There has been absolutely nothing to do. The government vessels are off on duty ; the miners away at the diggings ; the fishing season over ; half the tenements vacant ; no entries nor clearance at the custom house ; the governor is sticking type in his printing office ; and the attorneys are matching kopecks to see who shall win the next case. Down at the Indian "ranch" the dogs are dozing in the sun ; occasionally a Siwash will stroll to the beach, and straighten out the mats which cover his canoe ; a few of the mission boys at the far end of the village come in to visit their low-down relations ; groups of ravens are picking offal out of the landwash ; a few cows graze on the parade ; the black balls of the signal office anemometer scarcely turn in the wind.

Meanwhile the melting snow from the mountains trickles unceasingly into the sea, and the process of decay eats into the solid timbers of the old houses vacated by the Russians ; the rickety wharf all deserted, steams in the humid atmosphere, and the teredos bore insidiously into the piles below the water line.

The last time the steamer made fast to the dock, her stern-line pulled off a section of the worm-eaten piling, and the splash woke up a couple of Siwashes who had been dozing against the side of the warehouse ever since the trip before.

But "steamer day is an event." Then every thing is different. The stars and stripes are run up from the marine barracks and custom house ; all the public offices are open ; the marshal is on the *qui vive*, and the attorneys have two pens behind each ear ; the war vessel comes into port ; the governor shaves and cleans up to receive his guests ; tawdry klootchmen open up their basket-work, berries and curios at eligible stands ; and the distracted post-master is "just too busy for any thing ; " even the cows on the parade are too curious to graze for looking at the stir.

As soon as the brass gun of the expected vessel booms among the islands of the bay, the wharf is crowded. There are just 300 white people in town, and that is enough to make a crowd. If the wharf should give way, it would engulf the whole population—Siwashes excepted. There are no drays nor omnibuses nor wagons to be seen, for there are none in town, and only one horse to draw them ; no hotel runners, for there are no hotels ; no loud voiced newsboys, for there is but one paper in the place, and the editor is too modest to have it hawked under his nose ; no boot-blacks, no policemen, no peanut-vendors, no little flower-girls, no any thing that one might expect to see at the chief commercial port of one of the biggest territories in the world.* A few impatient passengers get ashore before the gang-plank is laid, and perhaps ten minutes later the entire complement of sightseers is scattered about the town. Into the Græco-Russian church with its green-painted minaret and dome; into the museum of the marine barracks where there is a collection of native curios which makes collectors envious ; up to the "castle" on an eminence, which was once the pretentious residence of the governors ; out to the Indian "ranch" along the shore front, and to the Indian mission on the curve of the beach, in the opposite direction ; up to the queer looking cemeteries on the ridge, white and native ; and to the old block-houses and the stockade, and trading stores, the public offices and the photograph gallery. Indeed there is "lots" to see in Sitka, and one can remain over one steamer and spend a month most agreeably, extending his observations to the environs, and for miles around. Miners and toughs who come by every steamer, camp out in gipsy fashion, or roll up in their blankets in some of the vacant rooms in the barn-like dilapidated government buildings, but fair boarding places can be found by sojourners after a little inquiry. At the stores one can buy almost any thing which is to be found at Victoria or Portland. Washing is done by the Russian families. There is no physician in the place except the naval surgeon, and

---

* A hotel, a restaurant and a private boarding-house have been opened since this chapter was written. Besides the Indian Mission School there is a public school for whites with forty-one pupils. There are five attorneys and a news depot. Eighty-two letters were advertised in the local paper for the month of May. Religious services are held by the Greek, Catholic and Protestant denominations. Sitka is waking up.

it occurs to the author that a fine opportunity is offered
for a worthy disciple of Æsculapius to establish himself in a
good business at Sitka, as the native Alaskans need the
services of a physician to an alarming extent.

During the twenty-four hours which the steamer is required by contract to remain in port, although she frequently stays two days, all the elite of the town—the "leading
ladies," the Creoles, the pure blood Russians, and the better
Klootchmen, crowd aboard to see their metropolitan sisters,
and inspect the latest fashions ; the merchants and officials
obtain their mail matter and invoices ; the naval officers "see
the boys" and receive their magazines and newspapers ;
if there is any fresh beef or fruit to spare, it is immediately
bespoken. Meanwhile the busy Siwashes on the dock are
unremittingly trundling freight, and small knots of privileged rustics wander all over the ship and inspect her fittings
and machinery. Sometimes there is opportunity to make
side excursions to points of interest, in respect to which the
blue jackets are of essential service, as they have a steam
launch and light boats and are always hospitable. Festivi-
ties, too, are in order, and invitations are issued for a
"grand ball" at the castle, *sans ceremonie*, toilets at discretion. The invitations are general, for the shore community
is not large enough to cut up into castes. If it were crit-
ically culled there wouldn't be waltzers enough to go round,
for the American population, all told, is but sixty. So
the floor is sifted over with spermaceti shavings, and an old
brass relic of a Russian chandelier is filled with candles and
hung up, while a couple of marines or waiters from the mail
steamer do excellent duty as musicians with banjo and accordeon. Slips and mishaps never mar such an occasion—
never ; they embellish it. "Select your Klootchmen!" and
"swing your Siwash!" fill up the measure of shuffling feet,
and the ball succeeds until the antiquated dust of all the
Romanoffs is stirred. 'Twas ever thus in the ancient days,
I'm told ; for even then, no crucial distinctions could be
made if the necessary components of a ball would be forth-
coming. But alas! not a vestige of the old glory remains
to illuminate the dark bare walls. Desolation reigns throughout the empty halls, and the wind whistles mournfully
through dozens of broken panes. Not a tenant holds the
venerable places in the castle except the U. S. signal man
aloft who keeps his lonely vigils in the cupola on the roof.
Up there, in the government sky parlor, the faithful
chronicler of the storms clings to his weather-beaten post.
Nothing moves him. Politics may change, civil service

reform may fail, silver coinage be repealed, or the rookery itself collapse and fall! Whatever may betide, blow hot, blow cold, whichever way the vane may turn, the four little cups on the top of his tripod go round and round in the unremitting whirligig of time.

In Sitka and northward, revelers, owls, and such, find small indulgence for orgies claimed for hours of darkness, for the sun is bright at 3 o'clock A.M., and he goes home early who goes " when daylight doth appear." In the longest days there is no interval of night so dark that all the stars are seen. Only the brightest of the planets outvie the twilight. So, long before the " wee sma' hours do come " the candles have burned down in their sockets, and the dancers in the castle repair to the parade for an Indian performance on the grass ; or sometimes there is a wedding in the church. Once in a while the fire company turns out for review, 48 men strong, with hose-cart, fire engine, and tin buckets improvised from oil cans.

I doubt if there is a more enchanting site in the world than Sitka's. It has been compared with Naples ; but Naples, though serenely sweet, is not so massive, nor near so grand. In the varied combination of its picturesque environment Sitka is both placid and stupendous, benignant and majestic, alluring and severe. It entices while it warns. It gathers its beautiful brood of verdant islets into its arms and folds them tenderly to its bosom, while momentarily it frowns in awful majesty from the beetling heights above. Behind is a battlement of snow-clad mountains. Volcanic peaks flank the range at either end—Edgecumbe and Vostovia—lifted high against the firmament of blue, and welted with great red ridges of hardened lava which radiate from their pure white tops—the contrast of colors showing aloft with striking effect. Edgecumbe, the nearest peak, some fifteen miles away, but seeming close at hand, is nearly 3,000 feet above the sea level, but looks as if it were part of a 5,000-feet peak which had been sliced off. This truncated apex is a crater, said by those who have visited it to be 2,000 feet in diameter by 200 feet deep.

The town of Sitka, most picturesque herself, though dingy, occupies the incurve of the crescent-shaped level, cuddling like a trustful child between the knees of the great giants, with her attendant satellites ranged in view among the glancing waves, some cultivated as gardens or used as pastures, and others natural gems of rock with verdure clad. And all her lap is filled with wealth of evergreens, back to the very bases of the mountains ; sparkling streams course through them ; and giant firs whose feet rest in the shadows of the valleys, lift their tremendous spires high into the sunlight of the upper air. The atmosphere is soft, like Italy's, suffused with pink and yellow laid on blue, and whenever the tall truncated cones catch the hues of sunset, the lava of their ice-crowned tops glows red hot ! Right in the harbor of Sitka is Japonskoi (Japanese) Island, where government pastures cattle. Eighty years ago a Japanese junk, drifting on the Kuro-Siwo from its native moorings, crossed the sea and rested there—a waif from Asia, to suggest to intellects obtuse the explanation of ethnical possibilities not at all mysterious or unaccountable. It is stated that the sympathetic Russians kindly cared for the castaway survivors of that dreadful drift and returned them to their country, as witnesses of a long-vexed problem solved. Some ten miles from town is Silver Bay, with a trout stream and a superb waterfall, which is often visited by excursionists who go in boats towed by a steam launch which tail out behind in a most exhilarating way. Indeed a steam launch of light draft, is indispensable to pleasure or business in those parts. Six miles north is Old Harbor, where the Russian Baronoff built the first fort in 1799, call- ing it Archangel. Three years later its garrison was massa- cred by Sitka Indians, and the present site of Sitka was occupied instead, and named New Archangel. The Hot Springs are ten or eleven miles south of town, on the main land, in a little bay which is protected by a break-water of pretty islands. There are three mineral springs—two of warm magnesia, and one of hot sulphur, the density of which is indicated by heavy incrustations in their basins. The temperature ranges from one hundred and twenty to one hundred and twenty-five degrees. Almost every visitor claims to have boiled an egg in them, but I have yet to learn where each contrives to get his egg. It might be well for future tourists who like positive tests to provide them- selves with eggs in Boston, New York, San 'Francisco or New Orleans, so as not to be disappointed when they finally reach the place. A few rods off is a clear spring of cold water, in which there may be trout convenient for the other popular test. For myself, when I visit the Yellowstone Park, or other noted place, I always catch my fish ready boiled. In 1860 the Russians built a hospital and bath, and the treatment was said to have had wonderful remedial powers in skin and rheumatic diseases. The buildings are now badly dilapidated and ought to be restored at once. If done, Sitka would have become more than ever a popular watering place, and an equivalent equal to the outlay would flow into the official treasury daily. In summer, excursion trips should be arranged to the springs at stated periods, so that visitors can depend upon them. Some four miles from Sitka is an old Russian redoubt, where there was also a prison, which is well worth a visit, not only as a relic of the former occupation, but for its beautiful scenery, the mountains rising 3,000 feet almost perpendicularly, on one side of the bay, and inclosing a lake (Ozersky) ten miles long, which is much resorted to by anglers. There are five Russian houses still standing which are used for a salmon cannery, and there are besides several other houses for the fishermen, and huts for the Siwashes. Substantial bridges, also built by the Russians, cross the rapids between the outlet of the lake and the bay, and form part of a long and winding promenade. Indeed one may say that all the vicinity of Sitka is suggestive of Russian America, which we, before its purchase, looked upon askance, as hyperborean and savage; but now are surprised to discover was so far advanced that the humble people of Cape Cod, or other shore settlements of the Atlantic, would have been appalled at its magnificence. Every thing built by the Russians was of a substantial character, and where the official comfort was concerned, with elegance.

The old Baronoffs lived high. They enriched themselves from the furs of the land, and subsisted on the appropriations of the crown. All they earned was clear profit, and whenever perchance a prince of the blood came over the Strait from Siberia, he was royally entertained; moreover, their spiritual welfare was zealously cared for by the church, which is able even now, so many years after the retirement of the Muscovites to maintain gratuitously its several missions at Sitka, St. Paul, St. Michael's, Anvic, Oonalashka, and Andreavsky. And so it happens that Greek priests still officiate for penitents of the great Republic, and the three little brass bells that were cast in Russia ring out from the tower of the Sitka sanctuary a Slavic melody for all Americans who respect the Sabbath. It is fortunate, indeed, that the little capital of Alaska was not left wholly bereft of Christian influences, else would its mongrel population have gone wholly to the bad; for so long as the suggestive spire stood in their midst, pointing heavenward, duty received a reminder and wickedness a check. At present there is a form of Protestant worship at the Indian mission, and ere many months elapse I trust a befitting chapel will be erected to meet the religious demands of a growing population. The public have long been made familiar with the architecture of this little church, its lofty dome, its shapely minaret, its gilt and gold and silver ornaments, and costly vestments, and holy pictures; and since it is now so well preserved in photograph and tourist's story, I can manifest no sincerer interest for the saintly relic than to bespeak for it the trifling sum necessary for its structural repair and preservation, or at least to replace the old barrel which is now used as a baptismal tub. It is a sin and a shame to let it drop piecemeal into ruin. The green paint is nearly worn from off the metal dome, and its wooden sides are weather-worn and stained; the doors are sprung, the bolts are rusted; the interior is well nigh despoiled by time and vandal hands; the voice of one of the bells is hushed, and in winter the main auditorium can not be used with comfort; yet I see that the gilding of the spire and roof continues bright, and by that token a new day is at hand.

The Russian population of Sitka pure and mixed, is about 250, and the church attendance is made up chiefly of Indians and Creoles, although Father Metropolsky is a well-instructed priest, pious and intelligent, and so might court the attendance of the better classes in the absence of teachers of other sects, especially and inasmuch as the services are conducted in the Slavonic language, which is both impressive and innocuous. The Indian communicants are always devout and neatly dressed, observing all the periods and crossing themselves at proper times with due observance of the formula; and as the services are conducted with formality and proper ceremony no essential rites can be overlooked. I agree with a most intelligent correspondent who has written: "There is a very silly and unnecessary antipathy existing between the missionaries here and this church, and instead of working harmoniously together in their efforts to Christianize the Indians, they work at cross purposes. If the Greek Church or any other can succeed in making the Indians clean themselves up one day in the week at least, well and good; it is a great step toward godliness, and it is the purest nonsense to try to Christianize any body before he is civilized to a certain extent." Ever since the American accession, the missionaries have antagonized the Greek Church, and the public officials fight the missionaries; and I could only wish that the long-suffering Siwash might look quietly on and pick up what drops in the mêlée to his own advantage.

It has taken a good while for the country to adapt itself

to the changed circumstances which followed its relinquishment by the Russians. The Muscovites left every thing in good order when they evacuated Sitka, indeed they wisely let go by degrees, and not all at once ; and they still retain some hold on the missions which they established. Had they not done so, nine years of utter neglect would have left the place a useless ruin. That there is a house still standing is largely due to the fact that they built of great logs, both hewed and round, and often two feet square ; the substantial structures which they have erected have not only withstood the high winds of winter, but the wearing tooth of time, very well for a climate whose rainfall is 55 ½ inches per year, soaking every thing with moisture. The principal buildings which are now occupied by the territorial and naval officers as custom-house, court-house, barracks, and government warehouse have at some time been coated with a dull yellow paint which still sticks to a degree ; some of the roofs are either of iron painted red, or they have grown rusty from rain. Once they were pretentious structures all, large, spacious, two-storied, with hard wood doors elaborately carved, and some regard paid to ornament in the shape of stained-glass panes inserted in parts to be effective ; but now the foundation timbers are eaten half through by rot, some of the 6-inch planking of the floors has been torn up for fuel ; piles of rubbish fill one-half of the apartments and with the exception of the marine barracks there is not one of all the lot with its window-glass unbroken or the plastering intact. A fire once cleared out several of the rooms in the custom-house, and there the charred débris still remains ; only three rooms in the entire great building are fit to be occupied and two of these are used by the judge and attorney. I believe the governor has to " rustle " for his quarters. The grand old castle which crowns a rocky eminence that overlooks the town, and was once the pride of all the Baronoffs and Romanoffs, is now the worst of all the Badly-offs ; and although it looks imposing in the uncertain twilight, nothing but immediate relief will save it from the assaults of time and weather. Once it was destroyed by earthquake, once by fire, and now the grand staircase up the rocky heights will scarcely stand another year, and after they collapse only scaling ladders can be used. A half-dozen unhappy barrels collect the rainfall from the roof ; the whole structure is sprung in every joint and tenon, and ere many moons have passed it will not be safe for the legendary " ghost of the hapless princess " which wanders thereabouts, to ascend to light her periodical beacon on the roof, without the help of the signal officer who has his crow's-nest there. The marines who guard the warehouse and magazine, keep an eye to the tottering walls when they make their turns, and pedestrians who pass under the projecting roof of the old trading-house, whence bullets were liable to rain upon the intruders, look aloft with more apprehensions of dry rot than hot shot. The block-houses which remain can scarcely stand, and but one side of the old stockade guards the plaza, shutting off the Indian " ranch." So it is throughout the town. With its population reduced two-thirds and its business nine-tenths, with half the shops and dwellings tenantless, there is not a building of any kind I venture to say, without a window broken. There are not more than two or three which indicate fresh paint on their fronts, and not a new structure of any kind except in the purlieus of the Indian " ranch," where the sight of a fresh slab is richness to the eyes. On every side the gruesome ravens croak, truly the " embodiment of spirits long departed." Noting the abundant traces of a previous occupancy, with the dead past buried all around them, antiquarians already begin to speculate how many hundred years ago these bastion towers were built, so dilapidated and gray they look ; industriously they decipher the inscriptions on the ancient coins ; and simple minded Yankees, when they see their flag floating in the air, wonder if this is really their own " God's country," or where they are. Nevertheless and withal, the town has still a habitable and homelike look. There are gardens filled with vegetables and flowers, geraniums in window pots, cows quietly grazing along the streets. Occasionally the thrum of a piano is heard, which is blessed music in the wilderness, though intolerable in town. Some of the Russian houses preserve their national characteristics, so that we have only to enter them to learn how the people live in Russia. As ladies have a better faculty of observation and tact to describe domestic economies, I will save myself the trouble of doing so by copying from my lady correspondent " Mintwood," who is accurate and vivacious. She says :

" As I am writing in one of them at this moment, I will describe it, as an illustration of one of the best Sitkan houses of Russian origin. It fronts directly on the bay with a charming outlook, and between the house and the bay is a large garden, in which a Russian neighbor has a fine colony of cabbages and some potato tops. The path from the gate leads up a gentle eminence between two rows

of gooseberry bushes, which are loaded with fruit, and supplemented in the rear with currant bushes, also in bearing
with green clusters. There is a row of pie-plant, in barrels, and a hot bed, the sash of which is a fish net. There
are lines in the garden on which are strung pieces of shining tin to frighten the ravens and crows. There are elder
bushes and two fruit trees ; one, a crab-apple, was quite full
of blossoms. A clump of wild roses bloom beautifully
under one window, and under another is a fragrant bed of
spearmint. In the back yard are four outbuildings, all of
them having evidently at one time been dwelling houses ;
two are of logs. The house itself, of one story and a loft,
has a vestibule, opening into a hall, at the right of which is
the large parlor, and at the left the large kitchen. In addition to these rooms there are two good-sized bedrooms.
The parlor has five windows, each window consisting of six
panes, each pane a foot square, in two rows. The lower
part of the window, of four panes, opens like a French window. The window sills are deep, and at one window there
is a green roller curtain. The parlor furniture consists of
an old mahogany Russian sofa, with a high back entirely in
veneer ; the hair-covered cushioned seat is dilapidated, and
is temporarily upholstered with a rubber blanket. There
are three chairs in various stages of infirmity, and a number
of four-legged stools of ingenious construction. There is a
mahogany table, and a ditto bureau, a modern and probably native made piece of furniture, of yellow cedar, quite
pretty, and consisting of closets and drawers. The skin of
a mountain goat covers a considerable space on the bare
floor, and a large box stove, for wood, that was manufactured in Philadelphia, has had a fire burning in it nearly
every day. The papered walls have their attractions—an
old Russian print of the Virgin Mary, and a local painting
of Sitka. The bedrooms have bedsteads—rickety—and
bureaus, and two pieces of broken looking-glass. The
kitchen is comfortably furnished ; an abundance of tables
and shelves, some dishes and glassware, an old brass
samovar, a heavy copper boiler, skillets, other culinary utensils, a worn-out cooking stove that still serves the user of it
well, nevertheless, and a pair of wooden buckets."

From the center of the town a macadamized road extends
along the curve of the beach, amply wide for vehicles to
pass abreast, lined by cosy dwellings on the landward side,
and commanding a fine view of the bay and islands and the
overhanging mountains. Perhaps some day the fashion-
ables of Sitka will use it for a carriage drive, but as yet few

vehicles have ever run over it. *Quien sabe?* who shall tell ? This road leads past the Indian mission, and to Indian River, just beyond, which is a favorite resort for visitors and towns-people as well. Since the occupancy of the town by the government marines, they have devoted lots of labor to building bridges, rustic seats and walks along this sparkling stream, which is broken into falls and picturesque reaches where trout disport ; and he who directed the work has done it admirably well, for every natural beauty has been left untouched, and as my friend already quoted declares, "it is just like walking through a magnificently wooded park which has gone wild for centuries, with only the walks left civilized." Some of the firs and hemlocks are simply immense, and the undergrowth is frightful to penetrate. In the midst of the forest I found a small potato patch which had been fenced, but it was hard in August to find either potatoes or fence. Some of the Indian boys dislike to come to the river to fish for fear of bears, but no bears ever yet seemed to take a liking to any of them. This river furnishes the only good drinking water to be had, and the good people of the town walk out along these beautiful paths with tin pails and demijohns to bring in drinking water. The barracks details fetch it in a canoe, and that this inconvenience exists in Sitka is but one illustration of the decay and amazing enervation of the town. If it did not rain here so much, and barrels and casks under eaves were not kept well filled most of the time, the water question would be a more difficult one than it is.

Hitherto the management of local or territorial affairs has not been happy. None of the appropriations made for the support of the civil government or for specific purposes appear to have been accounted for. Until two years ago the government itself was not a success. Its seat was never warm. There was no ownership in any thing. It did not even know what belonged to it. A merchant claimed the public warehouse as his private property ; another citizen claimed the dock, and the navy had actually to build a wharf for its own necessities. (N. B. When there is any litigation in Alaska about wharves, the teredo steps in and eats them up before a decision can be reached.) The last administration was unfortunate. The governor broke his arm and had a paralytic stroke, and the district attorney was killed in California by falling from a railroad train. When their successors took office, the district judge was found not to be a success, and attempts were made to prevent the confirmation of the new governor. Now, however, an auspicious era seems to have dawned. Immigration is pouring in apace. The newspaper recently started at Sitka is a wide-awake journal, devoted heartily to the development of the country, and from it the public can obtain information which can be relied upon. Governor Swineford means "straight business." Much depends upon his sagacity and discretion. He is laboring to secure a remedy for defects in the law governing territorial organization. There being no connection now between the different towns, in sending a prisoner from one point to another for trial, he is as liable to go via San Francisco as otherwise, taking three months for the transit, so that it is less expensive not to take than to make prisoners. What the government needs is a revenue cutter and one or two steam launches to serve as harbor police-boats and deputy sheriffs in these strange water-ways. Their moral effect alone would make all the difference in the world. It would insure good order and stability.

For whatever lies beyond Sitka, between it and Mt. St. Elias, 200 miles further west, I can not speak from my personal experience. Recently excursion trips have been extended to include those additional waters, within whose limits are the greatest number of high and imposing peaks to be found in any range in the world. In a pamphlet of 100 pages, beautifully printed and illustrated by the Northern Pacific Railway Company, to influence summer travel to Alaska, I find the following synopsis from the pen of Lieutenant Schwatka :

" Almost as soon as Cape Spencer is doubled, the southern spurs of the Mount St. Elias Alps burst into view, Crillon and Fairweather being prominent, and the latter easily recognized from our acquaintance with it from the waters of Glacier Bay. A trip of an hour or two takes us along a comparatively uninteresting coast, as viewed from the ' square off our starboard beam ; ' but all this time the mind is fixed by the grand Alpine views we have ahead of us, that are slowly developing in plainer outline here and there as we speed toward them. Soon we are abreast of Icy Point ; while just beyond it comes down a glacier to the ocean that gives about three miles of solid sea-wall of ice, while its source is lost in the heights covering the bases of the snowy peaks just behind. The high peak to the right, as we steam by the glacier front, is Mount La Perouse, named for one of the most daring of France's long list of explorers, and who lost his life in the interest of geographical science. His eyes rested on this range

of Alpine peaks in 1786, just a century ago. Its sides are
furrowed with glaciers, one of which is the ice-wall before
our eyes, and which is generally known as the La Perouse
Glacier. The highest peak of all, and on the left of this
noble range, is Mount Crillon, named by La Perouse, in
1786, after the French Minister of the Marine; while
between Crillon and La Perouse is Mount D'Agelet, the
astronomer of that celebrated expedition. Crillon cleaves
the air for 16,000 feet above the sea, on which we rest, and
can be seen for over a hundred miles to sea. It, too, is
surrounded with glaciers in all directions from its crown.
Crillon and La Perouse are about seven miles apart, nearly
north and south of each other. About fifteen miles northwest of Crillon is Lituya Peak, 10,000 feet high; and the
little bay-opening that we pass, between the two, is the
entrance to Lituya Bay, a sheet of water which La Perouse
has pronounced as one of the most extraordinary in the
world for grand scenery, with its glaciers and Alpine
shores. Our steamer will not enter, however; for the passage is dangerous even to small boats—one island bearing
a monument to the officers and men of La Perouse's expedition, lost in the tidal wave which sweeps through the con-
tracted passage like a breaker over a treacherous bar.
Some ten or twelve miles northwest from Lituya Peak is
Mount Fairweather, which bears abreast us after a little
over an hour's run from Lituya Bay. It was named by
Cook in 1778, and is generally considered to be a few hundred feet shorter than Mount Crillon. It is in every way,
by its peculiar isolation from near ridges almost as high as
itself, a much grander peak than Crillon, whose surroundings are not so good for a fine Alpine display. Fairweather, too, has its frozen river flowing down its sides;
but none of them reach the sea, for a low, wooded country,
some three or four miles in width, lies like a glacis at the
seaward side of the St. Elias Alps, for a short distance
along this part of the coast. The somber, deep green
forests add an impressive feature to the scene, however,
lying between the dancing waves below and the white and
blue glacier ice above. Rounding Cape Fairweather, the
coast trends northward; and, as our bowsprit is pointed in
the same direction, directly before us are seen immense
glaciers reaching to the sea. From Cape Fairweather
(abreast of Mt. Fairweather) to Yakutat Bay (abreast of
Mt. Vancouver) no conspicuous peak rears its head above
the grand mountain chain which for nearly a hundred miles
lies between these two Alpine bastions; but, nevertheless,

every hour reveals a new mountain of 5,000 to 8,000 feet in
height, which, if placed anywhere else, would be held up
with national or state pride as a grand acquisition. Here
they are only dwarfed by grander peaks."

THE SEALS OF PRIBYLOV

A treatise on Alaska, however ephemeral or unpretentious, would hardly be complete without some reference
being made to its fur-seal fishery, upon which almost the
only revenue of the territory was based up to the year 1884.
Professor Henry W. Elliott's official report to the government, made in 1882, comprising the result of many years investigation, is an exhaustive account of all there is to know
about the subject ; and from it I have gathered the facts appended.   This is an illustrated volume of nearly 200 quarto
pages, comprising a history of the fur-seal fishery from
earliest dates ; the discovery of the Pribylov group in 1786
by the hardy Muscovite whose name they bear collectively ;
the configuration and natural history of the Islands ; their
acquisition by the United States ; the formation and operations of the Alaska Commercial Company ; and a description of the inhabitants, their occupation and mode of life.
The breeding-places and habits of the seals and all their
phocine kindred, the walrus, sea-lion, sea-otter, hair-seal,
etc., and the methods employed to secure their hides, and
to prepare and ship them to market, and to dye them to
suit the wearers, are all given in the most considerate manner, with due regard to the sensibilities of the animals themselves, which, next to the ladies who hope to wear their
pelts, are unquestionably the parties chiefly interested. The
details are intensely interesting to the reader, and to the
seals excruciating, we may believe.
    Located fourteen hundred miles west-north-west from
Sitka, as the ship sails, and nearly two hundred miles from
Oonalashka, the nearest land, sea-girt and beset with outlying reefs, continually befogged in summer, and in winter
swept by cruel icy blasts, the Pribylovs are hard to find.   It
is said that navigators have even touched their cliffs with
their vessels' yard-arms before they were aware of their
close proximity.   And it is because of this isolation, as well
as because they afford the only good resting place in Alaska,
that the seals frequent them. They are all of volcanic
origin, bearing some not remote traces of dynamic action,

the crater of Otter island being " as distinctly defined, and
as plainly scorched as though it had burned out yesterday."
St. Paul island is thirteen miles in length by six in breadth,
composed of rough, rocky uplands, rugged hills, smooth
volcanic cones, parti-colored sand-dunes, grassy plats, and
wet and slippery flats, where the seals most congregate. It is
interspersed with pools and lagoons of good fresh water, in
which a pretty minute viviparous fish is found. St. George
is ten miles long by four and one-half miles wide, steep and
precipitous on all sides, except at three short reaches of
coast which the seals have appropriated for " rookeries."
Like St. Paul, it also has many pools of water. Its highest
land rises 930 feet, and St. Paul's 600 feet. Nearly half the
shore of St. Paul is a sandy beach, while on St. George there
is less than a mile of it all put together. Millions of sea-
fowl breed and hover perpetually over their ledges and inaccessible terraces, and all the available spaces are filled
with eggs in spring. There would be valuable guano deposits except that they are annually washed clean off by the
beating storms of winter, during which period the birds are
discreetly absent. Each island has its village of resident
overseers and employés, its killing-grounds, salting and
packing houses, and its little harbor where vessels may load
and discharge in favorable weather only. As for the rest,
on St. George there is a water-fall which drops 400 feet perpendicularly into the sea in spring ; a little running stream
to diversify the asperity of the physical contour ; and on
every prominent eminence a Greek cross erected there by
Russians, some of them as long as sixty years ago. There
is a good deal of grass—a dozen varieties of different
lengths and quality, and a multitude of pretty flowers, ferns
and mosses. Snow melts at a very low temperature, and
grass begins to grow at 34 degrees or 36 degrees even if it
be covered by melting drifts of snow and the frost has
hardened the ground for many feet beneath. Some success
has followed attempts at gardening, and lettuce, radishes,
turnips, and even small potatoes, have been grown in
favored spots. Countless sparrows come in early spring
and are gathered up for food by the thousands, just as the
Israelites gathered quails. These birds agreeably vary the
staple diet of seal meat, of which the little communities,
about 400 souls all told, consume some 1200 pounds a day.
The government allows them to catch 6,000 seals a year for
their subsistence. Excepting two or three mules for work,
the only animals on the islands are hosts of blue foxes, lem-
mings, which honeycomb the softer earth with their burrows,

mice, and stump-tail cats, which run wild and roam everywhere.   On favorable nights when the air is still and the
moonlight full, these incorrigible cats join in such an un-
earthly caterwauling that the natives turn out *en masse* to interdict them.   The shrieks of the tempest can not compare
with the ferocity of the chorus.   But for all, they decimate
the mice.   There are no reptiles on the islands, and no
mosquitoes nor venomous flies ; but there is a variety of fly
which settles down upon the grass of the killing-grounds
making the surface appear as if it were bedaubed with liquid
stove-polish, for the color they impart.   Their food is the
blood and offal of the slaughter.   The perfume of the
Pribylovs is intense, and one may perceive the odor far at
sea when the wind is fair.   On a hot day in the close cabins
of the village it would be overpowering to any body who was
not used to it.   No fish can be caught within the vicinity,
as the seals devour all that approach.

Six miles north from St. Paul Island is Otter Island, once
frequented by herds of sea otters, a sheer, cold and unbroken mural precipice, except at a low depression on the
north side.   Its walls average 300 feet in height.   It is
fairly over-run with blue foxes.   Walrus Island lies six miles
southwest, the abode of many of these huge animals, some
of which will weigh a ton.   It is a mere ledge barely lifted
above the wash of angry waves, only a fourth of a mile long
and 100 yards wide.   It literally swarms with wild fowl, and
is, therefore, very convenient for eggers, who, in other localities, have to climb up precipices, and swing from jutting
ledges to gather their plunder.   There is an island 200
miles north of St. Paul, but having no commercial connection
with it, called St. Matthew, which is of volcanic origin, and
fairly swarms with polar bears, which sometimes measure
eight feet long and weigh 1,200 pounds.   They are very
timid, and flee precipitately, old and young, upon the approach of man.   There are deserted Russian cabins on the
island, which were built and once occupied by bear-hunters,
who did a big business in meat, pelts and oil.   The traditional ferocity of these animals seems to have wholly petered
out in this sub-Arctic ursine community.

The Pribylov Islands were first peopled by a native colony
brought over from Oonalashka and other Aleutian neighbor-
hoods by the Russian fur-sealers in 1786, and were employed
in their service ; but they lived miserably in hovels which
were half dug-out.   Now, under the American regime, and
the fostering care of the Alaska Commercial Company, their
progeny are happy and well provided for in all those respects

which make a sealer's life worth the living. There are two hundred and ninety-eight people on St. Paul, of which fourteen are whites, one a woman ; on St. George ninety-two people, of whom four are whites. On both islands each family lives in a snug frame dwelling, painted, and lined with tarred paper, furnished with a stove and fuel, and out-houses complete. Streets are laid out, and regularly platted ; there is a large church at St. Paul, and a smaller one at St. George ; a hospital at St. Paul, with a complete stock of drugs, and physicians on both islands to take care of the people ; a school-house on each island, for which teachers are paid by the company for eight months in the year to instruct the youth, one of these teachers being a native Aleut who accomplished a four years course of study in Rutland, Vt.; and a store on each island, where once a year the trading ship brings the latest fashions, and every body enjoys a holiday opening. The church services are held in the Russian language, and their support is maintained entirely by native contribution. There are eighty families and eighty dwellings on St. Paul, and twenty-four at St. George, besides eight other structures, ecclesiastical and commercial, all painted and built by skilled mechanics, so that the settlements present an appearance up to the average of Eastern villages. The people all dress in modern attire, and eagerly discuss the newest fashion plates, but as yet silk "tiles" are unknown. Except during the sealing season, they have absolutely nothing to do but go to church and vegetate. Fully two hundred and ninety days of the year are occupied in observing the religious calendar. Many sleep away their time ; a few gamble ; some play the fiddle and accordeon. The population is very orderly. There are no policemen, no courts of justice, no fines, no crimes, and no instituted penalties for crimes. Quite frequently the islanders make a journey to their relatives on the mainland ; and to visit Oonalashka is like a rustic "doing" the metropolis. Oonalashka is no insignificant burg, be it known, for it discounts Sitka. There are tourists, little traveled, who think that Sitka is the land's end, but there are half a dozen towns at least lying west, along the coast and up the Yukon, which have a larger population.

The Alaska Commercial Company was organized by Messrs. Hutchinson and Morgan, both New England men, in 1869. With others who watched the negotiations for the Alaska purchase they came out early to the seal islands, and during the previous year had exclusive control of them.

The methods of the company are now complete, and it seems almost impossible to improve upon them. Abuses and breach of trust are almost impossible within the environment of restrictions by which they are hedged about, and it would be utterly impossible to catch more than the stipulated quota of seals without the fact becoming known at once. Only once have they caught the full complement (one hundred thousand) allowed by law, and then only inadvertently. Their rule is to make the number one thousand scant so as to avoid carping criticisms. The breeding grounds are protected, and obstreperous old males diligently kept off from them, but they are allowed to come to all other localities. One million seal pups are born every year, and of these there is a loss of fifty per cent. by whales, sharks, and predatory creatures, after they leave for their foraging grounds. While breeding they strictly fast. When they leave they go in independent gangs, and not all at once, and they range as far south as the forty-seventh parallel. Seals are in their prime at from four to five years of age, and only those which are desirable are selected for the annual drive. An average seal will measure six and a half feet long and weigh four hundred pounds, but they are caught up to six hundred pounds and seven and a half feet long. It is estimated, within the power of accurate calculation, that there are over three millions of seals on each island in the breeding season, not counting the non-breeders, "old bachelors," etc. The entire catch of one hundred thousand seals is now made in about thirty working days, included between the 14th day of June and the 1st of August. Seals do remain longer than the latter date, but their fur deteriorates rapidly. The sealers work under the direction of foremen, who receive the wages due for their work, according to the tale, and divide it among them, making up a number of extra shares over and above the men's, which go to the widows, the priest and the church. They receive forty cents per seal, and fifty cents to one dollar per day for incidental labor. It is estimated that more than four millions of sealskins have been taken from the Pribylovs since 1797. When the killing season has arrived, details of men run in between the sleeping seals and the surf-wash, and drive them slowly to designated slaughtering grounds, at a speed of half a mile an hour, halting them occasionally to rest and cool off, for heating injures their fur ; and it is a comical sight to see the long procession, urged on by shouts and clapping of whale thigh-bones, and gesticulating arms on the flanks and rear, wad-

dling, panting, gasping and shuffling along like so many
fat men, in the most awkward manner conceivable. Sometimes an old bull-seal, adipose and unwieldy, who can not
travel with the younger ones, falls to the earth supinely,
entirely exhausted, hot, and "clean done up." Another,
too weary to travel any more, will stand up in his tracks
and fight. These old recalcitrants are at once dismissed,
abandoned and ignored, as of little value, their under-wool
which gives price to the pelt, being much shorter, coarser,
and scantier than that of the younger seals. When a halt
is called and the men drop back from the line for a few
moments, the march at once ceases, and every seal fans
himself with his hind flippers, while his flanks heave with a
subdued panting sound. It is a grievous sight to behold,
but I have seen worse at a soldiers' parade on a 4th of July,
when the sun stood at a hundred in the shade, and there
was not lemonade enough to go round. When the seals
have partially cooled off, the march to death is resumed.
Finally the slaughter-ground is reached and the seals are
told off in squads of one hundred and fifty, and at a given
signal the executioners let go with clubs and lay them out
right and left, after which they are knifed and skinned at
the rate of one in every four minutes, although experts have
done the job in a minute and a half. The clubs are six
feet long, three inches in diameter at the but, made of hard
wood, and manufactured in New London, Ct., expressly
for this service. There is an excellent opportunity here to
indulge in sentimentalism, but I forbear to speak of the
languid eyes that plead before the uplifted club, and the
heart-rending moans which come from those not dead. My
real opinion is that there is little occasion to complain of
needless cruelty.

After the skins are flayed off, they are salted and piled in
kenches as high as a man can toss them, "hair to fat and
salt between," and having been allowed two weeks in which
to pickle, are tied up in bundles of two skins each, hair outside, and shipped to London *via* New York or Panama, to
be dyed; for few natural skins are less attractive than the
fur seals, the fur not being visible, but concealed by a
coat of stiff hair, dull gray, brown and grizzled. The art
of dying in its perfection is said to be possessed by only
one concern in London, although there are many other
dyers; and there is at Albany, in the state of New York, a
firm which does splendid work, but their dye color is said
to be lighter and not so rich as the Englishman's. The
cost of a fur comes from a combination of causes and

expenses which, it is affirmed, will keep the price up always to near its present figure. The Alaska Company has stations all over the Aleutian Islands west and north of Kodiak, and employs four steamers, and a dozen ships, barks and sloops, besides working boats. Its lease expires in 1890, but there is no doubt that it will be renewed.

Fur seals and sea otters are sometimes caught in large numbers off the Straits of Fuca and the west coast of Vancouver's Island, and in limited numbers by the Indians on the Alaskan coast. Last winter the fur seals seemed to be frequenting the waters of southeastern Alaska in increased numbers. Old residents along the shores say that the last large run was twenty years ago, and was followed immediately after by a run of sea otter, and they are hoping for a like result now. The Sitka paper says that a good many fur seal skins, both of pups and grown seals, have lately reached the Sitka market. In 1883 there were ten schooners engaged in British waters, employing forty sailors and 296 hunters, the latter chiefly Indians, who used 148 cedar canoes, and they took upward of 9,000 fur seals and 3,000 hair seals, valued at $93,000. The former are worth $10, and the latter fifty cents. Only ninety-six sea-otters were caught, marketable at $50 each.

This brief synopsis will suffice to convey an idea of an interesting industry and locality of which very little is known at large.

And now, leaving the seal islands, and the mountains and forests of Alaska, with their undergrowth and dampness, we are ready to turn our faces eastward, and homeward, where, climbing some crowning eminence which overlooks the tilled and tillable land, we view scores of blue lakes basking in the mellow haze, groves of party-colored foliage covering all the hillsides, fields dotted with conical straw piles and ricks of hay, meadows alive with grazing kine and herders, looking very red in the suffusion of the dawning light of day. And all the mirrored lakes reflect the form and color of the painted trees, as the looking-glass reflects the radiant bride, intensifying their crimson blush and heightening the effect of their tremulous emotion.

With unfeigned pleasure we exchange rankness for richness, and the tangle of the unkempt forest for the brightness of the cloth of gold, and a drier and more cheerful clime. The glory of the Indian summer pervades the land ; and while I gaze with rapture upon the golden landscape, a solitary pine rises in the foreground like a spirit of retrospection. Its generations have long since passed away, and the ashes of their fallen dead lie buried all around; but its stately shadow is projected westward toward the unsurveyed domain where its mighty kindred still stand erect in all their primal grandeur ; and like a prophetic finger it points infallibly to the value of the " SEWARD PURCHASE." Every sigh that soughs through its weathered fronds in regret of departed greatness, whispers hope for the future prospects of Alaska.

AN EXCURSION PARTY

APPENDIX.

Be it enacted by the Senate and House of Representatives of the United States of America in Congress assembled : That the territory ceded to the United States by Russia by the treaty of March thirtieth, eighteen hundred and sixty-seven, and known as Alaska, shall constitute a civil and judicial district, the government of which shall be organized and administered as hereinafter provided. The temporary seat of government of said district is hereby established at Sitka.

SECTION 2. That there shall be appointed for the said district a governor, who shall reside therein during his term of office and be charged with the interests of the United States Government that may arise within said district. To the end aforesaid he shall have authority to see that the laws enacted for said district are enforced, and to require the faithful discharge of their duties by the officials appointed to administer the same. He may also grant reprieves for offenses committed against the laws of the district or of the United States until the decision of the President thereon shall be made known. He shall be *ex officio* commander-in-chief of the militia of said district, and shall have power to call out the same when necessary to the due execution of the laws and to preserve the peace ; and to cause all able-bodied citizens of the United States in said district to enroll and serve as such when the public exigency demands; and he shall perform generally in and over said district such acts as pertain to the office of governor of a territory, so far as the same may be made or become applicable thereto. He shall make an annual report on the first day of October in each year, to the President of the United States, of his official acts and doings, and of the condition of said district, with references to its resources, industries, population, and the administration of the civil government thereof. And the President of the United States shall have power to review and to confirm or annul any reprieves granted or other acts done by him.

SECTION 3. That there shall be, and hereby is, established a district court for said district, with the civil and criminal jurisdiction of district courts of the United States exercising the jurisdiction of circuit courts, and such other jurisdiction, not inconsistent with this act, as may be established by law ; and a district judge shall be appointed for said district, who shall during his term of office reside therein, and hold at least two terms of said court therein in each year, one at Sitka, beginning on the first Monday in May, and the other at Wrangell, beginning on the first Monday in November. He is also authorized and directed to hold such special sessions as may be necessary for the dispatch of the business of said court, at such times and places in said district as he may deem expedient, and may adjourn such special session to any other time previous to a regular session. He shall have authority to employ interpreters, and to make allowances for the necessary expenses of his court.

SECTION 4. That a clerk shall be appointed for said court, who shall be *ex officio* secretary and treasurer of said district ; a district-attorney, and a marshal, all of whom shall during their terms of office reside therein. The clerk shall record and preserve copies of all the laws, proceedings, and official acts applicable to said district. He shall also receive all moneys collected from fines, forfeitures, or in any other manner except from violations of the custom laws, and shall apply the same to the incidental expenses of said district court, and the allowances thereof as directed by the judge of said court, and shall account for the same in detail, and for any balances on account thereof, quarterly, to and under the direction of the Secretary of the Treasury. He shall be *ex officio* recorder of deeds and mortgages and certificates of location of mining claims and other contracts relating to real estate and register of wills for said district, and shall establish secure offices in the towns of Sitka and Wrangell, in said district, for the safe keeping of all his official records, and of records concerning the reformation and establishment of the present status of titles to lands, as hereafter directed : *Provided,* That the district court hereby created may direct, if it shall deem expedient, the establishment of separate offices at the settlements at Wrangell, Oonalashka, and Juneau City, respectively, for the recording of such instruments as may pertain to the several natural divisions of said district most convenient to said settlements, the limits of which shall, in the event of such direction, be defined by said court; and said offices shall be in charge of the commissioners respectively hereinafter provided.

SECTION 5.   That there shall be appointed by the President four commissioners in and for the said district, who shall have the jurisdiction and powers of commissioners of the United States circuit courts in any part of said district but who shall reside, one at Sitka, one at Wrangell,* one at Oonalashka, and one at Juneau City.   Such commissioners shall exercise all the duties and powers, civil and criminal, now conferred on justices of the peace under the general laws of the state of Oregon, so far as the same may be applicable in said district, and may not be in conflict with this act, or the laws of the United States.   They shall also have jurisdiction, subject to the supervision of the district judge, in all testamentary and probate matters, and for this purpose their courts shall be opened at stated terms and be courts of record, and be provided with a seal for the authentication of their official acts.   They shall also have power to grant writs of habeas corpus for the purpose of inquiring into the cause of restraint of liberty, which writs shall be made returnable before the said district judge for said district ; and like proceedings shall be had thereon as if the same had been granted by said judge under the general laws of the United States in such cases.   Said commissioners shall also have the powers of notaries public, and shall keep a record of all deeds and other instruments of writing acknowledged before them and relating to the title to or transfer of property within said district, which record shall be subject to public inspection.   Said commissioners shall also keep a record of all fines and forfeitures received by them, and shall pay over the same quarterly to the clerk of said district court.   The governor appointed under the provisions of this act shall, from time to time, inquire into the operations of the Alaska Seal and Fur Company, and shall annually report to Congress the result of such inquiries and any and all violations by said company of the agreement existing between the United States and said company.

SECTION 6.   That the marshal for said district shall have the general authority and powers of the United States marshals of the states and territories.   He shall be the executive officer of said court, and charged with the execution of all processes of said court and with the transportation and custody of prisoners, and he shall be *ex-officio* keeper of the jail or penitentiary of said district.   He shall appoint four deputies, who shall reside severally at the towns of Sitka, Wrangell, Oonalashka and Juneau City, and they shall respectively be *ex-officio* constables and executive officers of the commissioners' courts herein provided, and shall have the powers and discharge the duties of United States deputy marshals, and those of constables under the laws of the state of Oregon now in force.

SECTION 7. That the general laws of the state of Oregon now in force are hereby declared to be the law in said district, so far as the same may be applicable and not in conflict with the provisions of this act or the laws of the United States ; and the sentence of imprisonment in any criminal case shall be carried out by confinement in the jail or penitentiary hereinafter provided for. But the said district court shall have exclusive jurisdiction in all cases in equity or those involving a question of title to land, or mining rights, or the constitutionality of a law, and in all criminal offenses which are capital. In all civil cases at common law, any issue of fact shall be determined by a jury, at the instance of either party ; and an appeal shall lie in any case, civil or criminal, from the judgment of said commissioners to the said district court, where the amount involved in any civil case is two hundred dollars or more, and in any criminal case where a fine of more than one hundred dollars or imprisonment is imposed, upon the filing of a sufficient appeal bond by the party appealing, to be approved by the court or commissioner. Writs of error in criminal cases shall issue to the said district court from the United States circuit court for the district of Oregon in the cases provided in chapter one hundred and seventy-six of the laws of eighteen hundred and seventy-nine ; and the jurisdiction thereby conferred upon circuit courts is hereby given to the circuit court of Oregon. And the final judgments or decrees of said circuit and district court may be reviewed by the supreme court of the United States as in other cases.

SECTION 8. That the said district of Alaska is hereby created a land district, and a United States land office for said district is hereby located at Sitka. The commissioner provided for by this act to reside at Sitka shall be *ex-officio* register of said land office, and the clerk provided for by this act shall be *ex-officio* receiver of public moneys, and the marshal provided for by this act shall be surveyor-general of said district, and the laws of the United States relating to mining claims, and the rights incident thereto, shall, from and after the passage of this act, be in full force and effect in said district, under the administration thereof herein provided for, subject to such regulations as may be made by the Secretary of the Interior, approved by the President :

Provided, That the Indians or other persons in said district shall not be disturbed in the possession of any lands, actually in their use or occupation or now claimed by them, but the terms under which such persons may acquire title to such lands is reserved for future legislation by Congress : *And provided further,* That parties who have located mines or mineral privileges therein under the laws of the United States applicable to the public domain, or who have occupied and improved or exercised acts of ownership over such claims, shall not be disturbed therein, but shall be allowed to perfect their title to such claims by payment as aforesaid : *And provided also,* That the land not exceeding six hundred and forty acres at any station now occupied as missionary stations among the Indian tribes in said section, with the improvements thereon erected by or for such societies, shall be continued in the occupancy of the several religious societies to which said missionary stations respectively belong until action by Congress.　But nothing contained in this act shall be construed to put in force in said district the general land laws of the United States.

SECTION 9.　That the governor, attorney, judge, marshal, clerk and commissioners provided for in this act shall be appointed by the President of the United States, by and with the advice and consent of the Senate, and shall hold their respective offices for the term of four years, and until their successors are appointed and qualified.　They shall severally receive the fee of office established by law for the several offices the duties of which have been hereby conferred upon them, as the same are determined and allowed in respect of similar offices under the laws of the United States, which fees shall be reported to the attorney-general and paid into the Treasury of the United States. They shall receive respectively the following annual salaries : The governor, the sum of three thousand dollars ; the attorney, the sum of two thousand dollars ; the marshal, the sum of two thousand five hundred dollars ; the judge, the sum of three thousand dollars ; and the clerk, the sum of two thousand five hundred dollars, payable to them quarterly from the Treasury of the United States. The district judge, marshal and district attorney shall be paid their actual, necessary expenses when traveling in the discharge of their official duties.　A detailed account shall be rendered of such expenses under oath, and as to the marshal and district attorney such account shall be approved by the judge, and as to his expenses by the attorney-general.　The commissioners shall receive the usual fees of United States commissioners and of justices of the peace for Oregon, and such fees for recording instruments as are allowed by the laws of Oregon for similar services, and in addition a salary of one thousand dollars each. The deputy marshals, in addition to the usual fees of constables in Oregon, shall receive each a salary of seven hundred and fifty dollars, which salaries shall also be payable quarterly out of the Treasury of the United States. Each of said officials shall, before entering on the duties of his office, take and subscribe an oath that he will faithfully execute the same, which said oath may be taken before the judge of said district or any United States district or circuit judge. That all officers appointed for said district, before entering upon the duties of their office, shall take the oaths required by law, and the laws of the United States, not locally inapplicable to said district and not inconsistent with the provisions of this act are hereby extended thereto, but there shall be no legislative assembly in said district, nor shall any delegate be sent to Congress therefrom. And the said clerk shall execute a bond, with sufficient sureties, in the penalty of ten thousand dollars, for the faithful performance of his duties, and file the same with the Secretary of the Treasury before entering upon the duties of his office ; and the commissioners shall each execute a bond, with sufficient sureties, in the penalty of three thousand dollars, for the faithful performance of their duties, and file the same with the clerk before entering upon the duties of their office.

SECTION 10. That any of the public buildings in said district not required for the customs service or military purposes shall be used for court rooms and offices of the civil government, and the Secretary of the Treasury is hereby directed to instruct and authorize the custodian of said buildings forthwith to make said repairs to the jail in the town of Sitka, in said district, as will render it suitable for a jail and penitentiary for the purpose of the civil government hereby provided, and to surrender to the marshal the custody of said jail and the other public buildings, or such parts of said buildings as may be selected for court-rooms, offices and officials.

SECTION 11. That the attorney-general is directed forthwith to compile and cause to be printed, in the English language, in pamphlet form, so much of the general laws of the United States as are applicable to the duties of the governor, attorney, judge, clerk, marshals and commissioners appointed for said district, and shall furnish for the

use of the officers of the said territory so many copies as
may be needed of the laws of Oregon applicable to said
district.

SECTION 12. That the Secretary of the Interior shall
select two of the officers to be appointed under this act,
who, together with the governor, shall constitute a commission to examine into and report upon the condition of the
Indians residing in said territory, what lands, if any, should
be reserved for their use, what provision shall be made for
their education, what rights by occupation of settlers should
be recognized, and all other facts that may be necessary to
enable Congress to determine what limitations may be imposed when the land laws of the United States shall be
extended to said district ; and to defray the expenses of
said commission the sum of two thousand dollars is hereby
appropriated out of any moneys in the treasury not otherwise appropriated,

SECTION 13. That the Secretary of the Interior shall
make needful and proper provision for the education of the
children of school age in the Territory of Alaska, without
reference to race, until such time as permanent provision
shall be made for the same, and the sum of twenty-five
thousand dollars, or so much thereof as may be necessary,
is hereby appropriated for this purpose.

SECTION 14. That the provision of chapter three, title
twenty-three, of the Revised Statutes of the United States,
relating to the unrecognized Territory of Alaska, shall
remain in full force, except as herein specially otherwise
provided ; and the importation, manufacture and sale of
intoxicating liquors in said district except for medicinal,
mechanical and scientific purposes, is hereby prohibited
under the penalties which are provided in section nineteen
hundred and fifty-five of the revised statutes for the
wrongful importation of distilled spirits. And the President of the United States shall make such regulations as
are necessary to carry out the provisions of this section.

Approved, May, 17, 1884.

APPENDIX B.

PACIFIC COAST EXCURSIONS.

The following round trip excursion rates will hereafter be made from St. Paul, Minneapolis, Duluth, Superior, Fargo, or intermediate points east of Fargo, to Portland :

In parties of 10, each....$165.00 In parties of 35, each....$130.00
"   "   15, "   .... 160.00   "   " 40, " ... 120.00
"   "   20, "   .... 155.00   "   " 45, " 110.00
"   "   25, "   .... 150.00   "   " 50 or more,
"   "   30, "   .... 140.00   each............... 100.00

For excursion rates to Tacoma and return, add to above rates $4.00

For excursion rates to Victoria and return, add to above rates $10.00

For excursion rates to Sitka, Alaska, and return, add to above rates $95.00.

Opportunity given on above tickets to stop over at all points of interest, including Livingston, for a side trip through the Yellowstone National Park, Lake Pend d'Oreille, and the tourists and sportsmen's resorts in the park regions of Minnesota.

PRICE OF TICKETS TO ALASKA AND RETURN.

INCLUDING BERTH AND MEALS ON STEAMER.

From San Francisco, via Victoria and Townsend, and
   returning same way....................$125
  " San Francisco, via Victoria, and returning via
   Tacoma, Portland and Columbia River...... 135
  " Portland, Oregon, via Astoria............... 100
  "   "   "   via Tacoma & Port Townsend }
  (N.P.R.R.to Tacoma,and O.R.& M.Co.str.to Pt.T'send) } 100
  " Port Townsend............................. 90
  " Victoria, B. C............................. 90

CALIFORNIA EXCURSIONISTS

Can return via Portland, Oregon, and the Northern Pacific Railroad to St. Paul, Minneapolis, or Duluth, Minn., by paying the agent of the Pacific Coast Steamship Company, 214 Montgomery Street, San Francisco, $15 for ticket, San Francisco to Portland, provided they hold an excursion ticket the return portion of which reads via the Northern Pacific Railroad. Should the return portion of the ticket read over one of the Southern lines, it will be exchanged on payment of $10 to return via the Northern Pacific on application to T. H. Goodman, General Passenger Agent of the Southern and Central Pacific Railroads, San Francisco, Cal. The same rule applies for excursionists reaching Portland via the Northern Pacific who may desire to return via San Francisco. The latter should apply to John J. Byrne, General Passenger Agent O. R. & N. Co., Ash street dock, Portland, Oregon, for exchange of railroad ticket or special excursion ticket, Portland to San Francisco.

Words of praise in commendation of the elegant steamers run by the Pacific Coast Steamship Company between Portland and San Francisco are unnecessary, as their excellence is well known and appreciated by the traveling public.

The rate of $15 referred to above includes state room and meals en route. Steamers leave Portland and San Francisco every five days.

STEAMER DAYS.

The demands of business have induced the Pacific Coast Steamship Company to double their service to Alaska, and steamers now run twice a month instead of monthly, as heretofore. The sagacity of this movement is indicated by the fact that the summer excursion lists are rapidly filling months in advance of the days of sailing. Dates of departure are herewith appended :—

Steamer.	Leaving Portland.				
Mexico	May 28	June 25	July 23	Aug. 20	Sept. 17
Idaho	" 14	" 11	" 9	" 6	" 3
	Leave Port Townsend.				
Mexico	May 3-31	June 28	July 26	Aug. 23	Sept 20
Idaho	" 17	" 14	" 12	" 9	" 6

If larger steamers are at any time required by the exigencies of trade, they will at once be substituted, though the above (the *Mexico* especially) are fine vessels. The Northern Pacific Railroad Company has arranged that any of its agents in the East can secure accommodations for Alaska excursionists by telegraphing to the office at St. Paul; diagrams, berth-lists, etc., furnished, and state rooms secured.

www.ingramcontent.com/pod-product-compliance
Lightning Source LLC
Chambersburg PA
CBHW030133030726
47498CB00007B/2684